INTRODUCTION TO
TOURISM TRANSPORT

D1477758

CABI TOURISM TEXTS are an essential resource for students of academic tourism, leisure studies, hospitality, entertainment and events management. The series reflects the growth of tourism-related studies at an academic level and responds to the changes and developments in these rapidly evolving industries, providing up-to-date practical guidance, discussion of the latest theories and concepts, and analysis by world experts. The series is intended to guide students through their academic programmes and remain an essential reference throughout their careers in the tourism sector.

Readers will find the books within the CABI TOURISM TEXTS series to have a uniquely wide scope, covering important elements in leisure and tourism, including management-led topics, practical subject matter and development of conceptual themes and debates. Useful textbook features such as case studies, bullet point summaries and helpful diagrams are employed throughout the series to aid study and encourage understanding of the subject.

Students at all levels of study, workers within tourism and leisure industries, researchers, academics, policy makers and others interested in the field of academic and practical tourism will find these books an invaluable and authoritative resource, useful for academic reference and real world tourism applications.

Titles available

INTRODUCTION TO TOURISM TRANSPORT

Sven Gross and Louisa Klemmer

Hochschule Harz – University of Applied Sciences, Germany

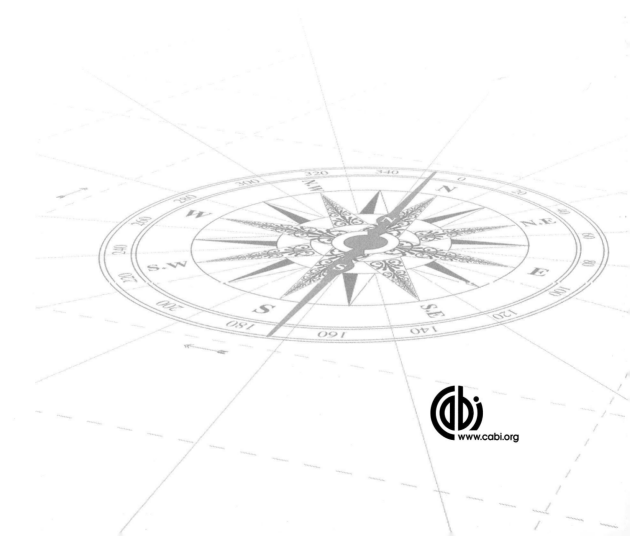

www.cabi.org

CABI is a trading name of CAB International

CABI	CABI
Nosworthy Way	38 Chauncy Street
Wallingford	Suite 1002
Oxfordshire OX10 8DE	Boston, MA 02111
UK	USA
Tel: +44 (0)1491 832111	Tel: +1 800 552 3083 (toll free)
Fax: +44 (0)1491 833508	Tel: +1 617 395 4051
E-mail: info@cabi.org	E-mail: cabi-nao@cabi.org
Website: www.cabi.org	

A catalogue record for this book is available from the British Library, London, UK.

Library of Congress Cataloging-in-Publication Data

Gross, Sven, 1969–
Introduction to tourism transport / by Sven Gross and Louisa Klemmer, Hochschule Harz –
  University of Applied Sciences, Germany.
    pages cm. -- (CABI tourism texts)
  Includes bibliographical references and index.
  ISBN 978-1-78064-214-7 (alk. paper)
  1. Tourism. 2. Transportation. I. Title.

  G155.A1G766 2014
  388'.042--dc23
                          2013045576

ISBN-13: 978 1 78064 214 7

Commissioning editor: Claire Parfitt
Editorial assistant: Alexandra Lainsbury
Production editor: Laura Tsitlidze and Claire Sissen

Typeset by SPi, Pondicherry, India.
Printed and bound by Gutenberg Press, Malta.

Contents

This book is enhanced with supplementary resources.
To access the customizable lecture slides please visit:
www.cabi.org/openresources/42147

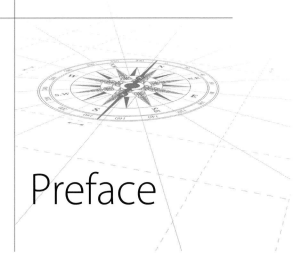

Preface

Travel is an inherent part of tourism, whether as a functional means of transportation, such as between origin and destination or within the destination, or as a key element of the holiday experience itself, as in cruising or travelling along scenic and/or historic routes. As tourism transport is dealt with rather superficially within a few paragraphs in most tourism textbooks, there is a paucity of academic texts dealing with tourism transport in any great detail. Therefore, this book is designed as an introductory text to provide students and other interested parties with the necessary background information to gain a comprehensive understanding of the transportation markets. Transportational modes will be defined, and the different types of transportation available within each mode, as well as their particular use within the tourism industry, will be elucidated from a mainly European and North American perspective. Historical developments of each market will also be presented in order to facilitate a deeper understanding of the subject matter before presenting current demand and supply trends. Furthermore, in order to understand the operational environment, applicable international institutional frameworks, selected national or regional agreements, and industry associations will be presented. We acknowledge that due to space limitation a more comprehensive understanding of planning and management issues cannot be addressed. However, for those who wish to gain a deeper understanding of the subject matter, references and further sources are provided at the end of each chapter. We hope the information contained in this book will find wide use among students and faculty alike, and simultaneously engage an interest for the exciting area of travel and tourism.

When writing a book, most authors depend on the support of various people and institutions. We too have been fortunate to receive help from various sources around the world during the two-year process. As numerous companies, consultants, associations, research institutions and universities, ministries, agencies and individuals have contributed important information to the content of this book, it is impossible to thank everyone individually; however, we would like to sincerely thank them all at this point.

There are certain people without whose support the completion of this book would not have been possible, and we would like to take this opportunity to express our utmost respect and gratitude to them. Special thanks go to our graduate research assistant Ms Luisa Wolter, who carried out much of the research and supported us with editorial work. We would also like to thank Ms Sandra Skolik, Ms Christin Faust, Ms Lucienne Röbisch and Mr Gerrit Welmering for their contributions.

We also wish to acknowledge and thank Alexandra Lainsbury and Claire Parfitt at CABI for their assistance and support throughout the editorial process. Further thanks go to the proposal reviewers as well as Gui Lohmann for his unselfish support through his vast collection of contributions on the subject of travel and transport literature; and Michael Lück for his insightful comments and the permission to use his photos.

Finally, it is particularly important to thank our families, without whose support this book would not have been possible.

Wernigerode, 2014
Sven Gross and Louisa Klemmer

It should be noted that all the information in this book has been compiled according to the current state of the literature, and we have credited original authors for their work to the best of our knowledge. Nevertheless, we cannot guarantee the accuracy, completeness or timeliness, and therefore no liability for the contents are taken, regardless of the purpose for which they are used.

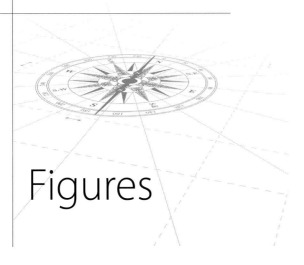

Figures

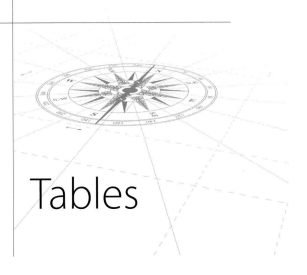

Tables

chapter 1

Introduction

Tourism and transport are intimately connected to each other, as the movement of people is one of the most important elements of tourism. For instance, the United Nations World Tourism Organization (UNWTO) defines tourism as a subset of travel since it entails the movement of people to countries or places outside their usual environment for personal or business/professional purposes (media.unwto.org, 2014). Theobald (2005) suggests the derivative of the word tourism, *tour-* can also be interpreted as a round-trip (based on the Latin word *tornare* and its etymological development) while *-ism* is the suffix that forms nouns of action; hence tourism can be seen as 'the act of leaving and then returning to the original starting point, and therefore, one who takes such a journey can be called a tourist' (p. 10). Furthermore, in Leiper's (1990) tourism system, transport is the key connection between the tourist's origin and the destination. Not without reason then, do many refer to the *travel and tourism* industry.

Just as the tourism product relies on natural and built landscapes, attractions and amenities as resources, so too does it rely on transportation to facilitate the movement of tourists. In fact, tourism not only relies on, but also causes and is affected by transportation. From a historical perspective we have witnessed the impact of transportation on the growth and development of tourism:

> History records that the transport system has exerted a profound effect on the development of travel from ancient times. [...] The movement of these early travellers from origin to destination was made possible by well engineered road systems, organised road transport based on horse and cart teams, organised sea travel in the Mediterranean and a hospitality sector. In more recent times the development of the steam train followed later by the car and the plane have added to humanity's ability to undertake travel to even the remotest corner of the globe.
>
> (Prideaux, 2000, p. 53)

It should not be surprising that although there is a mutual influence and dependence between tourism and transport, the dependence of tourism on transport is much greater than transport on tourism: all tourism involves travel, but not all travel involves tourism.

The following discussion of various tourism and transport services is based on the system of transportation modes; mainly air, ground and water based transportation. Furthermore, the main focus of this text is on the marketplace, where buyers and sellers come into contact to realize a voluntary exchange of goods and services (see Fig. 1.1).

The buyer's market is comprised of the consumers, in this case the tourists, while the providers are the producers or owners of the transport services. Within the framework of any market analysis, it is important to clearly delineate the market, its structure and its volume. The market can be delineated based on spatial, temporal, socio-demographic and product-specific aspects. The structure can be summarized by the number and size of market participants, while market volume can be described in terms of scope of the relevant market-traded services. Suitable parameters for determining market volume include typical data such as sales turnover and number of employees, among others. In addition to the general market analysis, it is important to consider the inter-relationships between the macro- and microeconomic environments as the market represents the interface of these two areas. Hence, the general institutional framework and examples of various actors and institutions that affect the transport service suppliers will be

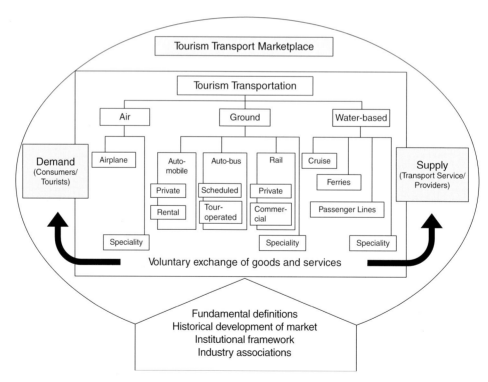

Fig. 1.1. Tourism transport marketplace to be examined. Source: Based on Goeldner and Ritchie, 2012

described once fundamental definitions and delimitations have been introduced. As it is often helpful to understand the historical development of a particular sector in order to gain a better understanding of the present situation, this too will be presented.

The microeconomic perspective will not be covered in this text, as it would go beyond the scope of the book. Besides, there are a variety of textbooks and management literature available which cover the various business functions of transport organizations (ranging from planning and development, sales and marketing, to financial planning) on which we will provide information in the sections on further reading.

First we will provide a definition of tourism and several definitions concerning transportation before further examining tourism transport.

DEFINITIONS OF TOURISM

Various approaches have been taken in defining tourism within the academic literature as well as by both national and international institutions and organizations. International examples include definitions by the Committee of Statistical Experts of the League of Nations, the International Union of Official Travel Organizations (IUOTO), and the Organization for Economic Co-operation and Development (OECD). Well-known national examples include definitions from the US Senate's National Tourism Policy Study, the Travel Industry Association of America (TIA), or the National Tourism Resources Review Commission from the USA; the Canadian Travel Survey from Canada; the National Tourist Boards of England, Scotland and Northern Ireland from the UK; or the Australian Bureau of Industry Economics (see Cooper *et al.*, 2005; Page and Connell, 2006; Wall and Mathieson, 2006; Goeldner and Ritchie, 2011). Cooper (2012) highlights that tourism has not only been defined from both a demand and supply side perspective, but that both conceptual and technical approaches have been taken. While conceptual supply side definitions of tourism exist, the diverse and fragmented nature of tourism makes it difficult to define and hence measure. More specifically, tourism is not only seen as an amalgamation of industries (including transportation, accommodation, food and beverage services, recreation and entertainment, and travel retail) but the degree to which companies cater to tourists or other consumers also varies extensively. The United Nations developed the Tourism Satellite Accounts (TSA) in order to try and standardize the measurement of these goods and services (making them comparable between countries as well as with other internationally recognized economic statistics) (see United Nations, 2010; Robinson *et al.*, 2013). A well-known and often quoted supply side definition is offered by the UNWTO where issues of technical measurement such as length of stay and purpose of visit have been addressed for legislative measurement objectives:

> A visitor is a traveller taking a trip to a main destination outside his/her usual environment, for less than a year, for any main purpose (business, leisure or other personal purpose) other than to be employed by a resident entity in the country or place visited. These trips taken by visitors qualify as tourism trips. Tourism refers to the activity of visitors.

(UNWTO, 2010a, p. 10)

This definition includes three important parameters: change of environment (which is composed of frequency and distance dimensions), length of stay and purpose. Furthermore, the UNWTO distinguishes between three basic forms of tourism (UNWTO, 2010a, p. 15).

- **Domestic tourism**: comprises the activities of a resident *visitor* within the country of reference, either as part of a *domestic tourism trip* or part of an *outbound tourism trip*.

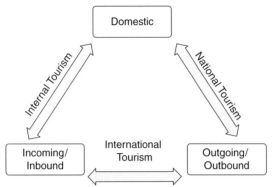

- **Incoming/inbound tourism**: comprises the *activities* of a non-resident *visitor* within the country of reference on an *inbound tourism trip*.
- **Outgoing/outbound tourism**: comprises the activities of a resident visitor outside the country of reference, either as part of an outbound tourism trip or as part of a domestic tourism trip.

As can be seen in Fig. 1.2, these three forms of tourism can then be combined into three further categories:

Fig. 1.2. Categorization of tourism (based on UNWTO, 2010b).

- **Internal tourism**: comprises domestic tourism plus inbound tourism, that is to say, the activities of resident and non-resident visitors within the country of reference as part of domestic or international tourism trips.
- **National tourism**: comprises domestic tourism plus outbound tourism, that is to say, the activities of resident visitors within and outside the country of reference, either as part of domestic or outbound tourism trips.
- **International tourism**: comprises inbound tourism plus outbound tourism, that is to say, the activities of resident visitors outside the country of reference, either as part of domestic or outbound tourism trips and the activities of non-resident visitors within the country of reference on inbound tourism trips.

A more detailed classification of international visitors by the UNWTO (2010b) can be seen in Fig. 1.3.

DEFINITIONS OF TRANSPORTATION

Important terminology concerning tourism transport includes several terms with which we are very familiar and hence often take their understanding for granted. However, to ensure a common understanding or baseline for the treated subject matter of this text, we will provide definitions for all fundamental terms.

- **Transport or transportation**: refers to the activity of moving an object (people or goods) from one place to another, or the system used for doing this. For the purpose of this book, we will define transport as the activity of travelling from one place to another.

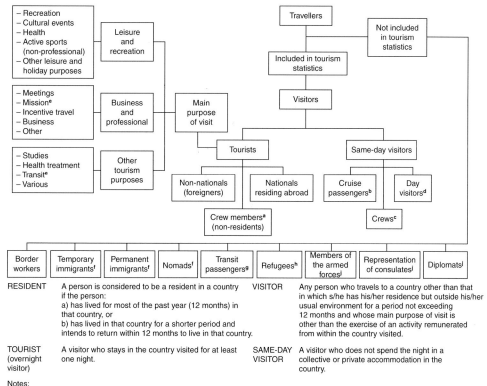

Fig. 1.3. Classification of international visitors (based on UNWTO, 2010b).

RESIDENT	A person is considered to be a resident in a country if the person: a) has lived for most of the past year (12 months) in that country, or b) has lived in that country for a shorter period and intends to return within 12 months to live in that country.	VISITOR	Any person who travels to a country other than that in which s/he has his/her residence but outside his/her usual environment for a period not exceeding 12 months and whose main purpose of visit is other than the exercise of an activity remunerated from within the country visited.
TOURIST (overnight visitor)	A visitor who stays in the country visited for at least one night.	SAME-DAY VISITOR	A visitor who does not spend the night in a collective or private accommodation in the country.

Notes:

[a] Foreign air or ship crews docked or in lay over and who use the accommodation establishments of the country visited.

[b] Persons who arrive in a country aboard cruise ships (as defined by the International Maritime Organization, 1965) and who spend the night aboard ship even disembarking for one or more day visits.

[c] Crews who are not residents of the country visited and who stay in the country for the day.

[d] Visitors who arrive and leave the same day for leisure and recreation, business and professional or other tourism purposes including transit day visitors en route to or from their destination countries.

[e] Overnight visitors en route from their destination countries.

[f] As defined by the United Nations in the Recommendations on Statistics of International Migration, 1980.

[g] Who do not leave the transit area of the airport or the port, including transfer between airports or ports.

[h] As defined by the United Nations High Commissioner for Refugees, 1967.

[i] When they travel from their country of origin to the duty station and vice versa (including household servants and dependants accompanying or joining them).

- **Transport infrastructure**: includes the material conditions such as routes (e.g. roads, tracks, etc.), means (e.g. vehicles), control systems (traffic control), handling facilities (bus, train or plane terminals), and transfer facilities.

- **Mode of transport**: refers to the environment in which the transport takes place: air, ground or water based transport (Duval, 2007). All vehicles which utilize the same environment belong to the same transport mode.

- **Transportation routes**: utilized by the transportation means.

- **Transportation means, type or carrier**: refers to the actual 'means of mobility realized within a particular mode' (Duval, 2007, p. 3). Examples include the aeroplane, boat or car as illustrated in Fig. 1.4. In conjunction with the transportation infrastructure, these means enable the implementation of transport services.

WHAT IS TOURISM TRANSPORT?

We have ascertained that transport is an inherent part of tourism. Now it must be noted that either it can play a functional or utilitarian role, such as the transport between origin and destination (flight on a leisure carrier, for example) or within the destination (such as an itinerary trip on a local bus) where the travel is merely a means to an end; or it can play a key role in the holiday experience itself. These roles can range from the transportation type as a tourist attraction (such as historic railways, steam trains or steam ships, for example); part of a recreational experience (such as biking, hiking or hot-air ballooning, for example); to providing the essential component of the tourism product where the transportation type is the actual holiday setting (such as in a cruise vacation or travelling along scenic and/or historic routes) (Lumsdon and Page, 2004; Page, 2009; Lohmann and Duval, 2011).

Lohmann and Duval (2011) illustrate the functional form of tourism transport between the origin and the destination, within the various destinations visited, and between the different destinations visited during a holiday trip in Fig. 1.5.

Furthermore, Lumsdon and Page (2004) address the different tourism transport experiences based on their level of intrinsic value. They describe a tourism transport continuum in terms of its level of intrinsic value as a tourism experience, where travel using a taxi, urban bus or metro system is classified as having low intrinsic value compared with a walking or cycling holiday or a heritage railway vacation which is classified as having high intrinsic value. A similar differentiation is made by Page (2009):

- Transport *for* tourism, where it is means to an end being very utilitarian, and the level of satisfaction is related to cost and speed of travel, so the mode of travel has no direct intrinsic value in itself [...]

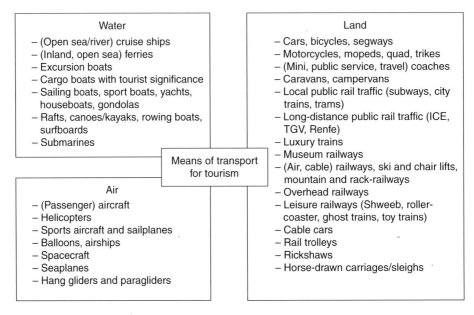

Fig. 1.4. Classification of transport means.

- Transport *as* tourism, where the transport mode is the containing context for travel such as a cruise and a basis for the tourist experience. Here the travel cost principle in transport for tourism does not apply where the transport is the main benefit, or at least many of the attributes associated with the mode of transport are beneficial.

(Page, 2009, p. 24)

The different means of transport are used to different degrees by both tourists and non-tourist consumers. Hence, usually tourists use leisure flights to holiday regions, sightseeing buses, and cruise ships, while city buses, trams and scheduled flights are more likely to be used to different extents by both tourists and local residents (Page, 2009).

A look at the historical development of transportation modes shows that the proliferation of many new forms of passenger transport also spurred the leisure demand. Examples include bicycles or motorcycles as recreational equipment, or the encouragement of early tourism development in the Alps through rack/cog railways and cable cars.

However, recreation and tourism are not only pioneers of new transportation forms, but also prevent some transportation forms from dying out. For example, many historical modes of transport, including horses, horse-drawn carriages, balloons, canoes, sailboats, trolleys, or even rafts, have survived as recreational pastimes or are utilized as a tourism product although they are no longer used as an everyday or regular mode of passenger transport. Moreover, through technological advances and innovations some recreational forms of transport have in fact enjoyed a revived interest and use. Examples include powered sailboats or mountain bikes (Heinze and Kill, 1997).

Tourism transportation means can be classified using several criteria: domestic or international, public or private, or whether they are land, water or air based, for example (see Fig. 1.5).

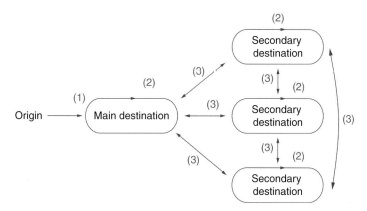

Fig. 1.5. Transport linking to, from and within destinations. From Lohmann and Duval, 2011, p. 5.

Both transit activities (arrivals and departures) and tourist activities in the target area require a safe and reliable transportation infrastructure. Particularly walking, cycling, hiking and horse-back riding are hard to imagine without extensive and well-marked trails. However, there are many tourism products (such as river cruises, canoe tourism, houseboat tourism) which heavily rely on good transportation routes and infrastructure (Gross, 2005).

Having introduced the basic concepts of tourism and transport, a more detailed examination of the main transportation markets will be given.

Part 1

Air Transportation

Air transport is an important element of the tourism system as just over half (52%) of all worldwide inbound travellers enter a country via air (UNWTO, 2013). As our focus lies on the interconnection of air transport and tourism, we will focus on air traffic and examine the airline industry more closely. As the different business models within the airline industry are of particular interest they will be dealt with in more detail.

chapter 2

Airplanes

LEARNING OBJECTIVES

- Become familiar with different air transport classifications.
- Identify characteristics of various airline business models.
- Outline the history of aviation.
- Understand the complex nature of aviation regulations and the associations which are involved.
- Outline worldwide airline demand and supply.
- Recognize the most important airline performance indicators.

DEFINITIONS

The term 'aviation industry' encompasses the aerospace industry, aviation organizations, and air transportation.

Aerospace industry

Encompasses all of the economic, organizational and technical air transport facilities required for the manufacture (for example, airframe and turbines) and delivery of aircraft, as well as infrastructure such as airports and air traffic control facilities (Pompl, 2007).

Aviation organizations

Consist of all institutions that constitute the legal and transactional framework necessary for the realization of air transportation and the production of the aerospace industry (Maurer, 2006; Pompl, 2007).

Air transportation

This includes all processes which encompass the transportation of persons or objects by air, including any direct or indirect services (Rössger and Hünermann, 1965, as cited by Pompl, 2007).

Based on the *Glossary of Transport Statistics* (2009) compiled by the International Transport Forum (ITF), Eurostat and the United Nations Economic Commission for Europe (UNECE), several basic terms concerning air transportation will be defined here.

Aircraft

While the *Collins English Dictionary* defines an aircraft as any machine capable of flying by means of buoyancy or aerodynamic forces, such as a glider, helicopter or aeroplane, the *Glossary of Transport Statistics* (2009, p. 136) defines an aircraft as 'Any machine that can derive support in the atmosphere from the reactions of the air other than the reactions of air against the earth's surface.'

Focus box

Lighter-than-air crafts (such as hot-air balloons) fly based on the buoyancy principle as air density decreases with increasing altitude. Heavier-than-air crafts can only fly based on a careful balance of the four aerodynamic forces of flight: lift, drag, weight and thrust. An aircraft's lift must be balanced by its weight, and its thrust must exceed its drag (MIT Department of Aeronautics and Astronautics, 1997).

Passenger aircraft

An aircraft configured for the transport of passengers and their baggage. Any freight, including mail, is generally carried in cargo holds in the belly of the aircraft.

Airline (commercial air transport operator)

An aviation enterprise operating aircraft for commercial purposes which (i) performs scheduled or non-scheduled air transport services, or both, which are available to the public for carriage of passengers, mail and/or cargo and (ii) is certified for such purposes by the civil aviation authority of the state in which it is established.

Commercial air flight

An air transport flight performed for the public transport of passengers and/or freight and mail, for remuneration and for hire.

Domestic flight

A flight having exclusively domestic flight stages.

International flight

A flight having one or more international flight stages.

Various criteria such as purpose, route length and regularity have been used within the academic literature to classify different types of air services (as illustrated in Table 2.1) as there are no internationally recognized definitions. However, from a tourism perspective we tend to categorize air transportation as either scheduled service, chartered flights or scenic flights (Page, 2009). There are several business models within the airline industry, which differ in terms of the carrier's product offering, value-added services, revenue generation and target customers (Cento, 2009). More specifically, these business models can be divided into network carriers, leisure carriers, low-cost carriers (LCCs), regional carriers and business aviation/aircraft charters (Koch, 2010; Conrady *et al.*, 2013; Robinson *et al.*, 2013).

Table 2.1. Selected criteria of air traffic classification. (Adapted from Conrady *et al.*, 2013.)

Criterion	Segment
Purpose of use	• distinction between commercial (airline services that are offered against payment on behalf of third parties) and non-commercial air traffic (primarily flights of companies with own aircraft in their own interest (own-account transport), transfer, sport and private flights, state flights)
	• distinction between public (accessible for the public within the framework of the general transport conditions) and non-public air traffic (e.g. pure charter transport, private air traffic)
	• distinction between civil and military air traffic
Transport object	• passenger, freight or postal air traffic
Route length	• short, medium and long haul
Geography	• regional, continental and intercontinental flights
	• domestic and international air traffic (the latter can take place within a continent or between continents)
Regularity	• scheduled and occasional services
Business model	• network carrier, leisure carrier, LCC, regional carrier, business aviation/air charters

HISTORICAL DEVELOPMENT

Flight has been a fascination for mankind since before Christ – tomb drawings of Pharaoh Ramses the III and Greek myths attest to this. During the Middle Ages flight continued to fascinate mankind, as evidenced by drawings of Leonardo da Vinci, for example. The first actual attempts to fly utilized balloons, as is further described in the chapter on speciality air transport.

The first regular passenger air service was established in Florida in 1914. The aircraft was a sea-plane able to carry one passenger at a time from St Petersburg to Tampa, crossing Tampa Bay in about 25 minutes (Airlines for America, 2013). However, the air transportation industry was not really established until after the First World War and has been accredited to the mail service. Although the US Post Office was granted funding for the proposed transportation of mail by air in 1916, at that time there were no planes suitable for these services. After the First World War, large planes capable of fast commercial airmail transportation were available and the US Congress granted the Post Office Department $100,000 to purchase, maintain and operate such planes, bringing to life the air transportation industry (Wensveen, 2007; Boyd, 2013). In fact, the US mail service largely subsidized the emergence of major US passenger airlines.

A similar development can be seen in Europe, where efforts were made to develop the aircraft as a means of transport with converted reconnaissance and bombing aircraft after the First World War. The aircraft became larger, more reliable and sturdier. However the first successful all-metal aircraft was the Junkers F13, which had its first flight. In the same year, the first national route in Germany was established between Berlin and Weimar by the Deutsche Luftreederei (DLR) to transport mail. Later that year, the first international route in Europe was established between Paris and Brussels by the French airline Lignes Aériennes Farman. During this time, many airlines emerged and disappeared again (Adam, 2012). Just as civil aircraft were developed from the existing military aircraft, military airports were gradually transformed into suitable commercial airports. In the 1920s, the first international airport was built in Croydon, London and it was during this time that there was a tremendous increase in the demand for air transport.

The first jet engines were developed concurrently in the 1930s by Frank Whittle in England and by Hans Joachim Pabst von Ohain in Germany. With the so called Heinkel/Ohain-Triebwerk the world's first flight with a jet airline was conducted on 27 August 1939 near Rostock in Germany. The jet engine was further developed during the Second World War and used in military aircraft. Although civil aviation was briefly interrupted during the war, progress continued in the decades following the war resulting in an expanding industry (Schulz *et al.*, 2010; Deutsches Museum, 2012a, b). Important milestones included early developments such as altimeters, speed and rate of climb indicators, or the use of radio, to more technological advancements such as flight recorders, terrain-avoidance systems and weather radars.

During the period from 1938 to 1978, tremendous growth in domestic as well as international air transportation could be observed in US air passenger traffic. The number of passengers, domestic and international, carried by US airlines rose from about 1 million in 1938 to nearly 267 million in 1978. Obviously, the number of both US and foreign airlines also increased during this period. Hence, not only was there an upsurge in direct airline employment, but also indirect employment increased dramatically (for example, in manufacturing of civil transport aircraft and engines, at airports and travel agencies and so on). Air transportation had thus become a major industry in the USA (Doganis, 2006; Wensveen, 2007).

The Airline Deregulation Act of 1978 brought major changes to the US airline industry as controls concerning airfares and routes on scheduled flights were abolished. Figure 2.1 gives an overview of the different stages of the deregulation process within the airline industry in the USA.

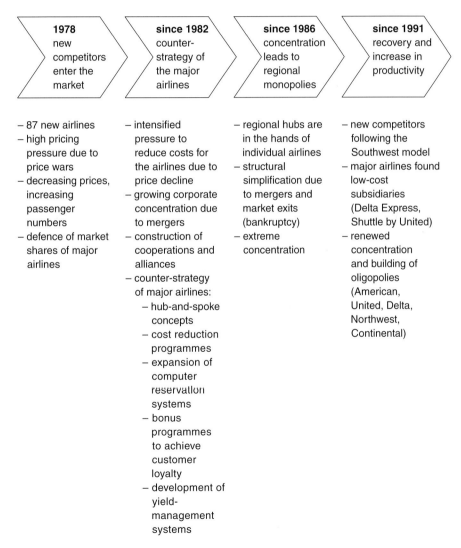

Fig. 2.1. Stages of the deregulation in the airline industry in the USA. From Maurer, 2006.

From 1955 onwards, airplanes were regularly crossing the Atlantic from Germany to the USA. By the end of the 1950s, passenger air traffic overtook maritime traffic across the Atlantic on this route.

Due to the large domestic market and the tremendous armament efforts, the USA realized scientific, technical and economic advantage both in the development of aircraft and the air transport market. Hence, the Europeans were forced to consolidate in both research and industry in order to compete successfully (Schulz, 2009). The A300 was the first wide-body aircraft with only two engines and had its first flight in 1972. In Europe the deregulation in the airline industry took place in various steps between 1988 and 1997 (see 'European air law', pp. 21–22).

In the Asia Pacific region the aviation industry remained regulated for much longer and was dominated by a few established national airlines that were owned or partly owned by the respective governments. However, the economic crisis in the early 1990s forced some Asian countries to liberalize their aviation policies and especially countries in South East Asia quickly recognized the potential commercial benefits of some degree of deregulation. Thus, Asian national airlines as well as private companies subsequently founded either LCC subsidiaries or new LCC companies in the early 2000s.

For much of the 21st century, the aviation industry has found itself in a financial crisis on a global scale. Although the major problems began with the economic downturn at the beginning of 2001, they reached almost disastrous proportions after the US terror attacks of 11 September 2001. For example, the US industry experienced net losses of $40 billion between 2001 and 2005 and only managed to become profitable again in 2006 with a total net profit of just over $3 billion. Many of the same forces affected non-US airlines, particularly international political and military events, as well as the SARS-related health crisis in 2003. As a group, the non-US airlines recorded losses from 2001 to 2003 but were able to achieve modest net profits in 2004 and 2005.

Nonetheless, the load factor (for definition and calculation of the load factor, see the end of this chapter, p. 42) has increased steadily since the end of the 1990s for the world airlines. A particularly strong increase can be observed since 2001 (see Fig. 2.2). The average load factors for the world airlines reached 78% in 2011, which is nine percentage points higher than in 2001 (ICAO, 2008, 2012a). To cope with the increase in air transportation, the formation of national and international regulations became necessary; these are explained in the following section.

INSTITUTIONAL FRAMEWORK

Air transportation is embedded in a wide-ranging framework of national and international legal policies, by-laws, agreements and permits (Gross, 2011). This section will therefore present only the most important regulations.

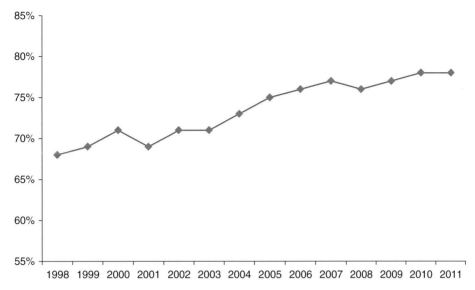

Fig. 2.2. World airline passenger load factors, 1998–2011. Based on ICAO, 2008, 2012a.

International air law

As commercial aviation grew, an international code of regulations became essential. Early on, the legal issues were handled by each nation individually; however, once the environment became increasingly international the lack of uniformity proved to be a considerable impediment (Wensveen, 2007). Therefore, several international organizations encouraged movements aiming at the international codification of commercial aviation law.

Multilateral agreements

In air traffic it is assumed that every state has unrestricted sovereignty over its airspace. This principle was established in the Paris Agreement of 1919 as well as in the Chicago Convention of 1944. The Chicago Convention has great significance for international air traffic and was adopted by 54 states at the International Conference on Civil Aviation, also called the Chicago Conference (Maurer, 2006; Wensveen, 2007; Odoni, 2009; Gross, 2011). The first article of this law states 'The contracting States recognize that every State has complete and exclusive sovereignty over the airspace above its territory' (ICAO, 2006, p. 2).

Furthermore, the Chicago Convention differentiates between scheduled airline traffic and unscheduled traffic. According to Article 6 of the agreement, scheduled airline flights may only be carried out over a country's territory if said country has granted a special permit. Unscheduled flights are generally permitted to approach into a country's territory, board and deplane passengers, and receive and dispatch cargo and/or post (Article 5). Interestingly, many states issue their own regulations, conditions or restrictions, as the legal system allows for this (Conrady *et al.*, 2013).

Two further important documents came out of the Chicago Conference: the International Air Services Transit Agreement (Two Freedoms Agreement) and the International Air Transport Agreement (Five Freedoms Agreement). These agreements determine certain traffic laws or freedoms of the air that were agreed upon during the conference. The International Air Services Transit Agreement settles two technical traffic laws, namely the first and second freedoms of the air (for details on the freedoms of the air see Fig. 2.3). Besides these two freedoms, the International Air Transport Agreement also defines freedoms three to five, which are also called commercial freedoms (Wensveen, 2007; Odoni, 2009; Gross, 2011). The Two Freedoms Agreement was widely accepted by various nations, whereas the Five Freedoms Agreement did not receive strong support from the representatives. Although the USA originally agreed to the Five Freedoms document, they later withdrew their decision (Wensveen, 2007). Today, there are nine freedoms of the air (see Fig. 2.3). The first five freedoms originate from the Chicago Conference and the eighth and ninth freedoms are based on the Chicago Agreement, while the sixth and seventh freedoms were formed in practice.

Further important multilateral agreements are the Tokyo Agreement from 1963 (prevention of prosecutable actions on board), the Haag Agreement from 1970 (illegally taking possession of airplanes), and the Montreal Convention from 1971 (combat against illegal actions against the security of civil aviation). Another significant multilateral agreement between the USA and the EU concerns the liberalization of transatlantic air traffic ('Open Skies Agreement'), which will be briefly explained below (Doganis, 2006; Conrady et al., 2013).

Open Skies Agreement

On 30 March 2008, the Open Skies Agreement[1] between the USA and the EU took effect. This agreement allows European airlines to fly from any point in the EU to any point in the USA. Until then, this was only possible from the respective homelands. Likewise, every US carrier is allowed to fly into every EU member state. This is especially an advantage for those EU member states that previously did not have a bilateral agreement with the USA as this agreement increases the number of possible destinations for many Europeans. Therefore, these European countries have been more affected by the Open Skies Agreement than those countries that had previously existing bilateral agreements with the USA (Cento, 2009; Conrady et al., 2013). Furthermore, 'other key factors of the agreement provide for cooperation in fields such as security, safety and environment' (Cento, 2009, p. 17).

While all airlines enjoy the rights of the fifth freedom of the air, within the US cabotage is still prohibited under the 'Fly America' policy and the US domestic market is thus closed for foreign airlines. The same goes for US airlines on the EU domestic market. Additionally, foreign entities are limited to owning a maximum of 24.9% of the voting shares of a US airline. However, US airlines are allowed to own up to 49.9% of the shares of a European airline. Due to some

First Freedom: A carrier may fly over the territory of another nation without landing. *Example:* Northwest (NWA) flies from the United States over Iceland to Norway.

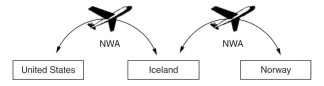

Second Freedom: A carrier may land in another nation for non-traffic-related purposes; i.e., only for a crew change or refuelling. *Example:* NWA flies from the United States to Norway but lands in Iceland for fuel.

Third Freedom: A carrier may drop off passengers from its own country in another nation. *Example:* NWA flies passengers from the United States to Norway.

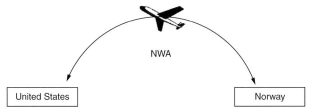

Fourth Freedom: A carrier may pick up passengers in another nation and carry them back to its own country. *Example:* NWA flies passengers from Norway to the United States.

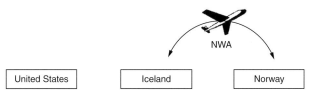

Fifth Freedom: A carrier may pick up passengers from a state other than its own and deliver them to a third state, also not its own. *Example:* NWA picks up passengers in Iceland and drops them off in Norway.

Fig. 2.3. The nine freedoms of the air. Based on Wensveen, 2007.

(Continued)

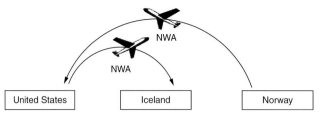

Sixth Freedom: A carrier may carry passengers from one state through its home country to a third state.
Example: NWA flies passengers from Norway to Iceland while stopping in the United States.

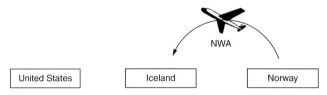

Seventh Freedom: A carrier may carry passengers from one state to a third state without going through its home country.
Example: NWA flies from Norway to Iceland without stopping in the United States.

Eighth Freedom: A carrier may operate domestic services in a foreign country with continuing service to or from one's own country (also known as cabotage).
Example: NWA flies between two cities in Norway or between two cities in Iceland.

Ninth Freedom: A carrier may operate within a foreign country without continuing service to or from one's own country (sometimes known as stand-alone cabotage).
Example: NWA flies between two cities in Iceland.

Fig. 2.3. Continued.

of these perceived inequalities, the Open Skies Agreement is currently still under negotiation (Cento, 2009; Odoni, 2009; Gross, 2011; Conrady *et al.*, 2013).

Bilateral agreements

In the context of bilateral air agreements (also known as 'Air Service Agreements') the involved countries concede each other air traffic rights. For granting the fifth freedom, the permission of the affected third country is needed (Gross, 2011). Worldwide, more than 4900 bilateral agreements can be viewed in the ICAO's Database of Aeronautical Agreements and Arrangements (DAGMAR), where all agreements since 31 January 1946 are registered (ICAO, 2013).

The principal questions which may be addressed in such agreements are (Odoni, 2009; Gross, 2011; Conrady *et al.*, 2013):

- Which airlines are allowed to carry out air traffic between the two countries?
- Which airports are allowed to be approached in international traffic?
- How often are the individual routes allowed to be operated and which capacities are allowed to be offered in international traffic?
- Which tariffs are allowed to be applied in international traffic?

The number of airports that can be operated in international traffic can be limited by bilateral agreements. In an extreme case, only one airport is allowed to be utilized by airlines from the contracting country ('single gateway rule'). The aim of this rule is to secure the home market for the national airlines (Conrady *et al.*, 2013).

European air law

Until the 1970s, the air traffic between the member states of the European Community was regulated by bilateral air transport agreements. After first attempts in 1974 and 1983, the European Court of Justice clarified that the restriction of competition on the European common market should also be abolished within the area of air traffic ('Nouvelles Frontières Decision'). Consequently, the airlines were no longer allowed to coordinate the tariffs within the IATA. The restrictive clauses of the bilateral agreements between the member states were also declared a violation of the terms of the EC Treaty. In order to guarantee the consistency of the guidelines, the European Union operates with regulations that are valid for all member states. Guidelines that require a transformation into national law and thus create leeway for implementation for the member states are therefore relatively rare in air traffic law (Conrady *et al.*, 2013).

The opening of the intra-community aviation market followed three stages of deregulation measures, which are known as the first, second and third packages. These packages became effective on 1 January 1988, 1 November 1990 and 1 January 1993, respectively.

1988: First package
- introduction of reduced rates
- introduction of 'double disapproval' for these rates (rates between partner countries are automatically approved as long as the governments of both countries do not reject the rate within 30 days)
- rejection of strict capacity ratios between the airlines involved in bilateral traffic (so that an equal distribution was no longer necessary)

1990: Second package
- extended margins for rates
- capacities of an airline can be increased to a certain extent during one season (up to a 75:25 allocation of capacities between the airlines of the involved countries)

1993: Third package

- abolition of all restrictions concerning routes and capacities
- freedom of establishment for EU airlines (free access to the market, with the exception of stand-alone cabotage, see Fig. 2.3)

Additionally to these three stages, on 1 April 1997, stand-alone cabotage became possible within the European Union (Maurer, 2006; Odoni, 2009; Conrady *et al.*, 2013).

ASSOCIATIONS

As the aviation industry is extremely large there are several organizations that participate in the regulatory and policy development process (see Fig. 2.4). Therefore, only some of the most important international associations from Europe and North America will be briefly highlighted below.

International Air Transport Association (IATA)

IATA is the global trade organization of the air transport industry and was founded in 1945 in Havana, Cuba. At that time, the organization had 57 members from 31 nations, mostly in

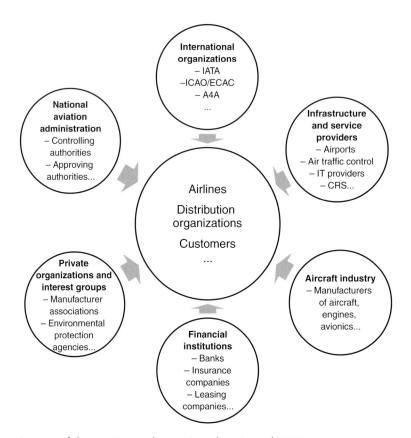

Fig. 2.4. System of the aviation industry. Based on Pompl, 2007.

Europe and North America. Today, IATA has about 240 members from 126 nations world-wide. Its members comprise the world's leading passenger and cargo airlines, which represent 84% of total air traffic (IATA, 2012a). 'It is the prime vehicle for inter-airline cooperation in promoting safe, reliable, secure and economical air services – for the benefit of the world's consumers' (IATA, 2012b).

Being an association, IATA provides a diverse service portfolio and operative support for its members. Among other things, the organization allows airlines to operate under clearly defined rules; it simplifies the travel and shipping processes for consumers; serves as an intermediary between airlines and passengers via neutrally applied agency service standards and centralized financial systems and provides training and consulting for anyone within the industry (IATA, 2012b).

International Civil Aviation Organization (ICAO)

Most nations of the world are represented by a national governmental aviation agency within the ICAO. More specifically, it has 191 member states and is a specialized agency of the United Nations created in 1944.

> 'The ICAO Council adopts standards and recommended practices concerning air navigation, its infrastructure, flight inspection, prevention of unlawful interference, and facilitation of border-crossing procedures for international civil aviation. In addition, the ICAO defines the protocols for air accident investigation followed by transport safety authorities in countries signatory to the Convention on International Civil Aviation, commonly known as the Chicago Convention' (US Consulate General, 2012).

European Civil Aviation Conference (ECAC)

ECAC was founded in 1955 as an intergovernmental organization and is the European equivalent to the ICAO. It has 44 member states and pursues 'the promotion of the con-tinued development of a safe, efficient and sustainable European air transport system' (ECAC, 2012). Its primary goals are coordinating civil aviation policies and furthering understanding on policy matters between its member states and other regions of the world (ECAC, 2012).

Association of European Airlines (AEA)

AEA is an industry organization founded in 1952 in Brussels, Belgium to represent the European airline industry. The association brings together 33 major European airlines and works in part-nership with the institutions of the European Union and other stakeholders in the value chain. AEA ensures the sustainable growth of the European airline industry in a global context and contributes to the policy decision-making processes (Association of European Airlines, 2012).

Airlines for America (A4A)

A4A was founded by a group of 14 airlines in 1936 in Chicago as the first trade organization of the principal US airlines. Today, it remains the only organization of its kind in the USA and comprises 67 airline and industry members, which transport more than 90% of all passengers in the USA. A4A is actively involved in technical, legal and political arenas and supports the industry efforts to fashion crucial policy and measures that enhance aviation safety, security and vitality of the system. Moreover, it enables US airlines to stimulate economic growth locally, nationally and internationally (Airlines for America, 2012).

A selection of other industry associations

- African Airlines Association (AFRAA)
- Air Transport Association of America (ATA)
- Airport Council International (ACI)
- Association of Asia Pacific Airlines (AAPA)
- Board of Airline Representatives in Germany (BARIG)
- Eurocontrol
- European Aviation Safety Association (EASA)
- European Low Fares Airline Association (ELFAA)
- European Regions Airline Association (ERA)
- International Air Carrier Association (IACA)

DEMAND AND SUPPLY

The following section will first present the demand side of air transportation, followed by a brief overview of the supply side, including the different products offered, aircraft types, suppliers and performance indicators.

Demand

Worldwide

Although there have been periods of declining air traffic volumes such as during the oil crises in 1973 and 1979, the first Gulf War in 1991, after 9/11 in 2001, during the Second Gulf War, or during the SARS epidemic in 2003 (Gross, 2011), overall we have witnessed a long-term increasing trend in international air traffic flow over the past decades. Moreover, following the crisis in 2009, passenger traffic rose by 14.8% worldwide in 2011. Overall, between 2000 and 2011 the passenger volume increased from 1.6 billion to over 2.7 billion. On average, these 2.7 billion passengers flew more than 1850 kilometres per route and thus generated a global transport volume of 5062 billion passenger kilometres (pkm; i.e. one person transported one kilometre), which is 6.5% more than in the year before. Thus, international air transport accounts for 62% of the overall generated transport volume (DLR, 2012).

Much of the world's air traffic is concentrated in the eastern USA, Western Europe and East Asia (Cooper, 2012). More specifically, by far the largest flow of traffic can be found on the North Atlantic route between the US and Europe. In 2011, 64.2 million passengers used the aircraft on this route, which is an increase of 5.1%. In addition, the second largest flow of traffic between Europe and the Far East also increased by 9% to a volume of 42.1 million passengers, followed by the flow of traffic between the Middle and the Far East with a volume of 35.9 million passengers. Furthermore, on the route between North and Central America 33.2 million passengers were registered and another 20.5 million passengers between Europe and Africa. Also, on the Pacific route between North America and the Far East an increase of 2.3% to 24.4 million passengers was observed. These and other important passenger flows between different world regions can be seen in Fig. 2.5 (DLR, 2012).

Europe

In 2011, 821.6 million passengers were transported by air in the 27 EU member states (EU27). Compared to the 2010 numbers, this is an increase of 5.8%. The air traffic in 2011 was composed of three elements:

- Domestic air traffic: more than 167 million passengers, 20% of the total air traffic volume
- Transnational intra-European air traffic: around 350 million passengers, 43% of the total air traffic volume
- Transnational extra-European air traffic: approximately 305 million passengers, 37% of the total air traffic volume

In comparison to the previous year, especially the intra- and extra-European traffic recorded a notable increase (see Fig. 2.6).

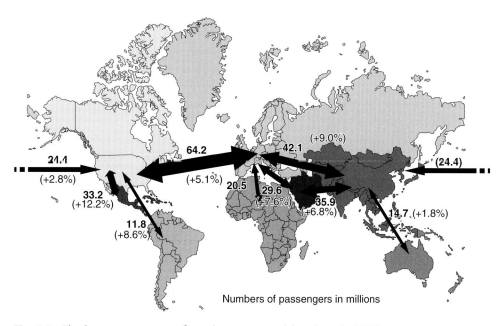

Numbers of passengers in millions

Fig. 2.5. The largest passenger flows between world regions in 2011.

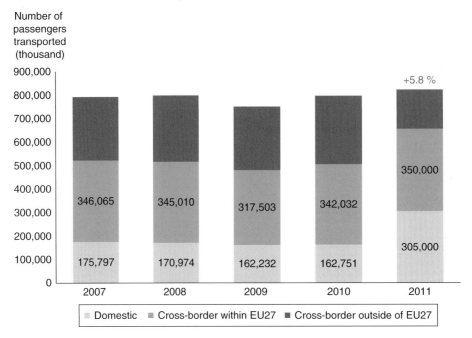

Fig. 2.6. Development of passenger volume in the EU27. Adapted from DLR, 2012.

The country-specific passenger numbers for each of the EU27 show that most countries had an increase and only a few countries experienced a decrease in passengers in 2011 (see Fig. 2.7). The UK had the highest volume with 202 million passengers in 2011, followed by Germany (177 million passengers), Spain (166 million passengers), France (133 million passengers) and Italy (118 million passengers). In general, the Eastern European countries achieved a lower passenger volume than their western neighbours. However, the highest growth rates were recorded predominantly in Eastern Europe: Estonia and Lithuania had growth rates of 37.8% and 15.9%, respectively.[2]

An analysis of the passenger flows reveals that the busiest route in Europe is between the UK and Spain with almost 31.6 million passengers. The flow between Germany and Spain follows with 22 million passengers, which is also Germany's busiest international traffic movement. The traffic between Germany and the UK (11.6 million passengers) constitutes the third largest flow, while the fourth largest traffic flow between Italy and Spain showed a remarkable growth of 11% to 11.8 million passengers in 2011 (DLR, 2012).

North America

In contrast to land-based transport, air traffic is by its nature internationally oriented in most countries, both in passenger and cargo transport. However, the US is an exception to the rule with 90% of its air traffic being domestic.

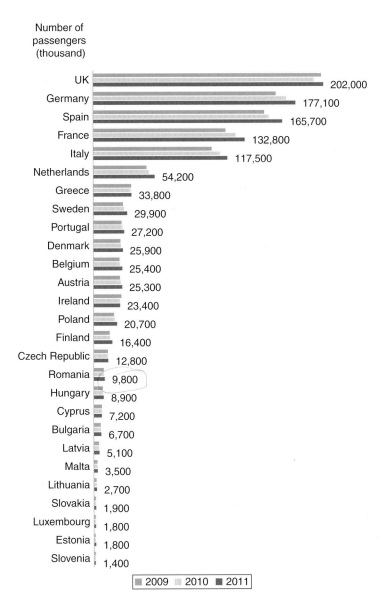

Number of passengers (thousand)

UK	202,000
Germany	177,100
Spain	165,700
France	132,800
Italy	117,500
Netherlands	54,200
Greece	33,800
Sweden	29,900
Portugal	27,200
Denmark	25,900
Belgium	25,400
Austria	25,300
Ireland	23,400
Poland	20,700
Finland	16,400
Czech Republic	12,800
Romania	9,800
Hungary	8,900
Cyprus	7,200
Bulgaria	6,700
Latvia	5,100
Malta	3,500
Lithuania	2,700
Slovakia	1,900
Luxembourg	1,800
Estonia	1,800
Slovenia	1,400

■ 2009 ▨ 2010 ■ 2011

Fig. 2.7. Passenger volumes in the EU27 between 2009 and 2011. Adapted from DLR, 2012.

In 2011, there were around 9.5 million performed aircraft departures[3] in the USA with about 518 million total emplaned passengers, almost 428 million of these at the top 50 airports in the USA. For the top 50 airports, this is a decrease of 14.3% from 2000 and 23.4% from 2010. A similar trend can be observed regarding all US airports, as these numbers also experienced a decrease of around 18% since 2000 and an even larger decrease of 23.5% has been observed since 2010. Among the US airports, Atlanta ranks first with almost 33 million total emplaned passengers in 2011, and it too saw a decrease of 9.2% from 2000 and 22.6% from 2010. By far the largest air transport market is the domestic market of the USA with 639.4 million passengers while Canada ranks ninth with 35.7 million passengers (see Fig. 2.8) (Bureau of Transportation Statistics 2012a, b; DLR, 2012).

When examining the largest worldwide air transport markets, North America is represented three times in the top ten. The route USA–Canada ranks second with 9.4 million passengers per direction. On rank four, the route USA–Mexico is represented with 8.5 million passengers in each direction, followed by USA–UK on rank five (5.9 million passengers per direction). In 2012, North America was still the region with the lowest growth rate, although this growth still represents a significant increase in terms of volume. However, other regions experienced growth in 2012 with the highest growth for international traffic registered in the Middle East, followed by Latin America and the Caribbean. African carriers also experienced a notable growth at 7.4% compared to 1.1% in 2011, making Africa the third fastest growing international market in 2012. The Asia/Pacific region, however, recorded a slower growth rate than in 2011, which is primarily due to lower economic results as well as the poor performance of Malaysian and Indian carriers (ICAO, 2012b).

Overall, the total scheduled passenger traffic grew at a rate of 5.5% (expressed in terms of revenue passenger kilometres, see definition at the end of this chapter) in 2012, which is a decrease of one percentage point compared to the growth rate in 2011. Nevertheless,

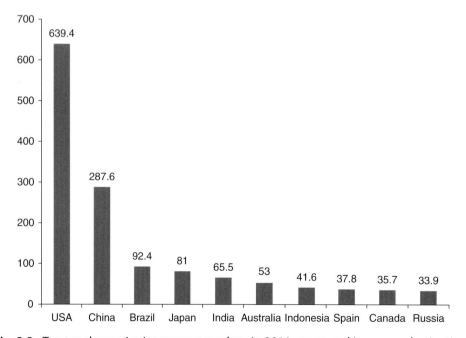

Fig. 2.8. Top ten domestic air transport markets in 2011, measured in source-destination passengers (millions). Adapted from DLR, 2012.

the traffic is expected to reach over 6 billion by 2030, according to ICAO's current projections (ICAO, 2012b).

Supply

The exact number of airlines worldwide is not known as it varies constantly. In 2010, Flight Global lists over 1500 global airlines (with more than 19 seats) and about 200 European airlines. Research conducted at the Harz University in Germany showed that there are at least 1600 globally active airlines. Furthermore, Boeing states that in 2012 there were 20,300 active commercial aircraft, the majority of which are so called single-aisle aircraft, while Airbus assumes a total of about 17,170 aircraft (Airbus, 2012; Boeing, 2013).

As mentioned in the definitions section, there are several different airline business models, which will be highlighted here (as illustrated in Table 2.1, p. 13).

Network carrier

The network carrier (also known as international passage airline, major airline, full-service network carrier, full-service carrier, traditional or established airline or legacy carrier) is the fundamental airline business model and provides a wide range of services. The oldest and most well-known flag carriers of the world such as Air France-KLM, Air New Zealand, American Airlines, British Airways, Lufthansa, United Airlines and Quantas belong to this category. Most of these airlines were founded partly using government funds and some are (at least to some extent) still state-owned airlines today. The following characteristics describe the network carriers (adapted from Maurer, 2006; Pompl, 2007; Cento, 2009; Koch, 2010; Conrady *et al.*, 2013).

- Global player: The network carrier operates in a global market, covering domestic, international and intercontinental markets with short-, medium- and long-haul flights. However, worldwide coverage has not really been achieved by any single airline, hence most network carriers make use of strategic alliances.
- Hub-and-spoke network: The business model is typified by this aircraft deployment method, which routes all traffic (so-called feeder flights) through one or more central hubs and synchronized connections within the hubs to cover as many connections as possible in an effort to make the overall system as efficient as possible.
- Fleet: The fleet is mostly heterogeneous, enabling variations in traffic volume and operating distance.
- Target group: As business travellers are more willing to pay higher prices, they are often more heavily targeted than leisure travellers.
- Product/service offer: Network carriers offer differentiated product and service concepts. Usually, two to three travel classes are offered (economy, business and first class) with varying degrees of pre-flight and onboard services (such as differentiated baggage allowance, lounge access, privileged boarding and dedicated services in business and first class, etc.). Since the

crisis experienced after 11 September 2001, several airlines introduced an alternative class known as premium economy (examples include Air Canada, Air New Zealand, Eva Air, Quantas and SAS).

- Multi-channel distribution: Both indirect (e.g. travel agencies, travel management companies) and direct (e.g. call centres, sales offices, websites) distribution channels are used. The presence in all established global distribution systems is self-evident.

- Frequent flyer programmes: The network carriers offer frequent flyer programmes with the main objective of creating customer loyalty.

- Yield management and pricing: Highly developed yield management systems are currently in use; prices may differ widely based on booking conditions (such as change, cancellation, or reimbursement policies) and can be based on time (booking and departure date), target group or geographical aspects (e.g. origin of sale and itinerary).

Interestingly, the ten largest airlines worldwide consist almost exclusively of US-American and European network carriers, with the exception of Southwest Airlines, which is an LCC. Recently, two Chinese airlines have also made it into the top ten list (see Table 2.2).

Table 2.2. The ten largest airlines worldwide (2012). (From Ishak, 2013.)

Rank	Airline	Country	Passenger traffic (RPK, millions)	Passenger number (millions)	Load factor
1	Delta Air Lines	USA	310,466	164.6	83.7%
2	United Airlines	USA	288,680	93.6	82.9%
3	American Airlines	USA	203,299	86.3	82.8%
4	Emirates	UAE	188,618	39.4	79.7%
5	Southwest Airlines	USA	165,753	134.1	80.3%
6	Lufthansa	Germany	149,780	74.7	78.1%
7	Air France	France	135,824	50.6	81.5%
8	British Airways	UK	126,436	37.6	79.9%
9	China Eastern Airlines	China	109,113	73.1	79.8%
10	China Southern Airlines	China	107,000	64.5	80.8%

Focus box

British Airways

British Airways was founded in 1974 by the British Overseas Airways Corporation (BOAC) and British European Airways (BEA). Today its hubs are in the major London airports (Heathrow, Gatwick and London City). British Airways flies to more than 400 destinations worldwide on a fleet of about 250 wide- and narrow-bodied Airbus and Boeing aircraft (this is including all joint business agreements, code sharing and franchise partners). Since the beginning of 2011 British Airways has been a subsidiary of the International Airlines Group to which the Spanish airlines Iberia and Vueling also belong.

From IAG, 2010; British Airways, 2012a, b; CAPA, 2012a.

Fig. 2.9. British Airways airplane. © Michael Lück.

Leisure carrier

The leisure carrier (also known as charter carrier, tourist carrier or holiday airline) was founded specifically for the transportation of tourists. In the past, seats were not generally sold directly to passengers by the airlines but rather included in package tours offered by tour operators; hence they were mainly referred to as charter airlines. Examples include Air Canada rouge, Condor, Transavia France, Oren Air and TUIfly. The term is misleading today as most flights offered by leisure carriers nowadays operate under the same principles as scheduled flights. The main characteristics of the leisure carrier are as follows (adapted from Maurer, 2006; Koch, 2010; Conrady *et al.*, 2013).

- Heavy dependence on tour operators (sometimes they are themselves part of a travel company such as TUIfly and Thompson Airways, which are part of the TUI group, or Condor and Thomas Cook Airlines, which are part of the Thomas Cook group) as the offer is aimed mainly at leisure travellers.
- Product offer: Most airlines offer only one class (economy) although some airlines offer a two or three class concept.
- Destinations: Mainly tourist destinations on the same continent.
- Routes: Mainly point-to-point with a relatively high seat load factor due to a consistent length of stay (mainly one, two or three week holidays).
- Fleet: Rather homogeneous fleet of predominantly small to medium sized aircraft with 150 to 250 seats (e.g. B737, A320 family).
- Distribution: Currently both via tour operators (as part of package tours) and directly to the end customer (via seat-only sales). Tickets are sold through different channels (e.g. travel agency, call centre, internet).

Focus box

Condor

Condor is the Thomas Cook AG leisure carrier and was founded on 21 December 1955 as the Deutsche Flugdienst GmbH by four partners: Norddeutscher Lloyd (27.75%), Hamburg-Amerika-Linie (27.75%), Deutsche Lufthansa (26%) and Deutsche Bundesbahn (18.5%). Around 1960, the Deutsche Lufthansa AG acquired 100% of the capital and a year later, the Deutsche Flugdienst GmbH absorbed Condor Luftreederei Hamburg changing its name to Condor Flugdienst GmbH. In 2002, the logo 'Thomas Cook powered by Condor appeared on Condor planes, highlighting the connection with Thomas Cook.

Currently, Condor is no longer part of Lufthansa, although still one of the world's leading leisure airlines, operating about 40 Airbus and Boeing aircraft with an annual transportation capacity of more than 6 million passengers. Condor operates a total of 11 departure airports in Germany to service over 70 destinations in Europe, Asia, Africa and America.

From Condor Flugdienst GmbH, 2012a, b.

Low-cost carrier

LCCs, also known as discount or budget airlines, focus on cost-reducing strategies (such as increasing seat density onboard, using smaller airports, or charging extra for food and beverages or baggage) in order to offer lower fares. Examples include easyJet, flydubai, germanwings, jetBlue, Ryanair and Flybe.

After the early pioneers were established, there are generally two further periods which are regarded as important development eras of LCCs: the early-to-mid-1990s in Canada, Europe and Oceania, and the 2000s in Asia, Eastern Europe and the Middle East (see Tabl Most LCC start-ups were launched during these two periods (Morrell, 2008; Cento Gross *et al.*, 2013).

Gross *et al.* (2013) claim that there are currently more than 100 active LCCs worldwide. The pioneer markets North America and Europe register the highest passenger volume, whereas the majority of currently active LCCs operate in Europe and Asia.

According to academic studies, LCCs do not conform to a particular business model although a number of typical characteristics have been identified (adapted from Gross and Schröder, 2007; Pompl, 2007; T2impact/Flight Insight, 2008; Cento, 2009; DLR, 2013; Gross *et al.*, 2013):

Table 2.3. The beginning of deregulation and low-cost developments by region. (From Gross *et al.*, 2013.)

Region or country	Year low-cost operations began (first airline/pioneer)	Implementation of deregulation
USA	1971 (Southwest Airlines)	1978
European Union	1986 (Ryanair)	1986
Australia	1990 (Compass Airlines, withdrew 1991)	1990
New Zealand	1994 (Kiwi Travel International Airlines, withdrew 1996)	1984
Canada	1996 (Westjet)	1996
Japan	1998 (Skymark Airlines)	1998
Malaysia	2001 (AirAsia)	2001
Brazil	2001 (GOL)	1998
South Africa	2001 (Kulula)	1999
EU expansion	2002 (Skyeurope, withdrew 2009)	2004
Gulf states	2003 (Air Arabia)	2003
India	2003 (Air Deccan, withdrew 2008, Jet Konnect)	2003
Thailand	2004 (Nok Air, Thai AirAsia)	2003
Singapore	2004 (Tiger Airways, Value Air)	2001
China	2005 (Spring Airlines)	Ongoing

- Service concept: No complimentary food and beverages on board (some airlines offer free simple drinks), one-class system[4], narrow seating, unreserved seating (or reservation for a fee), no lounge services at airports.
- Ancillary services and revenues: LCCs increasingly have revenue services besides ticket sales, e.g. credit card fees, (excess) luggage charges, in-flight food and beverages, commissions from hotels and car rental companies as well as from selling advertising space.
- Distribution channels: A strong focus on direct distribution, especially via the internet.
- Marketing: Simple branding that combines low costs with high brand value; simple price system and low prices, including very low promotional fares, are the most important marketing messages.
- Human resource management: Work hours at the legal maximum, lower pay for longer work hours with little or no fringe benefits, airline operation with legal minimum of personnel, simplified crew planning due to point-to-point traffic.
- Administration: Lean structures accomplished by outsourcing some departments and practising lean management.
- Strategic flight planning:
  - Point-to-point traffic
  - Use of smaller, less congested secondary or even tertiary airports that are less expensive regarding landing taxes and handling fees.
  - Frequent limitation to short-haul flights or maximum flight times of three to four hours.
  - Faster turnaround time to allow for maximum aircraft utilization.
  - (Usually) no connecting flights, but so-called 'self-hubbing' is increasingly important.
  - As little competition within the low-cost sector as possible, focusing on competition with the network carriers. In Europe, for example, 91% of the flight routes are serviced by a single LCC.
- Fleet: A recent study shows that 68% of the analysed airlines use only one type of aircraft (Gross *et al.* 2013). Another 26% use two and 8% use more than two different aircraft types. Ryanair, for example, only operates B737-800, Volaris only A319, Tiger Airways only A320 and Click Mexicana only Fokker 100. This simplifies flight and staff planning, and maintenance, as well as keeping training and development costs down.

With the help of these characteristics of the LCC business model, the airlines manage to achieve a cost advantage of up to 60% compared to the network carriers. Furthermore, the ancillary revenue is an important aspect for LCCs; it is estimated that the 2012 worldwide additional revenue within the airline industry was about €20.4 billion. More specifically, in 2012 Southwest Airlines had approximately €1.27 billion and Ryanair €1.06 billion in additional revenue (Sorensen, 2013). Fig. 2.10 shows the ancillary revenue and its relation to the profit margin. It can be seen that Air Asia and Allegiant are successful with their heavy focus on ancillary income. Although Ryanair achieves the highest amount in ancillary income in absolute terms, concerning ancillary income and profit margin it only ranks third among the analysed airlines.

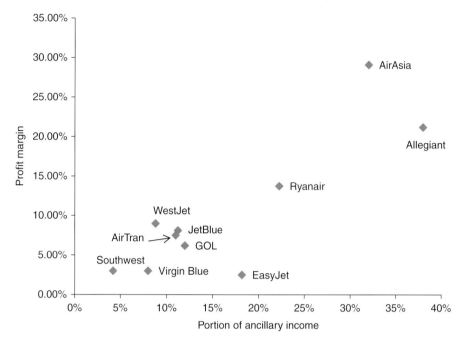

Fig. 2.10. Profit margins and ancillary income of LCCs (2009/10). For the analysis of LCCs in terms of their additional income, the selection criterion was the publication of annual reports for at least the past five years as well as the airline size (revenue, passengers). These figures were based on the publication *Airline Industry Guide 2009/10*. The following airlines have a financial end of year that differs from the calendar end of year: easyJet, September 2009; Ryanair, March 2010; Virgin Blue, June 2010. Adapted from Schröder and Freyer, 2011.

Focus box

Southwest Airlines

Southwest Airlines is the largest LCC not only in the USA, but also worldwide. The airline was founded in Texas and started operations in 1971. In the beginning, operations were limited to intra-state service and it was not until the deregulation of the aviation industry in the US that LCCs were able to operate within the entire country. In 2011 Southwest acquired AirTran Airways. Together both airlines currently serve almost 100 destinations in about 40 states, the District of Columbia, the Commonwealth of Puerto Rico and six close-lying countries. Southwest Airlines operates more than 3000 daily flights, which came to approximately 104 million passengers in 2011, with an average passenger load factor of 81%, which is slightly higher than the average of the IATA association airlines. As of 30 September 2012, Southwest and AirTran operated 692 Boeing jets.

From Southwest Airlines, 2012.

Regional carrier

Regional carriers (also known as commuter or feeder airlines) offer feeder flights between outer locations and the hubs of the network carriers (examples include Air New Zealand Link, Delta Connection and Lufthansa City Line) (Conrady *et al.*, 2013).

Further characteristics include (Koch, 2010; Gross, 2011):

- use of aircraft with a seat capacity between 19 and 120 seats (partially, use of propeller planes)
- use of medium and small airports, although in the case of feeder flights large airports are approached
- product and services targeted at business travellers
- elevated price level due to the target group and higher costs

Of the largest regional carriers worldwide, many are based in the USA/North America; for example, SkyWest, American Eagle Airlines and ExpressJet can be found in the top 100 passenger airlines (Ishak, 2013).

Focus box

SkyWest Airlines

SkyWest Airlines has its headquarters in St George, Utah and was founded in 1972. Since then, SkyWest Airlines has developed into a leading air service provider with a fleet of 323 aircraft and more than 1700 daily flights to over 150 destinations in North America. In 2012, SkyWest Airlines carried more than 26 million passengers and generated more than 14 billion revenue passenger miles. Most of the major US airlines cooperate with SkyWest (for example, American, Delta, United, and US Airways).

From SkyWest Airlines, 2013a, b.

Business aviation/air charters

Business aviation is a subcategory of general aviation and provides services to the business community. The terms business or corporate aviation are sometimes used synonymously although the Federal Aviation Administration does make a definitional distinction between the two: business aviation is defined by its purpose, while corporate aviation is defined as flights by professional pilots who do not own the aircraft they are flying. Business aircraft vary from helicopters and propeller-driven aircraft to turboprops and jets, generally seating anywhere from six to 18 passengers. While there are business jets capable of direct long-haul flights between Hong Kong and Paris or Los Angeles and Geneva, for example, most business aircraft fly average trips of less than 1000 miles (NBAA, 2012).

Perhaps surprisingly, Fortune 500 companies account for only about 3% of US business aviation with the vast majority of flights being attributable to a broad cross-section of organizations (including small to medium business enterprises, government organizations, universities or charities, for example). Furthermore, it is not top executives (approximately 22%) but rather sales and technical staff and middle management employees (approximately 70%) and even customers who account for the majority of business flights (NBAA, 2012).

While there are no large international brands offering such service, there are many regional providers (for example, Air Partner and Pro Sky). The International Business Aviation Council (IBAC) alone has a membership base of more than 7500 companies with 8600 operating aircraft (IBAC, 2013) and typical uses of business charters are illustrated in Fig. 2.11.

One of the advantages of using business aviation is the enormous time-saving potential for the customer. For example, within Europe, business charters are able to utilize over 1000 more airports than the network carriers, including regional and hub airports (GAT – general aviation terminal). Operators use several different types of aircraft, such as single- and twin-engine piston-powered airplanes, helicopters, turboprops or fast jets. This market is more fragmented than the market for large aircraft, which is dominated by the manufacturers Boeing and Airbus. The five largest manufacturers of the business jet market – Bombardier, Cessna, Dassault, Gulfstream and Raytheon – have a combined market share of 98% (HSH Bank, 2005; Wensveen, 2007).

While the classic business aviation model entails the chartering of an entire aircraft, air taxis sell single seats on flights that are operated according to client needs (merely paying for the required seats). However, this business model is currently not widespread.

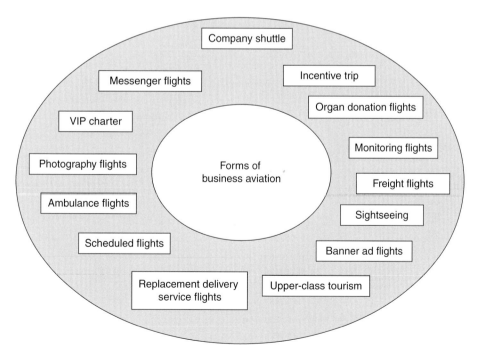

Fig. 2.11. Possible applications for business aviation. Based on Krüger and Reise, 2005.

Strategic alliances

The phenomena of global airline alliances have grown tremendously over the last two decades, with SkyTeam experiencing the fastest rate of expansion of the three major alliances. However, Star Alliance still remains the largest alliance (CAPA, 2012b, c).

Co-operations are common strategic arrangements in the aviation industry in order to achieve competitive advantages through synergistic effects and economies of scale, among other things. Such relationships can be of a horizontal nature (collaboration between companies providing the same product or operating within the same market), vertical nature (collaboration with companies along different stages of the value chain – suppliers, intermediaries, distributors or buyers) or diagonal nature (collaboration with companies from different industries). Horizontal collaborations between airline companies have transformed the competitive environment of the industry, as companies are able to benefit from economies of scale and scope by bypassing regulatory constraints. Vertical alliances include collaborations with other companies from the travel and tourism industry such as car rental firms, travel agents, tour operators or hotels, for example. Handling Agreements or General Sales Agency Agreements are typical vertical co-operations in the aviation industry. Collaborations between airlines and sports clubs (such as Air Berlin and Hertha BSC Berlin), retail companies (such as Emirates and the German discount supermarket chain Lidl) or other service providers (such as US Airways and MasterCard) are examples of diagonal relationships.

Important features of horizontal co-operations are (i) code-share agreements (which allow two airlines to market the same flight under their own codes, thus expanding the route network via flights operated by partner airlines); (ii) industry associations; and (iii) strategic alliances. The latter first appeared in the 1990s as 'deregulated market conditions along with the financial pressure on airlines and the Asian economic crisis in the 1990s saw the emergence of new global alliances' (Robinson *et al.*, 2013, p. 115). According to Doganis (2006) there are four major reasons for the advent of these alliances: marketing benefits of large scale and scope; cost synergies and reductions; the reduction of competition and bypassing regulatory barriers. The collaborative areas of strategic alliances address areas such as acquisition, maintenance, information technology, crew and aircraft sharing, retail and airport facilities, frequent flyer programmes, product standardization, flight planning and marketing activities (e.g. advertisement, common branding) (Wiezorek, 1998; Doganis, 2006).

Nowadays, the three global alliances illustrated in Table 2.4 dominate the aviation industry as they cover more than 50% of the global air transport. In addition, there are other but smaller co-operations, such as XinXing in China or WOW in the cargo sector (founded in April 2000 under the project New Global Cargo by Lufthansa Cargo, Singapore Airlines Cargo and SAS Cargo).

Alliances change continuously due to acquisition of new members, and members leaving the co-operation. Table 2.5 gives an overview of the three global alliances and their members in mid-2013. In the past years, several alliances were also terminated, for instance, Qualifiyer Group, Wings or Atlantic Excellence.

Table 2.4. Strategic alliances (mid-2013). (From OneWorld, 2013; SkyTeam, 2013; Star Alliance, 2013.)

	Star Alliance	One World	Sky Team
Year of formation	1997	1998	2000
Members	28	12	19
Countries	195	157	178
Destinations	1,328	841	1,024
Fleet	4,701	2,437	2,853 (+1,475 of related carriers)
Global share (measured by ASKs, 2011)[a]	25.8%	13.9%	15.6%
Annual passengers	727 million	341 million	569 million
Daily departures	21,900	8,837	> 15,000
Employees	460,238	299,967	452,590

[a] Unaligned carriers have a 27.9% share of available seat kilometres (ASKs) and LCCs 16.8% (CAPA, 2011).

Airline products

Major international aviation groups like the United Airlines Group, the Air France/KLM Group or the Lufthansa Group are large corporations offering a wide variety of products and services. They are also engaged in different business segments to, among other things, be more independent from the cyclical and sensitive airline business and generate additional income. The following example of the Lufthansa Group shows the different products a large aviation corporation can offer (Maurer, 2006):

- passenger transportation
- air cargo transport
- technology, e.g. overhaul of aircraft, maintenance of engines
- (in-flight) catering
- package tours and charter flights
- information technology for the travel and transport market, software for flight planning
- education and training, e.g. training for pilots and flight attendants
- insurance
- investments in the financial and service sectors
- business consulting.

Table 2.5. Global alliance members (mid-2013). (From OneWorld, 2013; SkyTeam, 2013; Star Alliance, 2013.)

Star Alliance	One World	Sky Team
Adria Airways	Air Berlin	Aeroflot
Aegan Airways	American Airlines	Aerolíneas Argentinas
Air Canada	British Airways	Aeroméxico
Air China	Cathay Pacific	Air Europa
Air New Zealand	Finnair	Air France
ANA All Nippon Airways	Iberia	Alitalia
Asiana Airlines	Japan Airlines	China Airlines
Austrian Airlines	LAN	China Eastern
Avianca	Malaysia Airlines	China Southern
Brussels Airlines	Qantas	Czech Airlines
Copa Airlines	Royal Jordanian	Delta Air Lines
Croatia Airlines	S7 Airlines	Kenya Airways
EgyptAir		KLM
Ethiopian Airlines		Korean Air
Eva Air		Middle East Airlines
LOT Polish Airlines		Saudia
Lufthansa		TAROM
SAS Scandinavian Airlines		Vietnam Airlines
Shenzhen Airlines		Xiamen Airlines
Singapore Airlines		
South African Airways		
SWISS		
TAM Linhas Aeras		
TAP Portugal		
Thai Airways International		

(Continued)

Table 2.5. Continued.

Star Alliance	One World	Sky Team
Turkish Airlines		
United Airlines		
US Airways		
Designated members:	Designated members:	Designated members:
No new decisions made (mid-2013)	SriLankan Airlines	Garuda Indonesia
	TAM	

Types of aircraft

Aircraft can be defined in different ways. Table 2.6 illustrates a range of criteria and the resulting classification of aircraft types. As can be seen, aircraft are differentiated by shape of the fuselage into narrow-body (single aisle) and wide-body (twin aisle). Moreover the term macro-body can be used for the newly developed Airbus A380, as it has two aisles and two passenger decks (it is currently the only aircraft with two complete passenger decks) (Gross, 2011).

Performance indicators for airlines

There are a number of important performance indicators that can be calculated for many different reasons. They can be the basis for management decisions and accounting/settlement within the IATA, capture the performance of an airline, be used for comparison with competitors' data (benchmarking) and the determination of weak points and potentials for the increase of productivity. In general, performance indicators can be divided into qualitative and quantitative indicators.

Qualitative indicators can, for example, be obtained by evaluating customer emails or letters concerning the service quality during a flight and calculating the quotient of positive and negative feedback, which will be a measurement parameter for customer satisfaction.

Quantitative indicators account for the output of an airline. These indicators can describe the offered capacity of an airline and the capacity actually sold and paid for. The ratio of these indicators results in the capacity utilization. The most important quantitative performance indicators are presented below (Maurer, 2006; Belobaba, 2009; McKnight, 2010; Gross, 2011).

AVAILABLE SEAT KILOMETRES (ASK). The available seat kilometres represent the offered capacity of an airline in passenger transport. It captures the available offer independently from the number of passengers on board.

ASK = offered seats × distance in kilometres
Example: 350 seats × 7000 km = 2,450,000 ASK

Table 2.6. Classification of aircraft. (Adapted from Maurer, 2006; Nubert, 2010.)

Criterion	Classification
Manufacturer	Boeing, Airbus, Bombardier, Fairchild Dornier, British Aerospace, Embraer SA, Sukhoi Civil Aircraft
Shape/diameter of fuselage	Narrow-body, wide-body, macro-body
Range capability	Short- (up to 1000 km), medium- (up to 5000 km) and long-haul aircraft (up to 13,000 km)[a]
Engine type	Turbofan, turboprop (propjet), jet
Number of engines	Single-, twin-, tri- and quad-engine
Ability to transport cargo	Freighter, combi, Quick Change, standard (cargo is transported in belly)
Airspeed	Subsonic and supersonic aircraft
Maximum take-off weight (MTOW)	A (20 t and more), B (14–20 t), C (5.7–14 t)
Type	Aircraft, rotary-wing aircraft, power gliders, airships, gliders, balloons

[a] This classification is one possibility, other authors may use different distances.

REVENUE PASSENGER KILOMETRES (RPK). This performance indicator describes the number of seats sold multiplied by the distance.

RPK = number of passengers transported × distance in kilometres
Example: 200 passengers × 7000 km = 1,400,000 RPK

PASSENGER LOAD FACTOR (PLF). The passenger load factor calculates the ratio of the revenue passenger kilometres and the available seat kilometres in percent. It is an important indicator for capacity utilization and often used to examine development in different markets, e.g. certain routes, regions or continents. One option to calculate the load factor would be:

PLF = (RPK / ASK) x 100
Example: (1,400,000 RPK / 2,450,000 PLF) × 100 = 57.14%

Another option would be to divide the total number of flown passengers by the actual seat capacity.

This chapter has given you an overview of the airline industry; however, as it is an extremely wide field we will also provide further material at this point (as in all further chapters) for those seeking a deeper understanding of the material.

NOTES

1. Apart from the Open Skies Agreement between the USA and Europe, similar agreements exist between other countries; for example, between the USA and Australia, the USA and Switzerland, the USA and Japan, Australia and Japan, New Zealand and Australia as well as the Multilateral Agreement on the Liberalization of International Air Transportation between New Zealand and Brunei Darussalam, Chile, Cook Islands, Mongolia, Samoa, Singapore, Tonga and the USA (Flightglobal, 2011; New Zealand Ministry of Transport, 2012/2013; US General Services Administration, 2013).

2. The difference in the data between Figs 2.5 and 2.6 is due to the specific use of the variable 'passengers transported'. Boarding and deboarding passengers are counted within each country-specific analysis. However, within a regional analysis passengers are only counted once, so that a passenger flying from Germany to the UK only appears once in the EU regional analysis, but twice in the country-specific analyses. Therefore, the country specific numbers from Fig. 2.10 cannot simply be summed and compared with Fig. 2.9 (personal contact via email on 9 September 2011 between Prof. Dr Sven Gross and Michael Hepting, DLR Air Transport and Airport Research, Cologne, Germany).

3. Total performed includes scheduled departures performed, minus those scheduled departures that did not occur, plus unscheduled service.

4. 79% of LCCs offer only one cabin class (economy class), while 21% include a premium cabin (premium economy or business class). 38% of the all-economy carriers offer only one fare, 23% two, 26% three and 13% offer four or more different fares (Gross *et al.*, 2013).

FURTHER READING

Belobaba, P., Odoni, A. and Barnhart, C. (2009) *The Global Airline Industry*. John Wiley & Sons, Chichester, UK.

Butler, G.F. and Keller, M.R. (2001) *Handbook of Airline Strategy, Public Policy, Regulatory Issues, Challenges, and Solutions*. McGraw-Hill, New York.

Conrady, R., Fichert, F. and Sterzenbach, R. (2013) *Luftverkehr – Betriebswirtschaftliches Lehr- und Handbuch*, 5th edn. Oldenbourg, Munich, Germany.

Doganis, R. (2006) *The Airline Business in the 21st Century*, 2nd edn. Routledge, London, UK.

Doganis, R. (2010) *Flying Off Course*, 4th edn. Routledge, London, UK.

Gössling, S. and Upham, P. (2009) *Climate Change and Aviation. Issues, Challenges, and Solutions*. Earthscan, London, UK.

Graham, A., Papatheodorou, A. and Forsyth, P. (2010) *Aviation and Tourism – Implications for Leisure Travel*. Ashgate Publishing, Aldershot, UK.

Gross, S. (2011) *Tourismus und Verkehr – Grundlagen, Marktanalyse und Strategien von Verkehrsunternehmen*, Oldenbourg, Munich, Germany.

Gross, S. and Lück, M. (2013) *The Low Cost Carrier Worldwide*. Ashgate Publishing, Aldershot, UK.

Gross, S. and Schröder, A. (2007) *Handbook of Low Cost Airlines – Strategies, Business Processes and Market Environment*. Erich Schmidt Verlag, Berlin, Germany.

Lawton, T.C. (2007) *Strategic Management in Aviation – Critical Essays*. Ashgate Publishing, Aldershot, UK.

Shaw, S. (2011) *Airline Marketing and Management*, 7th edn. Ashgate Publishing, Aldershot, UK.

Wald, A., Fay, C. and Gleich, R. (2010) *Introduction to Aviation Management*. LIT-Verlag, Berlin, Germany.

Wells, A.T. and Young, S.B. (2004) *Airport Planning & Management*, 2nd edn. McGraw-Hill, New York.

Wensveen, J.G. (2011) *Air Transportation – A Management Perspective*, 7th edn. Aldershot, UK.

Wittmer, A., Bieger, T. and Müller, R. (2011) *Aviation Systems*. Springer-Verlag, Berlin, Germany.

Trade journals/magazines and scientific organizations

Airline Business, Air Transport World, Journal of Airline and Airport Management, Journal of Air Transport Management, Journal of Airport Management, Journal of Revenue and Pricing Management, International Journal of Aviation Management, Low Cost & Regional Airline Business, Transportation Research, Research in Transportation Business and Management, Air Transport Research Society (www.atrsworld.org), German Aviation Research Society (www.garsonline.de).

Internet sources

www.aerlines.nl, www.destatis.de, www.dlr.de, www.adv.aero, www.aci-europe.co, www.airbus.com, www.airports.org, www.airtransportpubs.com, www.ashgate.com (Aviation), www.bitre.gov.au, www.boeing.com, www.bombardier.com, www.caa.co.uk, http://centreforaviation.com, www.embraer.com, www.eurocontrol.int, http://www.europa.eu.int/co/eurostat, www.faa.gov/data_research/aviation_data_statistics, www.flightglobal.com, www.iata.co, www.icao.co, www.med.govt.nz/sectors-industries/tourism/tourism-research-data, www.nbaa.org, www.skytraxresearch.com.

chapter 3

Speciality Air Transportation

LEARNING OBJECTIVES

- Appreciate the vast variety of different forms and experiences of passenger air transportation.
- Identify and describe the types, their history and the significant applications for tourism.

Although the focus of this book is on tourism and different forms of transportation, tourism is classified as a form of recreation and leisure. Hence, although not strictly a viable form of commercial transportation, we have included a small section covering some diverse and interesting options available to tourists.

BALLOONING

Ballooning can be traced back to the 18th century when the brothers Joseph and Etienne Montgolfier concluded that hot air was lighter than air at normal temperature after watching smoke rising up in the air from a fire. A small paper bag filled with hot air and smoke rising to the ceiling inspired the invention of hot-air balloons. Based on their findings, the Montgolfier brothers 'constructed a balloon of linen-lined paper with a circumference of 100 feet and released it on June 5, 1783' (Seth, 2006, p. 44). The balloon covered a distance of two miles, rising up to 6000 feet, and remained in the air for eight minutes. Thousands of spectators filled the grounds in Annonay, France to see the first air travellers, a sheep, a rooster and a duck, which returned safely (Gillispie, 1983; Seth, 2006; Bensaude-Vincent and Blondel, 2008).

The next balloon ride would carry human passengers during a flying event that took place in Paris in November 1783. Half a million visitors, including the King and Queen of France, witnessed

Pilâtre de Rosier and the Marquis of Arlandes fly over Paris; the flight lasted about 25 minutes and the balloon attained a height of 3000 feet (Marion, 2010). Around the same time, hydrogen was discovered and it did not take long before the Frenchman Cesar Charles flew in a hydrogen-filled balloon. Several attempts at flying different kinds of balloons followed in Europe and the USA, some of which unfortunately ended with fatalities. It is controversial whether the flight in 1783 was in fact the first manned balloon flight, as some claim that a manned balloon made of ox hide took off from the Russian city Ryazan in 1731 (as cited by Gross, 2011). However, the pilots were becoming bolder as Jean Pierri Blanchard and an American physician, Dr Jeffries, attempted to across the English Channel on 7 January 1785. Unfortunately the crossing could not be completed as the balloon started sinking halfway across the channel (Seth, 2006). Almost 100 years later in 1873, the American John Wise tried to actualize his dream of crossing the Atlantic to Europe in a balloon. Even though his attempt failed, Wise 'achieved the distinction of being the first man to fly a distance of 1,130 kilometres at one stretch' (Singh, 2010, p. 110).

However, it was not until the 1950s that ballooning experienced a revival when 'the US Navy contracted with the General Mills Company to develop a small hot air balloon for military purposes. The Navy never used the balloon, but the project created the basis for the modern hot air balloon' (US Department of Transportation, 2001, p. 1-1).

As can be seen in Table 3.1, balloons may be classified into several categories. Nowadays, balloon (gas or hot-air) rides are mainly offered as a leisure activity by specialized companies, intermediaries (such as mydays and Smartbox) or sports clubs. There are many different product offerings, ranging in purpose, duration and even themes. A balloon ride is often viewed as a special event, and is a popular form of present or prize. Companies, for example, may charter a balloon as a form of employee incentive prize. Balloons come in all different shapes and sizes, accommodating as many as 27 people in the basket (Ultramagic, 2013). Ballooning takes place almost all year round, with balloons primarily ascending shortly after sunrise or a few hours before sunset, providing customers rather unique experiences. Events such as the World Hot Air Balloon Championships, the Gordon Bennet Cup and various national balloon festivals attract large numbers of visitors. The history and development of balloons is also addressed in several museums, such as the Balloon Museum Gersthofen in Germany, the British Balloon Museum and Library in Berkshire or the Albuquerque Balloon Museum in New Mexico. Figure 3.1 shows the decreasing number of listed balloons in Germany.

AIRSHIPS

Hot-air balloons led to the development of airships in the 1870s. The German engineer Paul Haenlein constructed the first airship with an internal combustion engine in 1872 (Moedebeck, 2012). Air navigation started to become very popular and numerous constructions of airships with different steering mechanisms followed, peaking in summer 1900 when the German Ferdinand von Zeppelin flew his airship at approximately 20 miles an hour. His flying machine, simply called

Table 3.1. Classification of balloons. (Adapted from US Department of Transportation, 2001; Croucher, 2004; Seidel and Free, 2005; Deilbach and Stump, 2009; Ninomiya, 2010; Martínez, 2013.)

Type	Description
Gas balloon	<ul><li>inflated with a gas less dense than air or lighter than air</li><li>balloon is in a state of buoyant equilibrium at no altitude</li><li>direction and speed of the balloon determined by movement of air masses or wind</li><li>ascent and descent of the balloon only controlled by jettisoning ballast or by opening the valve and releasing gas</li></ul>
Hot-air balloon (Montgolfière)	<ul><li>uses heat to create a temperature differential between the atmospheric gas inside the balloon and the air outside</li><li>to ascend, propane gas is released into the envelope, which fires the burner and increases the temperature of the gas inside the balloon</li><li>descent can be controlled or reversed by releasing gas through opening the parachute valve</li></ul>
Rozière balloon	<ul><li>a double balloon system containing one gas balloon and one Montgolfière</li><li>with separate chambers for a non-heated lifting gas as well as a heated lifting gas that allow some control of buoyancy with much less use of fuel than a typical hot-air balloon</li></ul>
Solar balloon	<ul><li>gains buoyancy by heating the air inside by the sun's radiation, usually with the help of black or dark balloon fabric</li><li>the heated air inside the solar balloon expands and has lower density than the surrounding air</li></ul>
Moored balloon	<ul><li>often shaped like an airship, usually filled with helium</li><li>an inflated fabric structure, which is restrained by a cable attached to the ground or a vehicle</li><li>not free-flying</li></ul>
Super-pressure balloon	<ul><li>made of non-extensible fabric</li><li>designed to float stably with an internal pressure greater than that of the ambient atmosphere</li><li>gas inside expands and its temperature increases with the solar heating during the day</li><li>temperature and pressure drop at sundown</li><li>used for unmanned scientific experiments in the upper atmosphere</li></ul>
Cluster balloon	<ul><li>a harness attaches a balloonist to a cluster of helium-inflated rubber balloons – multiple, small, readily available and individually sealed balloons</li><li>jettisoning or deflating balloons allows the balloonist to control flight, arrest a climb or initiate a descent</li></ul>

Zeppelin, turned into a means of transportation as well as an instrument of warfare during the First World War by the Germans. In 1919, the British succeeded in crossing the Atlantic from London to New York and back with their airship P-34 (De Syon, 2002). Later, in the 1920s and 1930s, airships were refurbished in order to improve passenger transportation: sleeper-cabs, lavatories, kitchens, dining rooms and other facilities were built to accommodate up to 50 passengers (Knäusel, 2002). There are three types of airship, which are distinguished in Table 3.2.

Due to the expensive nature of airship transportation, it has not proven to be a very popular form of tourist attraction and tends to be rather exceptional. For example, a ride in an airship lasting up to 120 minutes costs about €765 per person (Zeppelin Luftschifftechnik GmbH & Co KG, 2013). Hence, although the company Zeppelin Europe Tours undertook a five-day

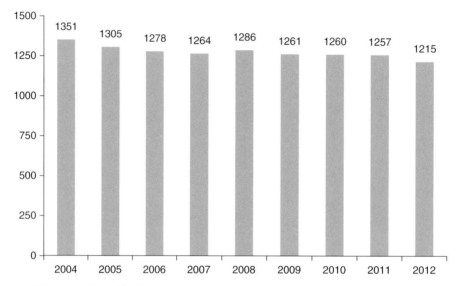

Fig. 3.1. Number of listed balloons in Germany (2004–2012). From Luftfahrt-Bundesamt, 2013.

Table 3.2. Types of airship. (Adapted from Becker and Höfling, 2000; Müller, 2005.)

Type	Description
Non-rigid airship (also called blimp)	• without an internal supporting framework or a keel • relies on a higher pressure of the lifting gas inside the envelope and the strength of the envelope itself
Rigid airship	• the envelope retains its shape by the use of an internal structural framework
Semi-rigid airship	• with a partial framework • often consists of a rigid or occasionally a flexible keel frame along the long axis under the aerodynamic hull envelope

trip between the UK and the Netherlands in a Zeppelin in 2008, there does not seem to be a great demand, as no further such trips seem to have taken place.

Similarly to hot-air ballooning, airship flights tend to be rather an exceptional experience and are even more exclusive and rare. Knorr suggests that passengers are for the most part retirees who either can afford such a trip or whose children have given it to them for their anniversary (personal contact via email on 24 June 2010 between Prof. Dr Sven Gross and Dorit Knorr, Assistant Marketing & PR at Deutsche Zeppelin-Reederei GmbH, Friedrichshafen, Germany). However, tourists are attracted to airship museums such as the Zeppelin Museum Friedrichshafen in Germany, the Spitsbergen Airship Museum in Norway or the Zeppelin Museum in Denmark. The German city of Friedrichshafen was the home town of Count Zeppelin and even offers a themed route and a visit to the Zeppelin shipyard. Figure 3.2 illustrates a blimp, which is the most common form of airship usage today.

Table 3.3 presents most of the airship manufacturers worldwide. The company Deutsche Zeppelin Reederei GmbH is one of the biggest suppliers and records around 12,000 passengers per year (Schultz-Friese, 2011).

In order to raise awareness regarding airships, the Airship Association was formed in 1971 and currently supports research and publications related to airships (Airship Association, 2012).

HELICOPTERS

A helicopter is a type of rotorcraft that derives its lift and thrust from rotors (Leishman, 2006). Interestingly, Leonardo Da Vinci designed a machine on paper with a rotor or *aerial screw*

Fig. 3.2. Blimp used for promotion.

Table 3.3. A selection of airship manufacturers and operators worldwide. (Based on company homepages and personal communications.)

Company	Location	Founding year	Type of airship	Quantity
Manufacturers				
21st Century Airships Team Inc.	Ontario, Canada	1988	n/a	14
GEFA-Flug GmbH	Aachen, Germany	1975	Hot-air airship	66
Augur RosAeroSystems	Moskua, Russland	1991	Blimp/ hot-air airship	n/a
Skyship Services, Inc. (formerly Airship Management Services Inc.)	Orlando, USA	1990	Blimp	1 currently operating (10 built)
The Goodyear Tire & Rubber Co	Ohio, USA	1898	Blimp	300[a]
US-LTA Corporation	Oregon, USA	1988	Blimp	n/a
Van Wagner Airship Group: founded through acquisitions of The Lightship Group (TLG) and the American Blimp Corporation (ABC)	Severna Park, USA	1987	Blimp	25
WDL Luftschiffgesellschaft mbH	Mühlheim, Germany	1972	Blimp	8 (2 rebuilt, 6 new built)
Worldwide AEROS Corporation	Montebello, USA	1987	Hybrid airship	n/a
ZLT Zeppelin Luftschifftechnik GmbH & Co KG	Friedrichshafen, Germany	1993	Zeppelin NT	5 (until 2017: 8)
Operators (a selection)				
Deutsche Zeppelin-Reederei GmbH	Friedrichshafen, Germany	2001	Zeppelin NT	2
Pestalozzi Luftschiff & Umwelt AG (2013 no flight operations)	Kloten, Switzerland	1989	Zeppelin	n/a

(Continued)

Table 3.3. Continued.

Company	Location	Founding year	Type of airship	Quantity
WDL Luftschiffgesellschaft mbH	Mühlheim, Germany	1972	Blimp	1
Charterer				
Airshipvision International SA	Paris, France	2003		
Announced or discontinued projects		**Former operators**		
SkyCat by World SkyCat Ltd	Sanswire Stratellite of Sanswire Networks	Skyship Cruise Ltd	Airship Ventures	
LEMV (Long Endurance Multi-Intelligence Vehicle) of Northrop Grumman for the US Army	DARPA-Project WAIRUS (Coproduction of AEROS and ABC)	Nippon Airship Corporation		
Blue Devil II Airship (BD2) project of the US Air Force	SkyHook JHL-40 of Boeing			

[a]The exact number of blimps ever built cannot be indicated. According to Haren (personal contact via email on 18 June 2010 between Prof. Dr Sven Gross and Jared Haren, Project Leader/LTA Systems Specialist at Goodyear Airship Operations, Mogadore, USA): 'The number of 308 airships represents all the airships that we built for the US Army/Navy and commercial use new or considered new. The question of how many airships has Goodyear "ever" built would be different. Our present envelope serial number D-655 is the 655th envelope since Vaniman's "Akron" of 1912. An envelope does not constitute a complete airship but they were used for a complete airship. For example, Goodyear built components, erected by the US Navy under Goodyear supervision. So in that realm the number changes to approximately 600 airships, for certain envelope numbers were not used or cancelled which is about 50+.'

in the 1480s (Pilotfriend, 2013). However, it was not until the 20th century that the actual development of helicopters finally succeeded. Airworthiness and controllability were paramount for the invention of the aircraft in the 1940s. Currently, we can distinguish between three types of helicopter:

- single rotor helicopter: one main and rear rotor
- helicopter with coaxial rotors: two main rotors counter-rotating, one upon the other
- helicopter with a tandem rotor: two tandem main rotors counter-rotating

There is a wide range of helicopter use in the tourism industry, including taxi services as part of a special event (such as weddings), or even for flight experiences in which the tourist can take over supervised control of the helicopter. However, helicopter sightseeing flights are by far the most popular form of tourist attractions regarding helicopters. Another aspect for which helicopters are used in tourism is for rescuing tourists in emergency situations, particularly in the mountains. Recently, a new and popular tourism product is heli-skiing, which involves taking tourists to a ski site by helicopter in order to reach trails which are not otherwise accessible. For example, the Canadian company Alpine Helicopters Inc. offers sightseeing flights in and around Banff National Park as well as heli-skiing flights (Alpine Helicopters Inc., 2013). Other popular destinations for heli-skiing include Austria, Slovenia, Italy, Switzerland and the Baltic States. However, in Germany and France this sport is prohibited (Gross, 2011).

An alternative to the real experience is a virtual 3D helicopter journey over selected destinations. AirPano, for instance, offers high resolution 3D aerial panoramas on their website. The visitor navigates the helicopter and can choose direction and locations. Manhattan, Hollywood, Iceland, Santorini in Greece, Paris or the Vatican City State, for example, are destinations that can be virtually visited (AirPano, 2013).

GLIDING

When it comes to aerial adventures, gliding is probably the most exciting, and includes sailplanes, motor gliders, seaplanes, microlights, paragliders, hang-gliders and gyroplanes. Pilots must have a licence for the operation of one of these aircraft and in most cases authorization for landing either on airfields or waterbodies is required (Gross, 2011). The sport of gliding is generally considered a recreational activity and is not generally viewed as a form of passenger transportation. Table 3.4 gives a description of the various types of gliding.

The tourism industry provides gliding activities either through providers based at the landing places, through tour operators or intermediaries such as Buyagift in the UK or Experience Gifts in the Netherlands, which offer vouchers. The Canadian tour operator, G Adventures, for instance offers gliding activities combined with accommodation and transportation (G Adventures, 2013). As gliding is rather a recreational activity, there is no data available on its demand in the tourism industry. However, in Germany there were about 200,370 participants in gliding activities in 2012 (Statistisches Bundesamt, 2013).

SPACE TRANSPORTATION

Space tourism not only includes flights into space, but also terrestrial and virtual space tourism as Fig. 3.3 illustrates.

The hype for orbital space tourism began in 2001 with Dennis Tito, the first official space tourist. As a crew member of the ISS EP-1, Tito spent nearly eight days in orbit during a visiting

Table 3.4. Different types of gliding vehicle. (Adapted from Whittall, 2002; JAA, 2004; FAA, 2006; Hughes and Lavery, 2008; FAI, 2012; BUGC, 2013.)

Type	Description
Sailplane	• aeroplane with very long wings and no engine • covers long distances due to its long wingspan and slick design
Motor glider	• fixed-wing aerodyne • equipped with a means of propulsion • capable of sustained soaring flight without thrust from the means of propulsion
Seaplane	• powered fixed-wing aircraft • capable of taking off and landing on water
Microlight	• aeroplane having no more than two seats • maximum weight for a two seat landplane: 450 kg • speed limit of 35 knots (65 km/h)
Paraglider	• lightweight, free-flying, foot-launched glider aircraft with no rigid primary structure • consists of a large parafoil • easily portable
Hang-glider	• lightweight and non-motorized foot-launch aircraft • delta-wing design with an airfoil suspended across a rigid tubing system
Gyroplane	• aircraft with a freely turning rotary wing or rotor blades • derives its thrust from an engine-driven propeller

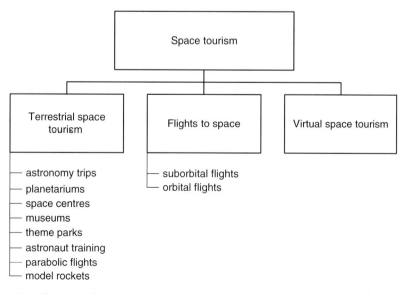

Fig. 3.3. Classification of space tourism. Adapted from Freyer and Gross, 2005.

mission to the International Space Station (Randolph, 2003). However, Tito was not the first space visitor, as the Saudi Arabian sultan Salman bin Abdulaziz al Saud flew aboard the STS-51-G in 1985, followed by the Japanese journalist Toyohiro Akiyama in 1990 who gave a live report from the Russian space station MIR, and the Briton Helen Sharman who funded her own trip to visit the MIR station in 1991 (Collins, 1992; Born, 2001; Crouch, 2001). There have been six more tourists to the ISS since Dennis Tito's flight: Mark Shuttleworth (2002), Greg Olsen (2005), Anousheh Ansaria (2006), Charles Simony (2007 and 2009), Guy Laliberte (2009) and Richard Garriott (2008) (SpaceAdventures, 2013a). In October 2012, the singer Sarah Brightman announced her intention to fly to space and is considered to be the next spaceflight client although her flight date has not yet been confirmed (SpaceAdventures, 2013b).

All seven space tourists to date have flown on the Russian Soyuz spacecraft, a government-owned vehicle, to the International Space Station (Jakhu *et al.*, 2011). To reduce the use of government-owned vehicles, the space exploration company Space Adventures has recently entered an agreement with Boeing to market seats on their new spacecraft, the CST-100, which is expected to be operational in 2016/7 (Space Adventures, 2013c). The International Institute of Space Commerce (2011) identified price elasticity in a price range of $5–20 million per flight and assesses the potential market for the period 2012–2022 (IISC, 2011).

Besides the orbital space flights, suborbital flights are also available. The main difference is that vehicles for suborbital flights attain a height of about 62 miles above sea level (orbital flights reach a height between 155 and 250 miles) from where tourists have a panoramic view of both space and the Earth. Due to the force of gravity, the aircraft returns back to the ground after a short time without actually orbiting the Earth (Crouch, 2001). In 2004, the first private manned rocket aircraft *SpaceShipOne* was built by the company Scaled Composites and won the Ansari X Prize and 10 million US dollars. It completed two suborbital flights within two weeks (Scaled Composites, 2004). According to the Federal Aviation Administration (2010) private companies such as Virgin Galactic, XCOR, Armadillo Aerospace, Blue Origin and Masten Space Systems are now taking more interest in suborbital spaceflight, due in part to ventures like the Ansari X Prize. Manned suborbital flights started in 2012 and can now be booked through Virgin Galactic and XCOR (Virgin Galactic, 2013; XCOR, 2013). An XCOR suborbital flight ticket costs about $95,000, including medical screening and G-force training (XCOR, 2013). In contrast, Virgin Galatic's starting price is at $200,000 (Virgin Galactic, 2013). The existence of spacelines brought along the development of spaceports, where space flights take off. Spaceport America was the first spaceport in the world built from the ground up, opened on 17 October 2011 and is home to the commercial passenger spaceline company Virgin Galactic (Spaceport America, 2012).

Various studies in the 1990s revealed that 70% of the Japanese, 61% of the North Americans, 43% of the Germans and approximately 35% of the British are interested in a space journey (Crouch, 2001). Crouch surveyed the literature and found that the global space tourism market is a strong function of price. Goehlich (2007) found that tourists are willing to pay more for an orbital flight than for a suborbital flight. Therefore, it can be expected that an orbital flight costing $100,000 would generate 100,000 passengers a year whereas a suborbital flight of the same price would generate only 20,000 passengers a year.

According to Futron Corporation (2002), the demand for space flights will account for approximately 15,000 suborbital and 60 orbital passengers a year. Even though the prognosis assumed that suborbital flights would already be offered in 2006 (which was not the case), the data give an overview of the potential demand for space flights (see Fig. 3.4).

As Fig. 3.3 illustrates, terrestrial space tourism is another form of enjoying space and offers much variety, including all trips of the category commercial space flight. Launches of the US space shuttle programme drew enormous crowds to the Florida launch site in Cape Canaveral. Also, several tour operators offer tours to locations around the world where solar eclipses can be experienced. Finally, terrestrial space tourism also incorporates space camps, theme parks and visits to planetariums and observatories (Gross, 2011).

Virtual space tourism 'utilizes the latest technology to give tourists the sense of visiting space without leaving the comfort of their armchairs' (Singh, 2004, p. 12). Although it still seems far-fetched at this point in time, besides watching a journey to the moon via webcam on the internet, technology in virtual space tourism extends to the possible development of chips by the US company Sun Microsystems that may be implanted in the neck of a person to generate virtual landscapes and scenes in the person's brain (Freyer, 2000; Born, 2001).

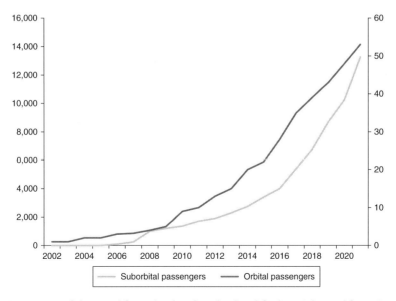

Fig. 3.4. Prognosis of demand for suborbital and orbital flights. Adapted from Futron Corporation, 2002, p. 3.

FURTHER READING

Barret, O. (1999) *An Evaluation of the Potential Demand for Space Tourism within the United Kingdom*. Bournemouth University, Dorset, UK.

Crouch, G. (2001) The market for space tourism. Early indications. *Journal of Travel Research* 40, 213–219.

Dick, H.G. and Robinson, D.H. (1992) *The Golden Age of the Great Passenger Airships: Graf Zeppelin and Hindenburg*. Smithsonian Books, Washington DC.

Duval, D. (2005) Space tourism. In: Novelli, M. (ed.) *Niche Tourism. Contemporary issues, trends and cases*. Elsevier, Burlington, Vermont, pp. 213–222.

Freyer, W. and Gross, S. (2005) Weltraumtourismus – Status quo und Zukunft der Entwicklung. *Wissenschaftliche Zeitschrift der TU Dresden* 01–02, 32–38.

Futron Corporation (2002). *Space Tourism Market Study* – orbital space travel and destinations with suborbital space travel. Available at: http://www1.futron.com/pdf/resource_center/white_papers/SpaceTourismMarketStudy.pdf

Goehlich, R.A. (2007) Space tourism. In: Conrady, R. and Buck, M. (eds) *Trends and Issues in Global Tourism 2007*. Springer-Verlag, Berlin, Germany, pp. 213–226.

Gross, S. (2011) *Tourismus und Verkehr – Grundlagen, Marktanalyse und Strategien von Verkehrsunternehmen*. Oldenbourg, Munich, Germany.

Knäusel, H.G. (2002) *Zeppelin – Die Geschichte der Zeppelin-Luftschiffe. Konstrukteure – Technik – Unternehmen*, 2nd edn. AVIATIC Verlag, Oberhaching, Germany.

Lappas, V. (2006) Space tourism. In: Buhalis, D. and Costa, C. (eds.) *Tourism Business Frontiers – Consumers, Products and Industry*. Elsevier, Oxford, UK, pp. 157–167.

Williamson, M. (2003) Space ethics and protection of the space environment. In: *Space Policy* 19, 47–52.

Wirth, D. and Young, J. (1980) *Ballooning – The Complete Guide to Riding the Winds*. Random House, London, UK.

Internet sources

http://astronaut.com, http://spaceshiptourist.com, http://spacetourismsociety.org, http://www.airships.net, http://www.bfa.net, http://www.fai.org/ballooning, http://www.interaeroleague.com, http://www.spacefuture.com, http://www.spacetransportation.org, http://www.raumfahrer.net, http://www.thespaceshipcompany.com, http://www.virgingalactic.com, www.zeppelinflug.de.

Part 2

Ground Transportation

Ground transportation accounts for an extremely large percentage of overall tourism movements. This part will highlight automobiles, buses and motor coaches, trains and a few speciality means of ground transportation.

chapter 4

Automobiles

LEARNING OBJECTIVES

- Identify, define and describe the passenger car as a product and understand its origins and different forms of usage.
- Assess the current state of the rental car industry in regards to tourism and its regulation.
- Analyse the demand and supply sides of the rental car industry, in order to understand the overall market.

DEFINITIONS

Automobiles are normally four-wheeled vehicles used for passenger transportation. Therefore, passenger cars, taxis and rental cars will be defined below.

Passenger cars

The European Commission's Directorate-General for Transport and Mobility (2012) defines a passenger car as a 'road motor vehicle for the carriage of passengers and comprising not more than eight seats in addition to the driver's seat.' Furthermore, the *Glossary of Transport Statistics* (2009), developed by the International Transport Forum (ITF), Eurostat and the United Nations Economic Commission for Europe (UNECE) points out, 'a passenger car includes microcars (needing no permit to be driven), taxis and passenger hire cars, provided that they have fewer than ten seats' (p. 47). This category may also include vans designed and used primarily for transport of passengers, as well as ambulances and motor homes. Excluded are light goods road vehicles, as well as motor coaches or buses and mini-buses/mini-coaches.

© S. Gross and L. Klemmer 2014. *Introduction to Tourism Transport* (S. Gross and L. Klemmer)

59

Taxis

According to the *Glossary of Transport Statistics* (2009, p. 47), a taxi is a 'licensed passenger car for hire with driver without predetermined routes' (Fig. 4.1). Its method of hire comprises flagging down on the street, picking up at a designated taxi rank or telephoning for collection.

Rental cars

Rental cars are available for temporary hire from companies that may rent automobiles, vans and trucks for a fee. The rental period ranges from a few hours to a few weeks. Usually, the business is organized around a network of numerous locations situated near airports or busy city areas. This form of organization allows the user to return a vehicle to a different location (Martinez, 2008).

Forms of passenger car usage

Various forms of passenger car usage have been developed over the last few years, where a differentiation can be made between three main categories, car sharing, car pooling and car leasing (Gross, 2011; Roseland, 2012):

Car sharing

According to the European business research and consulting firm Frost & Sullivan (2010) car sharing is:

> A mode of transport where vehicles are owned by a separate firm or an organisation and shared between a number of different people at different times. Carsharing can also be considered as an organised short-term rental car where users access a firm's vehicles that are maintained in a nearby network of vehicle locations called *Pods*.
>
> (Frost & Sullivan, 2010)

Fig. 4.1. NYC Taxi. © Elke Handke / pixelio.de. Available at: http://www.pixelio.de/media/446109 (accessed 14 February 2013).

A closer look at various definitions found in the literature uncovers that most published work provides a description of car sharing rather than a formal definition. The following features are shared by most of them:

- an organized group of participants
- a required membership
- one or more shared vehicles
- a decentralized network of parking locations (pods)
- self-accessing vehicles
- usage booked in advance
- rentals for short time periods

The Transit Cooperative Research Program (2005) sponsored by the Federal Transit Administration (part of the US Department of Transportation) recommends the following definition by the State of Washington as a standard, common definition for car sharing as it provides the most concise, effective way to address all the points mentioned above: 'A membership program intended to offer an alternative to car ownership under which persons or entities that become members are permitted to use vehicles from a fleet on an hourly basis'.

Car sharing has become fairly popular over the last few years and there are a variety of different models available which include free-floating systems such as car2go or Mu by Peugeot.

Car pooling

Car pooling describes an arrangement whereby several participants travel together in one vehicle, sharing the costs and often taking turns as the driver (Gross, 2011). A distinction can be drawn between formal and informal car pooling. Formal car pooling is the regular commute of two or more passengers in one vehicle, whereas informal pooling refers to mostly spontaneous offerings of an occasional ride to another person. In Europe, informal car pooling is organized via car pooling centres (known as *Mitfahrzentrale* in Germany, for example) although the most common formation is via online databases (Gross, 2011). The internet portal mitfahrgelegenheit.de is the biggest online agency in Europe with more than 3.8 million users (mitfahrgelegenheit.de, 2012).

Car leasing

Car leasing is a method used to obtain the use of an automobile without purchasing it outright. A financial institution purchases the car but its use is conveyed to the customer. In return, the customer makes a monthly rental payment for a set period of years. At the end of the lease term, the customer has the option to either return the car, to continue the lease, or to purchase the vehicle in return for the residual value (Wöhe, 2010).

Based on these definitions, Table 4.1 highlights the main similarities and differences of rental cars, car sharing, car pooling and car leasing.

Table 4.1. Forms of car passenger usage. (From Sahkdari, 2008; OPM Media GmbH, 2009; Frost & Sullivan, 2010; MOVECO GmbH, 2013.)

	Rental car	**Car Sharing**	**Car Pooling**	**Car Leasing**
Ownership	No ownership	No ownership	Retained	Retained
Organization	For-profit	For-profit, non-profit and co-operative	Non-profit	For-profit
Period of usage	1 to 90 days	Normally a few hours, uncommonly a few days or weeks	1 route	Normally several years
Membership	No	Sometimes	Yes	No
Possibility of taking over	During office hours	At any time	Departure time as agreed with driver	One-time, afterwards lessee can decide independently
Station	Central	Peripheral	Mostly central	Peripheral
Usage	One after another	One after another	Simultaneously	One after another
Costs	Depending on vehicle class, period, mileage	Membership fee, security, monthly fee, period, mileage	Fare per person	Normally first instalment, monthly rate

HISTORICAL DEVELOPMENT OF THE MARKET

The invention of the first automobile goes back to 1886, when Karl Benz drove his first car through the streets of Mannheim, Germany. The Motorwagen (Fig. 4.2) was a two-seated three-wheeler with a petrol-driven internal combustion engine. Its patent is considered to be the birth certificate of the car (Wolf, 1996; Stoyles and Pentland, 2006; Torok and Holper, 2008). In the same year, the German Gottlieb Daimler built a faster four-wheeled car with a high-speed motor running on gasoline. After several improvements were undertaken, the US car maker Henry Ford was the first to produce the automobile in mass quantities in 1908 (Berger, 2001).

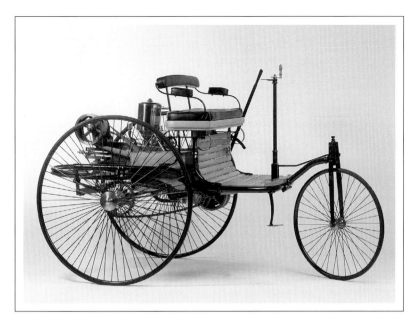

Fig. 4.2. Motorwagen. © Mercedes-Benz Classic.

The birth of the car rental industry is closely tied to Ford's introduction of the assembly line production of his Model T Ford (Boyd, 2008). One of the first rental car companies was founded in 1912 by Martin Sixt in Germany. With only seven cars he started the company Sixt Auto-fahrten und Selbstfahrer, specializing in day-trips and custom tours. During this time, his main clientele consisted of members of the British nobility and American tourists (Sixt AG, 2012).

Rental cars made a breakthrough in the United States after two young entrepeneurs named Joe Saunders and Walter L. Jacobs independently opened rental car businesses. Saunders began lending his car to local and visiting businessmen in Nebraska in 1916, utilizing a mile-age meter to charge 10 cents a mile to cover the wear and tear of his vehicle. By 1925, Saun-ders had expanded his car rental company to include operations in 21 states. Jacobs started his business with 12 Model T Fords in Chicago in 1918 (Burgdorf, 1993; Boyd, 2008). Within five years, Jacobs had expanded his operation to such an extent that the business generated annual revenues of about $1 million. Although Jacobs sold his car rental concern to John Hertz, President of Yellow Cab and Yellow Truck and Coach Manufacturing Company in 1923, he continued as Hertz's top operating and administrative executive. Only three years later in 1926, General Motors Corporation purchased the rental business known as Hertz Drive-Ur-Self System, when it purchased Hertz's Yellow Truck Company.

In contrast, the rental car business first had its heyday in Germany after the First World War, once there was positive economic development and the Golden Twenties started (Gross, 2011). The number of American tourists willingly to discover the country by automobile increased, resulting in a higher demand for rental cars. By 1939, the biggest German rental car company at that time (today known as EUROPCAR) had 30 rental car stations with 700 automobiles all over Germany. Due to the difficulty in acquiring spare parts for foreign automobiles during this time, almost all rental cars were Mercedes (Burgdorf, 1993; EUROPCAR Autovermietung GmbH, 2012).

Although the availability of spare parts was not a concern for the American rental car industry at this time, they suffered from an image problem as the cars were often associated with criminal activities during the Prohibition era (Römer, 2010). Boyd (2008) states 'many believed that [rental] cars were often used by bootleggers, bank robbers and prostitutes. [However,] after the 18th Amendment was repealed in 1933, the industry was able to regain a respectable reputation, and the business grew'. Further expansions were facilitated by a number of railways, which created so-called 'Railway Extensions' to counter the growth of private car ownership. These extensions enabled travellers to reserve cars at one station and pick them up at their destination (Boyd, 2008). Similarly, the burgeoning airline industry spurred car rental agencies to begin operating at major airports. In 1932, Hertz opened the first rent-a-car facility at Chicago's Midway Airport. Later that same year, to further facilitate the world's adjustment to travel by air, Hertz introduced the first 'Fly/Drive rental car program' (Hertz GmbH, 2012).

With the advent of the Second World War, all automobiles were commandeered in Germany and the business activities of the rental car companies essentially ceased. However, towards the end of the war, the companies were once again able to resume their work (Römer, 2010). The car rental industry also grew rapidly after the Second World War in the USA. As previously stated, this growth was linked closely with the boom in the airline industry. One of the most important milestones of the industry expansion was the further development of Herz's 'fly-drive' concept through franchises at airports in Atlanta and Milwaukee. While the majority of car rental companies focused on 'downtown' rental locations, Avis (which was founded by an Army pilot) centred almost all of its car rental operations on airport franchises aggressively advertising services through the airlines themselves (Boyd, 2008). Nowadays, the industry is closely linked to airline transportation, with most big rental car businesses operating offices at airports all over the world (Boyd, 2008; Straesser, 2010).

Since the 1960s, the industry has been extremely competitive. In fact, the increase in competition created innovative discount programmes and extreme price wars, which have forced out many smaller independent companies leaving major car rental chains in control of about 90% of the market (The Institute of Transport Management, 2012). Currently, the market is fairly saturated and in the firm control of major industry leaders such as Enterprise, Hertz and Avis.

INSTITUTIONAL FRAMEWORK

In contrast to other types of transportation, legislation and regulations for the rental car industry are limited as the companies do not offer passenger transportation, only the vehicles.

European institutional framework

According to the European Commission (2012) there is no legal framework regarding rental car operations. However, consumers are protected by other instruments with more general scope. Within the European Union, business-to-consumer commercial practices are regulated by the Unfair Commercial Practices Directive 2005/29/EC. Based on this regulation, rental car companies are bound to disclose the following information in their contracts:

- the main characteristics of the product, to an extent appropriate to the medium and the product;
- the price inclusive of taxes, or where the nature of the product means that the price cannot reasonably be calculated in advance, the manner in which the price is calculated, as well as, where appropriate, all additional freight, delivery or postal charges or, where these charges cannot reasonably be calculated in advance, the fact that such additional charges may be payable;
- the arrangements for payment, delivery, performance and the complaint handling policy.

Hence, all information must be fair and clear. Most importantly, the price quotation must include all 'unavoidable charges' (such as local fees and taxes, handling fees, etc.). Furthermore, the cost of any optional extras that the customer may require (such as child seat or additional insurance) must be shown clearly and not be presented in a misleading manner (European Commission, 2012).

North American institutional framework

In the USA, the rental car regulatory framework encompasses legislation and regulations (Feigenbaum, 2012). Like most large industries, this sector faces regulations mainly aimed at consumer protection. As in the European Union, rental car companies must have their cars licensed and insured. However, US rental car companies operate under laws within their respective states. Legislation in the different states varies considerably but there are a few categories of concern commonly addressed by states and cities:

- price disclosure: the total cost of renting a car (post taxes and fees) has to be stated in advertising and bookings.
- taxes: rental car companies have to collect state taxes. Therefore, the advertised prices often do not match the final invoice.
- liability: most states hold rental car companies partially liable for accidents, injuries and wrongful deaths caused by renters. Hence, good liability insurance is required to cover them.
- GPS monitoring: the abuse of installing tracking devices on rental cars to monitor the renters' movement rather than to locate lost, stolen or missing vehicles has led to the prohibition of their use in some states.

By comparison, in Canada and Mexico no government regulation exists for the rental car industry (Tomlinson, 2010; Marlen, 2011). Rules seem to differ from state to state and above all, from company to company. Therefore, the customer has to examine the conditions of rental closely before renting in both countries.

ASSOCIATIONS

Although there is an absence of extensive regulatory standards within the rental car industry, several industry associations participate in the regulatory and policy development process. However, as they represent the interests of operators their role mainly revolves around the promotion of the industry. Some of the international associations from Europe and North America are briefly highlighted below.

Association of Car Rental Industry System Standards (ACRISS)

The objectives of the Association of Car Rental Industry System Standards (ACRISS) include the development of clear common standards for car rental services in Europe, the Middle East and Africa; and supporting the increased use of reservation distribution systems. When first founded in 1989, the ACRISS was made up of the four rental car companies, Avis, Budget, Europcar and Hertz. Today, the association has 14 members, among them organizations of the tourism industry (such as IATA, Amadeus and Travelport). One of their major achievements has been the introduction of the ACRISS four-letter car classification code that identifies 400 vehicle types, which members utilize to define car models to ensure comparability of vehicles and rates. More specifically, a matrix of four columns exists (see Table 4.2), which are combined to form car codes by assigning one character from each column as follows (ACRISS, 2011):

- first character denotes the vehicle category – based on size, cost, power and luxury factor;
- second character defines the vehicle type – chassis type (van, wagon, SUV, etc.);
- third character defines the transmission and drive – automatic/manual and 2WD/4WD/AWD;
- fourth character defines the fuel type (petrol/diesel/hybrid) and whether air conditioned.

For instance, the car code FVMR stands for a fullsize passenger van with manual transmission that is air-conditioned (such as Ford Galaxy, Peugeot 807).

European Federation of Leasing Company Associations (Leaseurope)

Leaseurope, the European Federation of Leasing Company Associations, was founded in 1972 and is an international non-profit association based in Brussels, Belgium. Since 2006 it has represented the leasing and automotive rental industries in Europe and is composed of 44 member associations in 32 countries (representing about 2000 European leasing companies). Besides representing the common interests of its members in the dialogue with European and international institutions, Leaseurope produces publications, market trends analysis, position papers and industry statistics (Bundesverband Deutscher Leasing Unternehmen e.V., 2012; Leaseurope, 2013).

American Car Rental Association (ACRA)

The American Car Rental Association (ACRA) is a national association representing the US auto rental industry, and has given the industry a voice on public policy issues since 1978.

Table 4.2. Car classification code matrix. (From ACRISS, 2011.)

Category	Type	Transmission	Fuel/air-conditioned
M Mini	B 2–3 Door	M Manual unspecified	R Unspecified fuel/power with air
N Mini elite	C 2/4 Door	N Manual 4WD	N Unspecified fuel/power without air
E Economy	D 4–5 Door	C Manual AWD	D Diesel air
H Economy	W Wagon/estate	A Auto unspecified drive	Q Diesel no air
C Compact	V Passenger van	B Auto 4WD	H Hybrid air
D Compact elite	L Limousine	D Auto AWD	I Hybrid no air
I Intermediate	S Sport		E Electric air
J Intermediate elite	T Convertible		C Electric no air
S Standard	F SUV		L LPG/compressed gas/air
R Standard elite	J Open air all terrain		S LPG/compressed gas/no air
F Fullsize	X Special		A Hydrogen air
G Fullsize elite	P Pick up regular cab		B Hydrogen no air
P Premium	Q Pick up extended cab		M Multi-fuel/power air
U Premium elite	Z Special offer car		F Multi-fuel/power no air
L Luxury	E Coupe		V Petrol air
W Luxury elite	M Monospace		Z Petrol no air
O Oversize	R Recreational vehicle		U Ethanol air
X Special	H Motor home		V Ethanol no air
	Y 2 Wheel vehicle		
	N Roadster		
	G Crossover		
	K Commercial van/truck		

As a formal trade organization, it is composed of rental car companies ('regular' members) and associate members. The major car rental companies include such companies as Avis Budget Group, Enterprise Holdings, Hertz Corporation and Sixt. The association's role is to support and promote legislation that will benefit all its members. Its scope of duties comprises the following:

- educating its membership about recent developments in public policy and court decisions (through workshops, seminars, newsletters);
- lobbying at the state and federal level;
- analysing and reporting on federal, state and local laws;
- providing appropriate services as needed to support these goals.

ACRA is also responsible for organizing and participating in the annual Car Rental Show (ACRA, 2012; Car Rental Show, 2012).

Associated Canadian Car Rental Operators (ACCRO)

The Associated Canadian Car Rental Operators (ACCRO) was formed in 1980 and currently has more than 200 members. The association represents and promotes the industry in Canada and supports the commercial integrity of the industry. Objectives include the achievement of fair legislation for the automobile industry, the promotion of motor vehicle and driver safety and cooperation among members, affiliates and local, provincial and other national associations. Furthermore, ACCRO organizes educational seminars and an annual convention attended by operators and suppliers from across Canada and the USA. Moreover, it operates a buyers' group for independent car and truck rental operators with access to volume discounts on all industry products (ACCRO, 2012).

Most European nations also have a national car rental association (represented in Leaseurope). A few national examples include the Bundesverband der Autovermieter Deutschlands eV (Germany), the British Vehicle Rental and Leasing Association, the Polish Leasing Association, Asociación Española de Renting de Vehículos (Spain) and Fédération Nationale des Loueurs de Véhicules (France). Similarly, within the USA most states have their own rental car association, such as the New York Vehicle Rental Association or the Auto Rental Association of South Florida, for example. Mexico's national rental car association is called Asociación Nacional de Arrendadoras de Vehículos.

DEMAND AND SUPPLY

Demand

Due to the missing legislation and regulation in the rental car industry, the overall availability of statistics is relatively poor. Furthermore, statistics available concentrate only on transportation by private car. Therefore, only assumptions can be derived regarding the rental car market.

According to the International Transport Forum (ITF) at the Organization for Economic Co-operation and Development (OECD), private cars accounted for 10,377.9 thousand million[1] pkm in 2008 (OECD, 2011) within the ITF member countries, within the OECD member countries they accounted for 10,307 thousand million pkm, and 4410.1 thousand million pkm in the EU26 (Cyprus is not an ITF member country). Global trends are highlighted in Fig. 4.3 (it should be noted that the base year utilized for comparative purposes was 1990). Although private car transport in the EU member countries declined by an average of 0.7% in 2008, limited data available for 2009 suggest a return to growth in 2009 (OECD, 2011).

At the regional level, the European Commission provides transport statistics for the European Union while the North American Transportation Statistics Interchange reports information

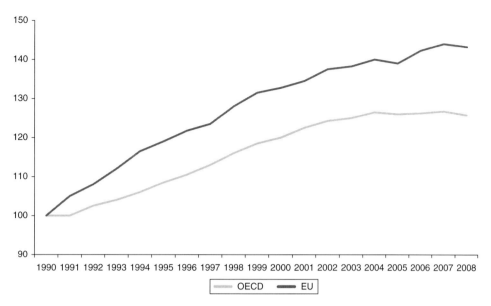

Fig. 4.3. Passenger transport by private cars. From OECD, 2011.

on transportation in Canada, the USA and Mexico. Overall, passengers within the EU27 travelled 4781 billion pkm by private cars in 2009; while this is an increase of only 0.4% from the previous year, private car transport performance has increased by almost 23% since 1995 and accounts for approximately 74% of total passenger transport activities within the EU27 (Eurostat, 2011). Comparatively, travellers in the USA and Canada travelled 4502 billion pkm and 266 billion pkm respectively in 2009; unfortunately there are no comparable current private car statistics reported for Mexico. While private car transport in Canada increased by 10% over the last five years[2], the USA saw a decrease in usage of approximately 19%. However, private cars still account for 80–82% of all passenger transport in the USA (depending on statistical methodology).

Hence, it is obvious that the number of people travelling by car is continuously increasing (especially in Europe) which may also have implications for the rental car industry. Unfortunately, due to the current lack of detailed statistics, it is impossible to measure this possible association. For example, although Leaseurope provides statistical data annually, comparisons across and between countries cannot be made due to inconsistencies within the data.

Europcar's Observatory of Lifestyle Trends in Travel and Transports (2008a) reported that 62% of Europeans had made use of a rental car in 2007, while 87% imagined that they may need to rent a car in the near future. Only 26% of the European men had not rented a car yet, whereas 41% of the women and 46% of the young people (between 18 and 29 years) were unversed in renting cars. Car rental is more predominant in larger cities with more than 20,000 inhabitants (68% versus 61% in rural areas). The main reasons for renting cars are practical, meaning Europeans rent a car for relocation purposes or when their own car is being repaired. However, domestic and international trips are also often cited reasons for renting cars. The motivations are mostly based on the flexibility (71%) and freedom (67%) which renting a car provides the user. More than half of the European respondents believe that car rental is essential for making the most out of a trip (see Table 4.3). These findings may be used to support the above-mentioned assumption that there is a parallel increase in car rental based on the increase in general car usage.

Figure 4.4 illustrates the seasonal spread of car rental demand in selected European countries. It is obvious that the rental car market in most western European countries peaks during July–August, Easter and Christmas.

Table 4.3. Motivations for car rental in Europe. (Adapted from Europcar Autovermietung GmbH, 2008a.)

Motivation in %	Europe	Sex		Age			Size of city	
		M	F	18–29	30–49	>50	>20,000 inh.	Rural area
Haven't made a car rental yet	38	26	41	46	28	33	32	39
For flat moving	23	39	34	32	43	33	38	31
My own car was being repaired	22	37	23	18	32	33	29	34
Vacation or a long trip abroad	17	14	13	13	15	13	14	12
Business travel	11	19	4	5	15	13	12	10
Short trip/a weekend away abroad	14	13	9	10	10	12	13	5
Short trip/a weekend away in my own country	16	12	8	10	13	8	11	8
Vacation or a long trip in my own country	8	3	12	2	2	2	2	1
Others	2	2	2	1	2	3	2	3

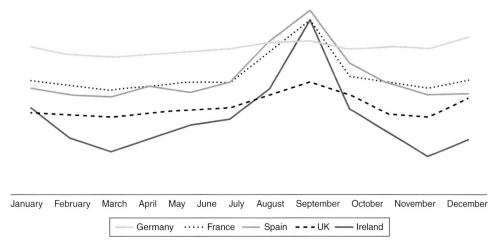

January   February   March   April   May   June   July   August   September   October   November   December

——— Germany   ····· France   —— Spain   ‐ ‐ ‐ UK   —— Ireland

Fig. 4.4. Seasonal spread of car rental demand in Europe. From Hertz for Car Rental Council of Ireland, 2010.

In the USA, the Department of Commerce for International Trade Administration and the Office of Travel and Tourism Industries (2012a) published a study analysing the overseas visitors' behaviour regarding the usage of rental cars during their stay in the USA. In 2011, approximately 8.2 million overseas visitors rented a car to travel within the USA (total overseas inbound visitors in 2011: 27.9 million; Office of Travel and Tourism Industries, 2012b). In comparison, in 2004 the number accounted for 6.2 million, which represents an increase of 32% in the demand for rental cars in the last seven years. Among the renters, 63% were male and on average about 43 years old. The females renting a car were slightly younger, being 40 years old on average. The top three activity participations of car renters were shopping, dining in restaurants and sightseeing in cities. Also for visiting national parks and touring countryside, rental cars come in handy and increased by about 1% in 2011 compared to the previous year (see Table 4.4).

Supply

There are several possible business models within the rental car market as illustrated in Table 4.5. However, often it is almost impossible to distinguish clearly between them (Gross and Stengel, 2010). The big rental car companies are called the generalists as their products and services are aimed at serving different target groups. In addition, there are rental car co-operations consisting of several smaller and mostly regional suppliers which benefit from each other. Another model is the so-called rental car broker. A rental car broker is an intermediary between rental car companies and consumers. Brokers do not own a fleet or station, instead the cars they rent are owned by the rental car companies. Car brokers often heavily rely on internet portals in order to conduct their business. Last but not least, low-cost suppliers also exist in the rental car industry.

Table 4.4. Activity participation of car renters while in the USA. (From Office of Travel and Tourism Industries, 2012a.)

Activity participation while in the USA (multiple response – top 10 of 25)	2010 (%)	2011 (%)	Point change
Shopping	90	90	0.5
Dining in restaurants	86	87	0.7
Sightseeing in cities	45	44	−1.0
Visit historical places	42	42	−0.5
Amusement/theme parks	42	41	−1.2
Visit small towns	37	36	−0.4
Visit national parks	29	30	0.9
Touring countryside	28	29	1.2
Water sports/sunbathing	28	27	−1.3
Cultural heritage sites	26	26	−0.6

The European rental car market is the second most important, following the US market. Within Europe, Germany is the largest submarket, followed by France, the UK and Spain (Europcar Autovermietung GmbH, 2008b).

Leaseurope releases annually data of its member associations and for 2012 there is data available for seven of its 34 member countries. The short-term car rental members reporting in the Leaseurope 2012 Annual Enquiry purchased around 555,000 cars during the year and, at year end, owned a fleet of approximately 522,000 cars (Leaseurope, 2013). In total, the association members represent more than 20.7 million rentals made during the year 2012 (see Table 4.6).

According to Euromonitor, the most important suppliers in Europe are the so-called Big Four which are Europcar, Avis, Hertz and Sixt. All together, they have a market share of 66% (see Fig. 4.5). However, it should be noted that there are methodological differences between the various sources, so that reported market share figures should be examined with care. By its own account, Europcar is the biggest rental car supplier in Europe since the takeover of the business of the two European brands Alamo and National by the American company Vanguard.

Table 4.5. Business models in the rental car industry. (Adapted from Gross and Stengel, 2010.)

Rental car companies

Generalist	Rental car co-operation	Rental car broker		Low-cost supplier	
		Holiday car rental supplier	**Internet broker**	**Car as an ad space**	**Low-cost brand**
• Alamo • Avis • Enterprise Rent a Car • Europcar • Hertz • Sixt • …	• CCUniRent System GmbH • Europa Service Autovermietung AG • LET'S rent a car Autovermietung GmbH • united rental-system GmbH • …	• Drive FTI • Holiday Autos • Sunny Cars • TUI Cars • DERTOUR • … *Portal* • thecarrental-portal.com mietwagen-markt.de m-broker.de …	• CarRental Broker • easyCar • CarDelMar • Happer-Cars.com • GetYour Car • …	• Lauda-Motion • Maxhopp • …	• Sixti • interRent • Avis Basic • …

Comparatively, the US market has been predominantly held by three major players after Hertz Global Holdings Inc. took over Dollar Thrifty Automotive Group Inc. in August 2012: Hertz has now a market share of approximately 38%, ahead of Enterprise's 31% and Avis's 29% (see Fig. 4.6).

The US rental car industry achieved record rental revenue in 2012 rising almost 15% in a two-year period. As illustrated in Table 4.7, 1.86 million cars were operated by approximately 18,300 companies (ARN Online, 2013).

It is expected that the US market will grow at a compound annual growth rate of 5.25% in the next three years (AM Mindpower Solutions, 2010). In Mexico, the compound annual growth rate is projected to account for 6.52% (Research and Markets, 2010).

In contrast, the revenue of Canada's rental car industry is comparatively small with about 4.775 billion Canadian dollars (equals approximately $4.878 billion) in 2010. However, there has been an increase of 4% after the revenues decreased in 2009 (CAD 4.560 billion) by 10% compared to 2008 (CAD 5.028 billion) (Statistics Canada, 2012b).

Table 4.6. Number of short-term car rentals of selected Leaseurope member countries in 2012. (From Leaseurope, 2013.)

Country	Association	Number of cars bought in 2012	Fleet size	Number of rentals made during 2012
Belgium	RENTA	24,718	17,779	433,227
France	Fédération Nationale des Loueurs de Véhicules	170,000	160,000	3,660,000
Italy	ANIASA	87,734	102,000	4,361,000
The Netherlands	BOVAG	19,141	26,975	–
Turkey	Tokkder	13,940	20,500	1,746,000
Ukraine	UUL	218	1,389	62,077 (2011)
UK	BVRLA	240,000	194,000	10,500,000
Total (without Luxembourg)		555,751	522,643	20,700,227

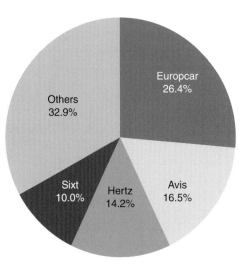

Fig. 4.5. European market shares of rental car companies. Source: Euromonitor, adapted from Statista, 2012.

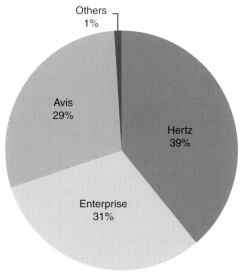

Fig. 4.6. US market shares of rental car companies. Based on Reuters, 2012.

Table 4.7. US rental car market in 2012. (From ARN Online, 2012, 2013.)

Company	US cars in service (avg.) 2012	Number of US locations	2012 US revenue est. (in millions)	2011 US revenue (in millions)	2010 US revenue (in millions)
Enterprise Holdings	941,064	6,202	$11,500	$11,100	$9,800
Hertz	366,000	2,700	$4,660	$4,241	$4,081
Avis Budget Group	300,000	2,500	$4,510	$4,500	$3,900
Dollar Thrifty Automotive Group	122,000	470	$1,563	$1,597	$1,628
Zipcar	8,800	151	$205	$178	$102
Fox Rent A Car	15,000	17	$170	$140	$110
Payless Car Rental System Inc.	11,000	44	$145	$135	$118
U-Save Auto Rental System Inc.	11,500	325	$118	$115	$100
ACE Rent A Car	9,000	92	$100	$100	$143
Rent-A-Wreck of America	5,600	184	$40	$38	$35
Triangle Rent-A-Car	4,000	28	$40	$40	$40
Affordable/ Sensible	3,300	180	$32	$32	$34
Independents	60,000	5,400	$545	$520	$500
Total	1,857,264	18,293	$23,628	$22,736	$20,591

NOTES

1. Many international data sources utilize the rather unwieldy 'thousand million' because of differences in the American and European billion. More specifically, a million million equates to a billion in Europe, while a thousand million equates to a billion in the USA. Although British English has adopted the American English interpretation, many parts of Europe still use the former system. Hence to avoid confusion and ease the comparison of large numbers between languages and countries, many sources utilize 'thousand million'.

2. The US Federal Highway Administration changed their methodology regarding calculations of annual vehicle miles travelled in 2007, hence there is a break in data comparability. Before the methodology change, private cars accounted for around 85–87% of total passenger transport activities in the USA between 2000 and 2006; the percentage decreased to approximately 80–82% after the new methodology was adopted.

FURTHER READING

Boyd, L. (2008) *Brief History of Buses and Rental Cars in the US*. Available at: http://library.duke.edu/digitalcollections/adaccess/guide/transportation/carandbus.

Goeldner, C. and Ritchie, J.R. (2011) *Tourism – Principles, Practices, Philosophies*, 12th edn. Wiley, Hoboken, New York.

Gross, S. (2011) *Tourismus und Verkehr – Grundlagen, Marktanalyse und Strategien von Verkehrsunternehmen*. Oldenbourg, Munich, Germany.

Gross, S. and Stengel, N. (2010) *Mietfahrzeuge im Tourismus – Grundlagen, Geschäftsprozesse und Marktanalyse*. Oldenbourg, Munich, Germany.

Gross, S., Sonderegger, R. and Grotrian, J. (2007) Transferring the low cost strategy to ship, bus and rental car companies. In: Gross, S. and Schröder, A. (eds) *Handbook of Low Cost Airlines – Strategies, Business Processes and Market Environment*. Erich Schmidt-Verlag, Berlin, Germany, pp. 293–314.

Kazanjian, K. (2007) *Exceeding Customer Expectations – What Enterprise, America's #1 car rental company, can teach us about creating lifetime customers*. Currency Doubleday, New York.

Lohmann, G. and Zahra, A. (2011) The influence of international tourists' travel patterns on rental car fleet management in New Zealand. In: Prideaux, B. and Carson, D. (eds) *Drive Tourism: Trends and emerging markets*. Routledge, New York, pp. 159–171.

Lourens, M. (2007) Route tourism – a roadmap for successful destinations and local economic development. *Development Southern Africa* 3, 475–489.

Minelli, B. (2008) *How To Save Big Money on Car Rentals – Uncovering the Secrets They Don't Want You to Know*. AuthorHouse, Bloomington, Indiana.

Olsen, M. (2003) Tourism themed routes – A Queensland perspective. *Journal of Vacation Marketing* 4, 331–341.

Palmer-Tous, T., Riera-Font, A. and Rosselló-Nadal, J. (2007) Taxing tourism: The case of rental cars in Mallorca. *Tourism Management* 28, 271–279.

Prideaux, B. and Carson, D. (2007) A framework for increasing understanding of self-drive tourism markets. *Journal of Vacation Marketing* 4, 307–313.

Prideaux, B. and Carson, D. (2011) *Drive Tourism: Trends and Emerging Markets*. Routledge, New York.

Schwieger, B. (2011) *Second Generation Car-Sharing*. Südwestdeutscher Verlag für Hochschulschriften, Saarbrücken, Germany.

Trade journals/magazines and scientific organizations

Kraftstoff – Business-Magazin für die Autovermietung, Der Autovermieter, Internationales Verkehrswesen, taxi heute – Das bundesweite Fachblatt für den erfolgreichen Taxi- und Mietwagen-Unternehmer, Travel and Tourism Research Association (www.ttra.com).

Internet sources

www.aaa.com, www.acriss.org, www.bitre.gov.au, www.bundesverband-der-autovermieter-deutschlands.de, www.datamonitor.com, http://tinet.ita.doc.gov, www.alamo.com, www.avis.com, www.hertz.com, www.enterprise.com, www.europcar.com, www.leaseurope.org, www.sixt.com.

chapter 5

Buses and Motor Coaches

LEARNING OBJECTIVES

- Identify, define, and describe the differences between buses and motor coaches and the services they provide.
- Assess the current state of the bus and motor coach industry in regards to tourism.
- Determine whether the motor coach industry could provide a competitive alternative to other modes of tourism transportation in light of economic and environmental trends.

The terms bus and motor coach are used inconsistently and interchangeably in the English language. While not everyone makes a distinction, some sources differentiate based on physical characteristics of the vehicles, while others distinguish between the types of services provided. We will highlight official definitions, as well as the different types of services provided by this mode of transport, before providing the definitions utilized for the purpose of this book.

DEFINITIONS

Bus

The *Glossary of Transport Statistics* (2009), developed by the International Transport Forum (ITF), Eurostat and the United Nations Economic Commission for Europe (UNECE) defines a bus as a 'passenger road motor vehicle designed to carry more than 24 persons (including the driver), and with provision to carry seated as well as standing passengers' (p. 45). Furthermore it states, 'the vehicles may be constructed with areas for standing passengers, to allow frequent passenger movement, or designed to allow the carriage of standing passengers in the gangway' (p. 45). Alternatively, the *Public Transportation Fact Book* (APTA, 2011), developed by the American Public Transportation Association (APTA) defines a bus as:

> a mode of transit service (also called motor bus) characterized by roadway vehicles powered by diesel, gasoline, battery, or alternative fuel engines contained within the vehicle. Vehicles operate on streets and roadways in fixed-route or other regular service. Types of bus service include local service, where vehicles may stop every block or two along a route several miles long. When limited to a small geographic area or to short-distance trips, local service is often called circulator, feeder, neighbourhood, trolley, or shuttle service. Other types of bus service are express service, limited-stop service, and bus rapid transit (BRT) (p. 38).

Motor coach

The *Glossary of Transport Statistics* (2009) defines a motor coach as a 'passenger road motor vehicle designed to seat 24 or more persons (including the driver) and constructed exclusively for the carriage of seated passengers' (p. 46). When compared to the definition of a bus, one can see that while similar, the coach does not allow the carriage of standing passengers in the gangway. While APTA does not seem to make a distinction between bus and motor coach, the term 'over-the-road-bus' can be found in the US code and is defined as 'a bus characterized by an elevated passenger deck located over a baggage compartment' (6 USC § 1151). In a benchmarking study of the motor coach industry in the USA and Canada, Nathan Associates Inc. (2008) expanded upon this definition and offered the following definition of a motor coach: 'a vehicle designed for long-distance transportation of passengers, characterized by integral construction with an elevated passenger deck located over a baggage compartment. It is at least 35 feet in length with a capacity of more than 30 passengers' (p. 1).

Minibus or minicoach

As the name implies, these are smaller versions of their large counterparts and the *Glossary of Transport Statistics* (2009) defines these as 'passenger road motor vehicle designed to carry 10–23 seated or standing persons (including the driver)' (p. 46). Furthermore, it is pointed out 'the vehicles may be constructed exclusively to carry seated passengers or to carry both seated and standing passengers'.

Trolleybus

A trolleybus is a special form of bus as it is electrically propelled from overhead wires along its route. One could argue that it is similar to a tram, the difference being that it is a rubber-tyred vehicle and does not operate on rails. While this form of transportation is still in use in some areas, it does not constitute a significant proportion of bus transportation. A trolleybus or trolley coach is defined by APTA (2011) as: 'a mode of transit service using vehicles propelled by a motor drawing current from overhead wires via connecting poles called a trolley poles from a central power source not on board the vehicle' (p. 39).

Based on these definitions, it soon becomes clear that there are no overarching international definitions offering clear-cut distinctions between the bus and motor coach. However, based on the European definitions, buses are constructed to allow for the carriage of standing passengers while coaches are designed for passengers to be transported while seated. While the term motor coach is frequently utilized within the US bus industry (although written as motorcoach), no official definition utilizing this term could be found. However, the definition found in the US code does highlight the different services offered.

Types of bus and motor coach services

Different types of vehicles are used for various types of bus or motor coach transportation services, which generally fall into one of three categories: regular services, special regular services or occasional services (Nathan Associates, 2008; Steer Davies Gleave, 2009; Gross, 2011).

Regular services (domestic and international) are ticketed, regular-route services that operate at specified times along fixed routes, with predetermined boarding and alighting points, open to all, also known as public transit or commuter service.

Special regular services operate on defined routes and at defined times, but provide for the carriage of a certain group of passengers to the exclusion of others (such as workers, students or soldiers). This type of service can also include special published, regular-route services to special events, such as fairs or sporting events.

Occasional services are services that do not meet the definition of regular or special regular services. They provide the carriage of a preformed group (brought together on the initiative of the customer or the carrier itself) which has exclusive use of the bus or motor coach under a fixed contract. This type of service includes the packaged retail tour, sightseeing services and services organized for special events such as conferences or cultural or sporting events. Packaged retail tours are prearranged trips, usually including accommodation, meals, sightseeing and transportation, offered at a fixed price to leisure travellers by a motor coach transportation company (including a tour company that leases/owns and operates motor coaches).

Interestingly, there is a further categorization of bus and urban transit services in North America under the North American Industrial Classification System (NAICS) utilized by the federal statistical agencies in Canada, Mexico and the USA to classify business establishments. Under NAICS the bus industry is grouped into six categories: urban transit systems; inter-urban and rural bus transportation (scheduled intercity); school and employee bus transportation; charter bus industry; other ground passenger transportation (shuttle); scenic/sightseeing transportation. Figure 5.1 illustrates the distinctions made between different types of bus services and where the NAICS classifications could be integrated into the system (it should be remembered that theoretically buses or coaches can be chartered for use in any type of service; however, for our purposes here we are categorizing them for tourism services).

Based on the definitions and descriptions of services provided, we offer the following definitions of a bus and motor coach.

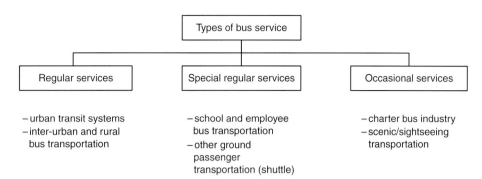

Fig. 5.1. Types of bus service and the North American Industrial Classification (NAICS). Compiled by the author.

A bus is a passenger road motor vehicle geared towards short trips with provision to carry seated as well as standing passengers, characterized by separate entrance and exit doors, limited comfort and legroom, and handles for standing passengers.

A motor coach is a passenger road motor vehicle intended for longer journeys, constructed exclusively for the carriage of seated passengers, characterized by separate luggage compartments and offering extended legroom, comfort and on board amenities. A more luxurious environment for long-distance travel is provided by including amenities such as reclining seats with headrests, tray tables, air-conditioning, reading lights, television screens, VCR/DVD, stereo and public address systems (the PA system is often used during sightseeing tours, for instance) and on-board toilets.

To summarize, transportation utilizing buses or motor coaches can be categorized as either public transportation or group tour services. Public bus services (sometimes referred to as public transit or mass transit) are regular scheduled services open to the general public, accessible at any bus stop along the route, where passengers pay a fare as they come aboard or present a prepaid bus ticket or bus pass. As a general rule, buses are utilized for public transportation, although some coach use is evidenced in the form of intercity services, which tend to be longer journeys with relatively few stops (also known as express service, limited-stop service, and bus rapid transit), and in rural areas where distances travelled also tend to be longer (see the Focus box for an example of vehicle usage in Canada based on service provided). While tourists may utilize public bus services as a means of transportation in and around a destination, for example, there are many coach operators who specifically cater to the needs of tourists. Coach tour services consist of a packaged or retail tour, ranging anywhere from a few hours to a vacation lasting several weeks. Such tours are offered by the bus operators themselves, or by intermediaries such as tour operators or wholesalers, who make the travel arrangements and charter the bus on which the tour will take place. Coaches (and to some extent minicoaches or minibuses) are utilized for travel to vacation destinations, for airport transfer services, or for escorted tours in and around the destination. Hence, such tour services are not open to the public, in the sense that they cannot be freely accessed en route; they are generally open to a certain group who have prepaid for an excursion such as a sightseeing tour, special event or party shuttle, or long-distance travel to a specific destination (national or international).

Focus box

Type of vehicle usage based on service provided in Canada 2010

| | Service provided | | | | | |
	Urban transit	Inter-urban and rural	School and employees	Charter bus and sightseeing	Other transit – shuttle	Total
Number of companies	88	20	1,023	154	193	1,371
Vehicle type:						
Motor coach	29	2,528	797	2,053	148	5,168
School bus	124	519	33,706	509	300	37,884
Urban transit bus	15,930	189	805	148	271	18,837
All other rolling stock	3,818	76	3,156	329	960	7,617
Total	19,901	3,312	38,464	3,039	1,678	69,507

From Statistics Canada, 2012a.

Although we have made the generalization that public transportation is provided by buses and tour services generally utilize motor coaches, there are obviously exceptions. For example, while many city-sightseeing tours use coaches with tour guides, most of you will also be familiar with the traditional London double-decker buses utilized in many cities around the world for sightseeing tours (Fig. 5.2). Passengers purchase a ticket which entitles them to travel along a regular route highlighting the key places of interest where they can 'hop on and hop off' as much as they like along the way, giving them the opportunity of individual-based exploration at the various tourist attractions. As this particular service is characterized by frequent stops with multiple entry and exit possibilities, buses offer design advantages in comparison to the coach, and the London double-decker buses offer additional marketing benefits.

Fig. 5.2. Double-decker bus – Gray Line Tours, Canada. © Michael Lück.

HISTORICAL DEVELOPMENT OF THE MARKET

As early as the mid-17th century, Blaise Pascal recognized the need for passenger transport, as the majority of the population could not afford their own carriages. Although carriages could be rented on a daily (and later even an hourly) basis, they were much too expensive for ordinary citizens. Pascal is credited with inventing the first vehicle resembling a bus in the form of a horse-drawn carriage capable of carrying eight passengers. Together with the Marquis de Crénan and the Duke de Roannez, Pascal founded a transport company that operated a regular scheduled service within Paris beginning in 1662 utilizing seven such carriages. The first route ran from the gates of St Antoine close to the Bastille to the Palais de Luxembourg and a fare of 5 sous was charged; hence the carriages were known as *carosses à cinq sols* (Huss and Schenk, 1982; Gould, 2010). By the end of the 17th century, similar horse-drawn coach transport was being utilized in Paris, London and Berlin. The first coach line was founded in Nantes, France in 1826, and was soon followed by another in Paris in 1828 named Generale des voitures dites omnibus by its founder Baudry. Interestingly, *voiture omnibus* means vehicle for all, and the term omnibus is today still sometimes used. Around the same time horse-drawn carriages or omnibuses began operating along designated routes in the USA, such as the one operated by Abraham Brower along Broadway in New York City in 1827. Interestingly, if someone wanted to get on, they could signal the driver by waving their arm in the air, much like hailing a modern-day taxi. When they wanted to get off, they alerted the driver by pulling on a little leather strap that was connected to his ankle (Bellis, 2011b).

Although steam-powered coaches were also developed around the turn of the century, they were less popular among the public due to high noise levels and a fear of explosions. Although there is some evidence that steam omnibuses were used for leisure trips by the travel agency Thomas Cook, more extensive use seems to have been limited to France. However, the idea of a self-propelled vehicle was born, and the age of the automobile arrived in 1886, when Karl Benz drove his first gasoline-powered automobile through the streets of Mannheim, Germany. By 1895, Benz implemented the gasoline-powered engine to develop the first motorized omnibus (Fig. 5.3), which was utilized for the transportation of factory workers in Germany. The town of Llandudno in Wales was the first to utilize Benz's invention for organized tourism during the summer season of 1898 (Huss and Schenk, 1982). During the early 19th century motorized buses started to become a more commonplace part of cityscapes in both Europe and North America. According to Walsh (2010), following modest growth in the early 1900s, bus usage by the general public soared during the Second World War in America and attained its highest-ever share of the market. After the Second World War,

Fig. 5.3. First motorized omnibus by Benz. © Mercedes-Benz Classic.

leisure trips and long-distance holiday travel by coach were also becoming more and more popular in Europe. For example, in 1954 the bus and coach industry in Germany enjoyed a 17% market share among main holidays lasting longer than five days (Gross, 2011) and trips to destinations such as the Costa Brava in Spain and the Italian Riviera were very popular. However, in the last half of the 20th century, the market share began to fall each decade due to faster, more comfortable, and more convenient options for long distance travel such as the airplane or the private automobile; so that the market share of coach travel among main holidays with a duration of five days or more had shrunk to approximately 8% by 2012 (FUR, 2013). However, according to the European Travel Commission this negative trend was not witnessed only in Germany; coach trips in Europe declined by as much as 19% in 2009 and made little recovery in 2010 (ETC Market Intelligence Group, 2011).

INSTITUTIONAL FRAMEWORK

In contrast to other types of transportation there are no comparable international conventions for the bus and motor coach industry. Although there are common rules and regulations binding passenger transportation on buses and coaches within international organizations such as the European Union and NAFTA, there are still significant differences in the regulatory environments between member nations.

European institutional framework

Within the European Union, the regulatory arrangements range from very liberalized to prohibition on operations. In a study of coach passenger transport prepared for the European Commission, Steer Davies Gleave (2009) reported that the UK and Sweden are very liberalized, allowing competition between operators, and although the Italian and Polish markets have also been liberalized, some administrative barriers remain. Spain and Romania both have concession systems, where operators bid for the right to operate routes. While the concessions in Spain tend to be rather long, they are limited to a period of three years in Romania. The most restrictive regulatory systems exist in Greece and Germany. In Germany, for example, regular domestic services, which would run parallel to an existing rail link, have been generally prohibited to protect the rail service from competition since 1934 (Federal Ministry of Transport, Building and Urban Development, 2012). However, changes to the current legislation that would greatly liberalize the German coach market came into effect in 2013. Travellers will then be able to use long-distance bus services for a length of run of more than 50 kilometres and exceeding a journey time of one hour. This limitation protects the local traffic and regional rail transport from competition. Deregulating the long-distance bus routes helps to minimize the number of passenger cars on the roads (one single bus replaces about 30 passengers cars) and offers an inexpensive alternative to rail transportation. By the end of 2019, all long-distance buses must be accessible to disabled people. Additionally, newly built buses must offer two seats for wheelchair users, starting 2016.

Interestingly, the German tourist coach sector is highly developed and less regulated and in fact, most member states impose few if any regulatory requirements on the operation of occasional services.

Within the European Union, the market for international carriage of passengers by bus and coach is regulated by the EEC Regulation No. 1073/2009, which incorporates previous Regulation Nos 684/92 and 12/98. Based on this regulation, bus and coach carriers from within the Community are free to operate passenger transport services (regular, special regular and occasional services) between any member states without discrimination on the grounds of nationality or place of establishment provided that the carrier:

- is authorized to undertake regular services in accordance with the market access conditions in national law in the EU country of establishment;
- fulfils the conditions of all EU rules on admission to the occupation of road passenger transport operations;
- meets all EU legal requirements and standards regarding drivers and vehicles.

However, different kinds of coach and bus services have specific requirements they must fulfil to access the international EU road transport market. For example, regular services require a national authorization; special regular services (e.g. the transport of workers or schoolchildren) do not require national authorization as long as they are covered by a contract between the organizer and the transport operator; while occasional services (e.g. transport to an event such as a concert in another member state) require the submission of a form for that particular journey. Furthermore, a system of Community licences was introduced for those operators licensed within their State of establishment, who are entitled to carry passengers by coach and bus and meet the conditions for admission to the occupation and road safety criteria. The licence is issued in the name of the carrier by authorities of the member state of establishment and is renewable for a period of up to ten years. The conditions under which non-resident carriers may operate national road passenger transport services within member states were regulated under the Council Regulation (No 12/98) in December 1997. The same regulation permits coach operators with a Community licence to temporarily operate cabotage services within other member states without having a registered office in that state.

Common rules regarding road transport operations are set out in EC Regulation No. 1071/2009, while rules regarding maximum daily and fortnightly driving times, as well as daily and weekly minimum rest periods, were set out in Regulation 561/2006 (as amended by Regulation 1073/2009). Known as the '12 day derogation rule', the regulation was aimed at improving working conditions and road safety. It applies to coach drivers on a single occasional service of international carriage (international coach tour) and states that drivers will be able to work for up to 12 consecutive days but the journey must be a single trip, not several different trips; and the driver must be compensated after the 12 days working with longer rest periods. Furthermore, drivers must continue to take daily rests and breaks in line with the existing requirements (which are summarized in Table 5.1). Hence, a coach driver can only work for up to 12 days consecutively with the following provisions.

- The extended working period is calculated from a 'regular' weekly rest period; a rest that is at least 45 h long.
- The driver is working a single occasional service (such as a coach tour) during which at least 24 consecutive hours must be spent in a member state or a third country other than the one in which the journey started.
- After the extended working period, the driver takes two regular rest periods together (i.e. 90 h) or one regular weekly rest period (minimum of 45 h) and one weekly reduced rest period (not less than 24 h). If a reduced rest is taken, the reduction in rest must be compensated by an equivalent period of rest taken en bloc before the end of the third week following the derogation period. (The compensating rest must be attached to a period of rest of at least 9 h – in effect, either a weekly or a daily rest period.)

Table 5.1. Current limits on drivers' hours as specified by EU rules as of 2011. (From Vehicle & Operator Services Agency, 2011.)

Breaks from driving	A break of no less than 45 min must be taken after no more than 4.5 h of driving. The break can be divided into two periods – the first at least 15 min long and the second at least 30 min – taken over the 4.5 h.
Daily driving	Maximum of 9 h, extendable to 10 h no more than twice a week.
Weekly driving	Maximum of 56 h.
Two-weekly driving	Maximum of 90 h in any 2-week period.
Daily rest	Minimum of 11 h, which can be reduced to a minimum of 9 h no more than three times between weekly rests. May be taken in two periods, the first at least 3 h long and the second at least 9 h long. The rest must be completed within 24 h of the end of the last daily or weekly rest period.
Multi-manning daily rest	A 9-h daily rest must be taken within a period of 30 h that starts from the end of the last daily or weekly rest period. For the first hour of multi-manning, the presence of another driver is optional, but for the remaining time it is compulsory.
Weekly rest	A regular weekly rest of at least 45 h, or a reduced weekly rest of at least 24 h, must be started no later than the end of six consecutive 24-h periods from the end of the last weekly rest. In any two consecutive weeks a driver must have at least two weekly rests – one of which must be at least 45 h long. A weekly rest that falls across 2 weeks may be counted in either week but not in both. Any reductions must be compensated in one block by an equivalent rest added to another rest period of at least 9 h before the end of the third week following the week in question.

After 1 January 2014, the regulation further requires that coaches involved in tours availing of derogation must be equipped with a digital tachograph, and when driving between 10pm and 6am, no more than 3 h of driving is done between breaks unless the vehicle is multi-manned.

Furthermore, there are several EU level technical directives that influence the construction of passenger vehicles, covering issues such as the approved weights and dimensions of the vehicles, seating and safety belt requirements and engine emissions, for example. Passenger rights in bus and coach transport have recently been implemented and are governed by Regulation No. 181/2011, which covers general provisions such as non-discrimination against passengers based on nationality, minimum rules regarding travel information for all passengers before and during the journey, rights in cases of cancellation or delay, loss of or damage to their luggage, and compensation and assistance in the event of personal injury or death due to accidents. Moreover, the rights of and assistance to disabled persons and persons with reduced mobility are also addressed in this regulation, including non-discriminatory access to transport, the right to compensation for loss of, or damage to, wheelchairs or other mobility equipment, submission and handling of complaints, and disability-related training of bus and coach staff[1].

North American institutional framework

The North American Free Trade Agreement (NAFTA) has regulatory implications for the Canadian, Mexican and US bus and motor coach industry on issues such as operating and safety standards, cabotage rules, and ownership and investment. The NAFTA surface transportation provisions were designed to eliminate restrictions limiting access and investment in transportation companies. Furthermore, the Land Transport Standards Subcommittee (LTSS) was established in order to facilitate the raising of standards and compatibility among the three countries while also acting as a forum for consultation and co-operation. Transport Canada regulates the bus and motor coach industry in Canada, although both the federal government and the provinces share jurisdiction in this area. While the Motor Vehicle Transport Act (MVTA) is a federal act, the legislation allows provinces to apply their own rules and regulations subject to conditions set within the Act. The Motor Carrier Policy Group and the Road Safety Group are the two institutions directly concerned with matters relating to the MVTA within Transport Canada. While Canadian carriers have been operating throughout the USA since 1982, Mexican carriers still face several restrictions. Although cross-border restrictions have been lifted for charter and tour buses, a reciprocal lifting of restrictions on regular route carriers has yet to be implemented (US Department of Transportation, 2011a). US regulations require all Mexican-domiciled carriers entering the USA to have a drug and alcohol-testing programme, a system of compliance with US federal hours-of-service requirements, adequate data and safety management systems, and valid insurance with a US registered insurance company.

In the USA, the Federal Motor Carrier Safety Administration (FMCSA) and the National Highway Traffic Safety Administration (NHTSA) each have important safety roles within the Department of Transportation regarding bus and motor coach operation. Current bus and coach regulations are based on the Motor Carrier Act of 1935 which first introduced regulations governing safety, finance, insurance, accounting and records. Interestingly, it was not until 1986 that minimum commercial driver's licence standards were developed in the Commercial Motor Vehicle Safety Act (CMVSA). Another important milestone in the American bus regulatory system was the Motor Carrier Safety Improvement Act of 1999 through which the current regulatory body FMCSA was created as part of the Federal Highway Administration. Today, the FMCSA is part of the Department of Transportation and is responsible for issuing, administering and enforcing regulations pertaining to the bus and motor coach industry. As the FMCSA's primary mission is to prevent commercial motor vehicle-related fatalities and injuries, they set minimum safety standards that motor coach companies must follow for the buses/vehicles they operate as well as the physical qualifications and operating rules for their drivers. According to the FMCSA, their activities

> contribute to ensuring safety in motor carrier operations through strong enforcement of safety regulations; targeting high-risk carriers and commercial motor vehicle drivers; improving safety information systems and commercial motor vehicle technologies; strengthening commercial motor vehicle equipment and operating standards; and increasing safety awareness. To accomplish these activities, the Administration works with Federal, State, and local enforcement agencies, the motor carrier industry, labor safety interest groups, and others.
>
> (FMCSA, 2011)[2]

Federal general and permanent rules are classified in the Code of Federal Regulations (CFR) where Title 49 contains the transportational regulations, and parts 325 to 383 particularly apply to passenger carriers[3].

While some states allow those over 18 years of age to operate buses within state borders, the USDOT sets minimum qualifications for bus drivers regarding interstate operations. According to the FMCA, drivers must be at least 21 years old, pass a physical exam once every two years, and have an acceptable command of the English language. Furthermore, under federal and state laws any carrier operating interstate service in the USA is required to have a USDOT number assigned by the FMCA to facilitate monitoring of performance and driving history of operators and carriers. New entrants are subject to a new-entrant safety monitoring procedure for an 18-month period. The safety assurance process identifies 16 regulations covering issues regarding both the driver and the vehicle, which the FMCA deems essential elements of basic safety management controls necessary to operate in interstate commerce. A carrier's failure to comply with any one of the 16 regulations results in an automatic failure of the safety audit and prohibits carriers from further operations.

Federal regulations regarding the maximum hours bus and coach drivers can work were set out in 49 CFR, part 395:

> a) No motor carrier shall permit or require any driver used by it to drive a passenger-carrying commercial motor vehicle, nor shall any such driver drive a passenger-carrying commercial motor vehicle:
> 1) More than 10 hours following 8 consecutive hours off duty; or
> 2) For any period after having been on duty 15 hours following 8 consecutive hours off duty.

b) No motor carrier shall permit or require a driver of a passenger-carrying commercial motor vehicle to drive, nor shall any driver drive a passenger-carrying commercial motor vehicle, regardless of the number of motor carriers using the driver's services, for any period after

1) having been on duty 60 hours in any 7 consecutive days if the employing motor carrier does not operate commercial motor vehicles every day of the week; or

2) having been on duty 70 hours in any period of 8 consecutive days if the employing motor carrier operates commercial motor vehicles every day of the week

(70 FR 50073, Aug. 25, 2005)

Although these are federal regulations that apply to interstate commerce, most states have adopted identical or very similar hours-of-service regulations that apply to intrastate commerce. Further actions aimed at improving road safety include the development of a Motorcoach Safety Action Plan by the Department of Transportation in 2009, which included initiatives such as the requirement of electronic on-board recording devices to monitor driver's duty hours and manage fatigue; prohibiting texting and limiting cellular phone use; the installation of seat belts on motor coaches; the evaluation of safety and performance requirements; enhancing knowledge requirements of personnel; and enhancing oversight of carriers (US Department of Transportation, 2009a). The restriction on the use of hand-held mobile telephones by drivers of commercial motor vehicles, including a ban on texting while operating in interstate commerce (75 FR 59118) has been in effect since October 2010. The Compliance, Safety, and Accountability system is a relatively new safety measurement implemented in December 2010 aimed at bus and truck safety through early intervention and replaces previous programmes[4].

As evidenced by both EU and NAFTA legislative measures, there is a desire in both Europe and North America to harmonize market access and operational rules governing bus and coach passenger transport services. While this goal has yet to be fully achieved, measures have been implemented to move towards a more efficient, safe and high quality international bus and coach passenger service.

ASSOCIATIONS

Associations at the international, regional, national and local levels represent the bus and coach industry. Some of the international associations from Europe and North America are briefly highlighted below.

International Road Transport Union (IRU)

According to their website, the IRU represents the interests of bus, coach, taxi and truck operators worldwide, ranging from large transport fleets to individual owner-operators. When first founded in Geneva in 1948, the IRU was made up of national road transport associations from eight European countries: Belgium, Denmark, France, the Netherlands, Norway, Sweden,

Switzerland and the UK. Today, the association represents approximately 180 members in more than 70 countries spread over five continents and acts as an industry interest group at international, regional, national and in some cases even local level with public authorities. The IRU promotes the facilitation of road transport worldwide while working towards its sustainable development. Creating partnerships between its members and related organizations, monitoring possible impacts and lobbying intergovernmental bodies, international organizations and other stakeholders on behalf of the industry are just a few of the strategies implemented in pursuit of these goals. Providing vocational training, information and practical services to road transport operators is also part of the organization's service to its members (IRU, 2012).

RDA International Coach Tourism Federation

The RDA is the leading association for coach and group tourism in Europe and was founded in Germany in 1951 as the Reise-Ring Deutscher Autobusunternehmungen eV. With approximately 3000 members the RDA still has a very strong German focus although it has alliances with international associations in more than 40 countries. Members include coach companies, tour operators, tourism associations, destination marketing organizations, visitor attractions, culture and events suppliers, carriers and hotel and even restaurant operators. As the promotion of coach and group holiday travel is the primary aim of the RDA, it engages in public service and lobbying activities at national and international levels. Services to its members include special events such as workshops and seminars to help members network and share experiences, and it also offers relevant educational material specific to the industry. The RDA workshop, for example, is an annual trade exhibition for service providers and has become the leading purchasing and sales exhibition in its field. The majority of the events are geared towards small and medium sized tourism enterprises, as this is most representative of its membership base (RDA, 2012).

United Motorcoach Association (UMA)

UMA (as it became known in 1996) is a non-profit corporation that has its origins in the United Bus Owners Association (UBOA) founded in 1971. UMA is a North American association of motor coach owners and industry suppliers with more than 1000 members in both the USA and Canada, including small companies that provide tours and charters, as well as larger fleets that operate intercity route services, larger tours and cross-country trips. The association's role is to protect and promote the interests and welfare of the motor coach industry owners and operators, including the exchange of administrative, operative, and technical information between members, establishing supplier networks, and the representation of members in legislative and regulatory matters (UMA, 2012).

American Bus Association (ABA)

The Washington DC based trade association was founded as early as 1926 as the Motor Bus Division of the American Automobile Association, but adopted its current name in 1977 (after two previous name changes, including the National Association of Motor Bus Operators in 1930, and the National Association of Motor Bus Owners in 1960). Today ABA represents approximately 1000 members in the USA and Canada, including motor coach and tour operators as well as an additional 2800 member organizations representing the travel and tourism industry, as well as suppliers of bus products and services. The organization promotes the business interests of privately owned motor coach and tour operators through government advocacy, by organizing trade events, by providing networking and business development opportunities, educational seminars, management and professional development programmes, and by providing cost-saving programmes such as preferred pricing and discounts from service providers for members. The association is best known for its list of top 100 events in North America, which is compiled every year and includes festivals, parades, fairs, exhibits, shows and other events well-suited for group travel.

At the European level, most nations also have a national bus and/or motor coach association in addition to some regional level associations. A few national examples include the Belgian Federation of Bus and Coach operators (FBAA), the Bundesverband Deutscher Omnibusunternehmer (Germany), the Confederation of Passenger Transport UK, the Danish Coach Owners' Association, Feria Internacional del Autobús y del Autocar (Spain), Les Autocars de France, and the Portuguese Bus and Coach Association. Similarly there are regional level organizations within North America such as Motor Coach Canada, the Mexican Chamber of Passenger and Tourism Road Transport or the National Association of Motorcoach Operators in the USA. Moreover, most states within the USA also have their own motor coach associations, such as the North Carolina Motorcoach Association or the Florida Motorcoach Association, for example.

DEMAND AND SUPPLY

Demand

Due to the fragmented nature of the bus and coach transport sector in terms of regulation, size and type of operators, as well as the range in services offered, the overall availability and reliability of statistics is relatively poor (COST 349, 2005; Steer Davies Gleave, 2009). Furthermore, coach and bus statistics are grouped together in most national statistics. If on rare occasion statistics are available for individual services, the coverage may differ (regular services, special regular services, occasional services, or urban versus inter-urban, for example) and the definitions of those services are unfortunately not consistent between nations and hence impact the comparability of statistics. The International Transport Forum (ITF) at the Organization for Economic Co-operation and Development (OECD) publish data on global transport trends based on data provided by its 52 member countries from which a general overview regarding different transportation modes can be gleaned. For instance, within the ITF member countries buses and coaches accounted for 1607.4 thousand million[5] pkm in 2008 (OECD, 2011), within the OECD member countries they accounted for 1362.1

thousand million pkm, and 505 thousand million pkm in the EU26 (Cyprus is not an ITF member country). Global trends are highlighted in Fig. 5.7 (it should be noted that the base year utilized for comparative purposes was 1990). Although bus and coach transport in the ITF member countries grew by an average of 1.3% in 2008, limited data available for 2009 reveal that the industry was negatively impacted by the economic crisis (OECD, 2011). Furthermore, in the overall development of global mobility, the bus industry is forecasted to lose the greatest share of pkm in comparison to other modes of transport (OECD, 2011).

At the regional level, the European Commission provides transport statistics for the European Union while the North American Transportation Statistics Interchange reports information on transportation in Canada, the USA and Mexico. Overall, passengers within the EU27 travelled 510.4 billion pkm by bus and coach (including trolleybus) in 2009; while this is a decrease of almost 4% from the previous year, bus and coach passenger transport performance has remained relatively stable at around 500 billion pkm over the last ten years in Europe (see Fig. 5.4).

Comparatively, travellers in the USA and Mexico travelled 490 billion pkm and 452 billion pkm respectively in 2009; unfortunately there are no comparable current bus statistics reported for Canada as they utilize number of trips rather than pkm. While bus transport[6] in the USA remained relatively stable over the last ten years[7], Mexico saw a steady increase in usage of approximately 27%. In Europe, buses and coaches have accounted for around 8% of total passenger transport activities over the last ten years. More specifically, during 2009 buses and coaches accounted for 7.8% of total intra-EU passenger transport activities within the EU27,

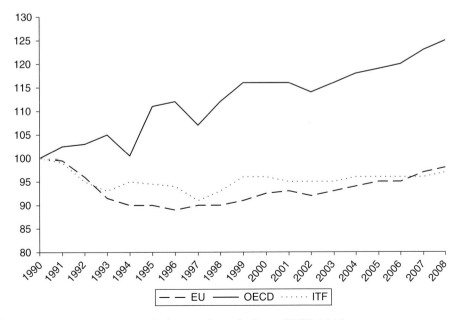

Fig. 5.4. Passenger transport by bus and coach. From OECD, 2011.

rivalling air transport which accounted for 8% (Eurostat, 2011). Interestingly, although air travel overtook bus and coach travel in terms of pkm between 2004 and 2005, the air pkm have dropped recently and the two modes currently account for almost equal pkm (see Fig. 5.5).

This is by no means the case in the USA where air transport accounts for about 12% of total pkm compared with buses and coaches that account for between 3 and 6% of all passenger transport depending on statistical methodology. Although transport demand is often positively correlated with GDP, some evidence has been found indicating that coach travel tends to be higher in states with below average GDP per head. For example, if one considers the modal split of passenger transport on land only, buses and coaches account for 8.8% of ground transportation in the EU27, while reaching 12.1% in the EU12 countries, the newest EU entrants consisting of eight central and eastern European countries (see Table 5.2).

A study of passenger transport by coach prepared for the European Commission attempted to review and analyse the European coach industry including domestic long distance, international regular service, special regular service and occasional transport (Steer Davies Gleave, 2009). Based on an overall market share comparison between coach, bus, rail and car transportation, it was estimated that buses and coaches account for approximately equal shares of the overall pkm travelled within this mode (see Fig. 5.6). More specifically, based on an indicative estimate of EU coach demand by service category, regular service was projected to account for almost 3 billion passenger journeys, special regular services for just over 2 billion passenger journeys, and occasional service for approximately 1.5 billion journeys (see Table 5.3).

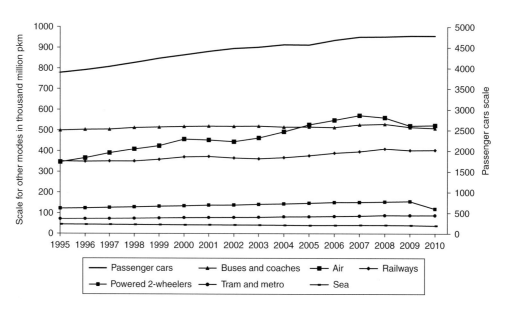

Fig. 5.5. EU27 performance by mode for passenger transport. From Eurostat, 2012.

Table 5.2. EU-wide bus and coach passenger transport in 2010 as percentage of overall land transportation and percentage of main form of transport for holiday trips of four nights or more. (From Eurostat, 2010b, 2013a.)

Country	Overall passenger transport on land (pkm in %)	Main means of transport for holiday trips of >4 nights (%)[a]	Sub-total membership
EU27	8.8	6	
EU15	8.3	–	
EU12	12.1	–	
Austria	10.6	7	EU15
Belgium	13.6	7	EU15
Bulgaria	17.0	25	EU12
Cyprus	18.4	–	EU12
Czech Republic	18.7	18	EU12
Denmark	9.9	6	EU15
Estonia	14.5	17	EU12
Finland	9.9	5	EU15
France	5.8	2	EU15
Germany	6.1	7	EU15
Greece	16.5	11	EU15
Hungary	25.1	7	EU12
Ireland	12.8	2	EU15
Italy	12.2	5	EU15
Latvia	15.3	18	EU12
Lithuania	8.2	15	EU12
Luxembourg	11.4	4	EU15
Malta	18.9	–	EU12

(Continued)

Table 5.2. Continued.

Country	Overall passenger transport on land (pkm in %)	Main means of transport for holiday trips of >4 nights (%)[a]	Sub-total membership
Netherlands	3.9	5	EU15
Poland	6.4	14	EU12
Portugal	10.9	8	EU15
Romania	12.9	–	EU12
Slovakia	15.5	23	EU12
Slovenia	10.8	6	EU12
Spain	12.3	15	EU15
Sweden	7.2	–	EU15
UK	5.1	3	EU15

[a]Data only available for 2008.

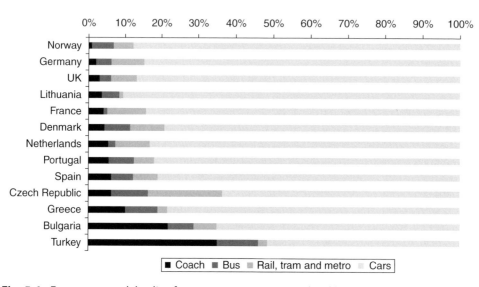

Fig. 5.6. European modal split of passenger transport on land by country for 2008. From Steer Davies Gleave, 2009.

Table 5.3. Estimates of EU coach transport demand by type of service. (From Steer Davies Gleave, 2009.)

	Journeys (millions)	Passenger kilometres (millions)
Regular	2,912	81,226
Special	2,226	52,572
Occasional	1,484	129,185

However, the occasional service by far accounted for the greatest number of pkm (129 billion) probably because tourism services such as the packaged retail tour fall into this category and generally cover greater distances than the other services. It should be noted that these figures are estimates as there is little robust statistical data regarding passenger transport by coach separated by type of service, especially occasional transport (Grant *et al.*, 2009; Steer Davies Gleave, 2009). While not directly comparable, a study commissioned by the American Bus Association estimated that the motor coach industry provided approximately 723 million passenger trips in the USA and Canada in 2009, or approximately 95 billion pkm (Nathan Associates, 2008). Moreover, it was estimated that charter, tour and sightseeing services accounted for over half of the distance travelled by motor coaches.

Unfortunately, reliable statistics for bus and coach tourism are almost impossible to quote at the global level, and very limited at the regional and even national levels because such data are presently not collected regularly, if at all[8]. For example, although the UNWTO reports global information regarding tourism travel statistics including mode of transport for inbound tourism, and the tourism satellite accounts make provisions for three subdivisions of land transport including railway, road and other, no provisions are made for more detailed level reporting. Hence, the 2011 edition of the UNWTO publication Tourism Highlights reports that 41% of travellers arrived at their destination by road, the percentage of coach and bus use is unfortunately not evident. Nonetheless, based on tourism statistics published by Eurostat, land transport was the principal means of transport for holiday trips of four nights or more for 71% of Europeans in 2008, of which bus or coach transport constituted a mere 6% (Eurostat, 2010b). However, as illustrated in Fig. 5.6 the market share of buses and motor coaches varies greatly by country. Moreover, in a recent Eurobarometer survey, 39% of respondents in Turkey (currently an associate member of the EU) reported using the bus as their primary method of transport for their main holiday trip in 2009 (European Commission, 2010c). Travellers in Germany are representative of the 6% European average in bus use as the main mode of transport for their main vacation, translating to a market volume of 5.3 million motor coach holidays (of five days or longer) as well as 12–15 million short trips annually (see Focus box). According to the 2009 US National Household Travel Survey (NHTS, 2010), only 2–3% of travellers utilize the bus for holiday travel; moreover, the bus captures 3% of leisure travel at the average intercity trip length of 244 miles, decreasing to 2% with a trip length of 500 miles, and vanishes to under 1% for trip lengths over 1000 miles.

There is limited market research in the area of motor coach tourism, particularly in relation to market segmentation and customer need assessments as well as the creation of benchmarks and yearly monitoring of trends (Lumsdon, 2006). However, as discussed earlier in this chapter, the horse omnibus came about because of a perceived need for transport among the poor and middle-class; to this day, bus and coach transport is still considered to be a low cost means of transportation and as such offers a viable alternative to people unable to afford more expensive modes of transportation.

Focus box

Snapshot of coach market in Germany

- approximately 5.3 million coach holidays (5 days or more)
- approximately 12 million short break trips (2–4 days in duration)
- approximately 70 million occasional services (day trips, excursions, school trips)
- average trip lasted 9.3 days
- average age is 56 years
- share of age over 60 years is 59.9%, and between 14 and 29 years is 24.0%

From RDA, 2013.

Statistically, groups that often have low incomes and low affordability for high-end travel include the young, the old, women and minorities; although the motor coach industry caters to all, young and senior travellers have traditionally represented the largest demand segments within the industry (Becker *et al.*, 2006; Steer Davies Gleave, 2009; Gross, 2011). In fact, it was suggested that about 50 to 70% of motor coach travellers in the USA were seniors (Hung and Petrick, 2009). Case studies of four European countries also indicate that particularly the young and senior travellers are well represented in coach travel (see Table 5.4). Similarly, annual market studies of the bus and coach industry in Germany have consistently found the average coach traveller to be around 60 years of age. Moreover, it was found that approximately 25% of travellers over the age of 60 took a coach trip in the last three years (Gross, 2011), while coach holidays account for 8.5% of all German holidays abroad. The limited research on coach tourism has shown that some of the benefits travellers seek are good value for money, a sense of safety and convenience provided by the expertise of a tour company, and the provision of companionship and friendship while travelling. However, there is a general lack of concrete information regarding coach tourism users and this would be an interesting area for future research. Particularly in light of the desire for more sustainable and efficient modes of transportation, it has been shown that travelling by bus or coach creates the smallest carbon footprint among counterparts such as the train, ferries, cars or airplanes. More specifically,

Table 5.4. Profile of coach users and trips in selected EU member states. (From Steer Davies Gleave, 2009.)

Member state	Proportion of coach users aged		Motive for travel				
	<30	>50	Visit friends/ relatives	Holiday	Work/ business	Education	Other
Greece	63%	14.5%	–	–	–	–	–
Spain	48%	21%	23%	28%	18%	14%	17%
Sweden (regular services)	31%	45%	47%	15%	4%	5%	29%
Sweden (occasional services)	55%	38%	15%	12%	3%	1%	70%
UK (regular services)	33.5%	47.5%	22%	25%	3%	2%	48%
UK (occasional services)	14.3%	71.1%	3%	35%	0%	0%	63%

coaches emit 0.03kg of CO_2 per pkm, which is half that of trains and a fraction of the amount emitted by cars and airplanes which emit 0.11 kg and 0.18 kg of CO_2 respectively (Smart Move Campaign, 2013).

Supply

There are several possible parties involved in the provision of coach tourism: independent bus/coach operators providing tour services (which can range from very small to very large companies or take the form of consortiums of independent coach companies); classic tour operators (ranging from general tour operators offering coach tourism as one of many products, to specialized bus tour operators); and tour wholesalers who charter buses to provide the transportation for their tours (see Fig. 5.7).

Generally the average size of coach operators within Europe and North America is small, although there are also a number of very large coach operators. As illustrated in Table 5.5, there were approximately 680,000 buses and coaches in the EU in 2008 operated by

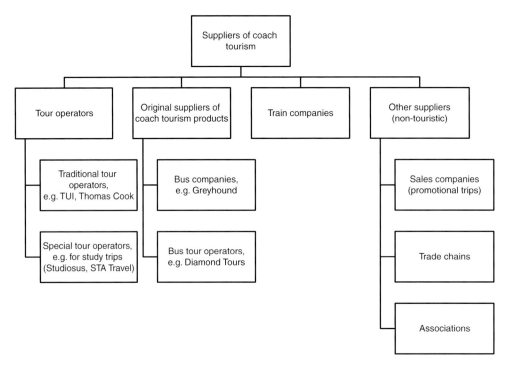

Fig. 5.7. Suppliers of coach tourism. Based on Pompl, 1997.

approximately 43,000 companies (Steer Davies Gleave, 2009). Comparatively, there were just over 3000 companies operating approximately 29,000 motor coaches in the USA, while 295 Canadian companies were operating just over 4000 motor coaches (Nathan Associates, 2008); based on these statistics, a carrier operated an average of ten motor coaches. Although the 28 largest companies (operating 100 coaches or more) accounted for a mere 1% of all suppliers, they operated nearly a third of the motor coaches in the industry. Comparatively, approximately 2700 companies operated fewer than ten motor coaches (with an average of three motor coaches) and accounted for almost a quarter of all operations (Nathan Associates, 2008). Furthermore, of 1729 companies providing bus charter services (not including local services) in the USA, approximately 79% operated fewer than ten vehicles (Highbeam Business, 2012). As a European example, in the UK there were 5610 companies advertising coach services in 2009 while the total coach fleet consisted of approximately 22,000 vehicles; indicating fewer than four vehicles per company (Steer Davies Gleave, 2009).

The National Express Group is one of the largest providers of bus and coach service operating in Europe and North America. While it is the largest scheduled coach service provider in Europe, it focuses on the school bus market in North America (Durham School Services). In Europe it operates the largest and probably best known brand Eurolines, which is a consortium of between 28 and 32 independent coach companies operating together to form Europe's largest regular coach network. ALSA is the largest private bus operator in Spain and since

Table 5.5. Overview of European and North American bus and coach industry.

	Estimate of fleet size		Number of companies	
	Coach only	**Bus and coach**	**Coach only**	**Bus and coach**
EU15	180,185[a]	457,352[a,d]	21,842[a]	29,818[a]
EU12	68,694[a]	221,714[a,e]	7,379[a]	13,400[a]
Total EU	**248,879[a]**	**679,066[a,f]**	**29,221[a]**	**43,218[a]**
Canada	4,211[c]	84,163[b]	295[c]	1,385[g]
Mexico	–	333,287[b]	–	–
USA	29,325[c]	843,308[b]	3,137[c]	–

[a] Steer Davies Gleave, 2009 (2008 data).

[b] North American Transport Statistics Database, 2012 (2008 data).

[c] Motorcoach Census 2008; Nathan Associates, 2008 (2007 data, as subsequent US and Canadian data was cumulated in 2008 and 2009 updates).

[d] According to the EC Statistical Pocketbook 2011, there were 572,000 buses and coaches registered in the EU15 in 2008.

[e] According to the EC Statistical Pocketbook 2011, there were 245,000 buses and coaches registered in the EU12 in 2008.

[f] According to the EC Statistical Pocketbook 2011, there were 817,000 buses and coaches registered in the total EU in 2008.

[g] Canadian Passenger Bus and Urban Transit Industries, 2009.

2005 also belongs to the National Express Group. The group employs approximately 38,000 people and operates more than 21,000 vehicles. Similarly, FirstGroup plc operates in the USA, Canada, and the UK and its most recognized brand is probably Greyhound, which is almost an American icon for many tourists and provides scheduled intercity bus transportation services in the USA and Canada. Coach America is also a consortium of over 20 local companies in North America providing scheduled bus routes, coach tours, charter and sightseeing tours. In fact, Metro Magazine publishes an annual list of the top 50 motor coach companies in North America; the two largest companies by far are FirstGroup America and Coach USA/ Coach Canada, who operate a total of 9175 and 1717 buses and coaches respectively. More specifically, FirstGroup America operates 1950 motor coaches while Coach USA and Coach Canada operate 1202 motor coaches. Academy Express is the next largest company operating 639 motor coaches, followed by two Canadian companies: Pacific Western Transportation Ltd (390 coaches) and Royal Hyway Tours (355 coaches). Trailway is North America's oldest independent group of privately owned motor coach companies and operates more than 2000 coaches throughout North America and parts of Europe. While the services provided by the motor coach industry are diverse, nearly all operators provide charter services (96%) and tours (52%),

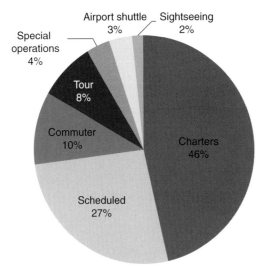

Fig. 5.8. Percentage of service provided by coach operators. From Nathan Associates Inc., 2008.

while the proportion offering sightseeing, shuttle services and scheduled and commuter services is limited (Nathan Associates Inc., 2008). However, many operators provide a mixture of services (see Fig. 5.8).

It was estimated that the combined turnover of the bus and coach industry in Europe was approximately €29 billion in 2008, of which around €15 billion can be attributed to the coach industry. Furthermore, it was estimated that over 1.5 million people were employed by the bus and coach industry in Europe, of which approximately 1.1 million were drivers (Steer Davies Gleave, 2009). Based on the US Tourism Satellite Accounts, inter-urban bus transportation, inter-urban charter bus transportation, and scenic and sightseeing services accounted for almost $6.5 million in terms of direct tourism output in 2010 (US Department of Commerce, 2011). Furthermore, motor coach based tourism generates as many as 1,056,750 jobs in communities across the USA, paying almost $40.6 billion in wages and benefits (John Dunham & Associates, 2012).

Focus box

Economic impacts of bus tourism

Motor coach travellers can generate significant economic transactions for a destination. For example, a fully loaded coach can contribute close to $12,000 per day trip to a destination in meals, lodging and other spending. In a study conducted in three destinations in the northeastern USA, it was estimated that the economic impact on a destination community by a one-day motor coach group is between $2,536 to $4,563; an overnight group can create an economic impact between $5,094 and $11,264; and a visit by a two-night or more group creates an impact between $9,021 and $16,080 (ABA, 2010). More specifically, approximately 43.7 to 63.9% of the gross amount spent remained in the destination's economy. Local restaurants, retailers, hotels and attractions reported that the estimated share of overall quarterly business generated by bus groups ranged from 18.3 to 40%.

Each bus passenger was reported to spend

- $15 at restaurants,
- $35 at retail locations,
- $268 at hotels, and
- $35 on attractions.

The International Road Transportation union introduced an international classification system for tourist coaches which is similar to that used in the hotel industry and ranges from one star coaches to four star luxury touring coaches. The scale is graded according to technical, performance and comfort standards, including such criteria as engine power, transport capacity, year of manufacture, comfort of seats (including distance between seats, reclining angle, armrests, etc.) and minimum requirements regarding cooling and heating, windows, lighting, acoustics and luggage, for example. Standards regarding equipment include criteria such as availability of toilets, air-conditioning, video, or kitchenette. An example of a national classification system is that of the Gütegemeinschaft Buskomfort in Germany, which utilizes five stars and is mainly based on comfort standards.

NOTES

1. While we highlight the main rules and regulations governing bus and coach operations in Europe, more extensive information can be found at the Europa portal under http://europa.eu/legislation_summaries/transport/road_transport/index_en.htm

2. For more detailed information regarding the FMCSA rules and regulations see http://www.fmcsa.dot.gov/rules-regulations/rules-regulations.htm

3. The regulations governing charter service provisions by recipients of federal funds are laid out in CFR 49, part 604 available at http://edocket.access.gpo.gov/2008/pdf/08-86.pdf

4. See http://csa.fmcsa.dot.gov for more detailed information.

5. Many international data sources utilize the rather unwieldy 'thousand million' because of differences in the American and European billion. More specifically, a million million equates to a billion in Europe, while a thousand million equates to a billion in the USA. Although British English has adopted the American English interpretation, many parts of Europe still use the former system. Hence to avoid confusion and ease the comparison of large numbers between languages and countries, many sources utilize 'thousand million'.

6. No distinction is made between bus and coach in the database. Furthermore, although distinct categories of service are provided for in the database, only Canada made use of these and they unfortunately stopped reporting bus data in 2003.

7. The US Federal Highway Administration changed their methodology regarding calculations of annual vehicle miles travelled in 2007, hence there is a break in data comparability. Before the methodology change, buses accounted for around 3% of total passenger transport activities in the USA between 1996 and 2006; the percentage increased to approximately 6% after the new methodology was adopted.

8. Personal communication with Oleg Kamberski, Head of Passenger Transport & Taxis, International Road Transport Union, on 31 January 2012.

FURTHER READING

Becken, S. (2005) Towards sustainable tourism transport: an analysis of coach tourism in New Zealand. *Tourism Geography* 1, 23–42.

Dean, C.J. (1993) Travels by the excursion coach in the United Kingdom. *Journal of Travel Research* Spring, 59–64.

Dürkop, D. and Gross, S. (2012) Tourist cards – experiences with soft mobility in Germany's low mountain ranges. In: Tiller, T.R. (ed.) Proceedings of Conference BEST EN Think Tank XII. University of Technology Sydney, Sydney, Australia, pp. 318–324.

European Commission (2009) Study of passenger transport by coach (Final Report). Brussels, Belgium.

Gross, S. (2011) *Tourismus und Verkehr – Grundlagen, Marktanalyse und Strategien von Verkehrsun-ternehmen*. Oldenbourg, Munich, Germany.

Gross, S. and Schröder, A. (2007) Low cost airlines and coach tourism – threats and opportunities for German tour operators. In: Gross, S. and Schröder, A. (eds) *Handbook of Low Cost Airlines – Strategies, Business Processes and Market Environment*. Erich Schmidt Verlag, Berlin, Germany, pp. 249–261.

Guiver, J., Lumsdon, L. and Morris, K. (2007) The role of scheduled buses in reducing car journeys in tourist areas. In: Peeters, P.M. (ed.) *Tourism and Climate Change Mitigation. Methods, Greenhouse Gas Reduction and Policies*. Stichting NHTV Breda, Breda, The Netherlands.

Guiver, J., Lumsdon, L., Weston, R. and Ferguson, M. (2007) Do buses help meet tourism objectives? The contribution and potential of scheduled buses in rural destination areas. *Transport Policy* 4, 275–282.

IBIS World (2009) *Charter Bus Services in the US*. Melbourne, Australia.

Lumsdon, L. (2006) The design of tourist buses. *Annals of Tourism Research* 3, 748–766.

Page, S.J. (2009) *Transport and Tourism – Global Perspectives*, 3rd edn. Prentice Hall, Harlow, UK.

Plimsoll World (2011) *Bus & Coach Operators Industry Analysis – Europe*. Stockton-on-Tees, UK.

Steer Davies Gleave (2009) Study of passenger transport by coach. Study prepared for the European Commission, Directorate General Energy and Transport, Brussels, Belgium.

White, P. and Farrington, J. (1998) Bus and coach deregulation and privatization in Great Britain, with particular reference to Scotland. *Journal of Transport Geography* 02, 135–141.

Trade journals/magazines and scientific organizations

BusToCoach – European on-line magazine, Coach Tourism Professional, EuroBus, Omnibusrevue and Bus Aktuell, Travel and Tourism Research Association (www.ttra.com).

Internet sources

http://epp.eurostat.ec.europa.eu/portal/page/portal/eurostat/home, www.bdo-online.de, www.bustocoach.com/en, www.bitre.gov.au, www.busandcoach.travel, www.buses.org, www.buskomfort.de, www.eact.travel, www.eurostat.org, www.rda.de, www.iru.org, www.mindbranch.com (more than 70 studies about 'Bus and Coach', but they are all with costs), www.uma.org.

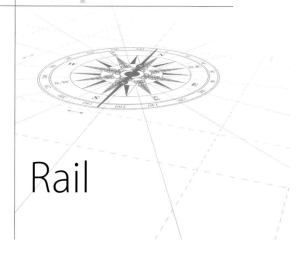

chapter 6

Rail

LEARNING OBJECTIVES

- Identify and describe the different types of rail transportation and their relative importance to the tourism industry.
- Describe the impact of early rail operations and the present state of the industry.
- Critically assess rail governance and appraise the impact of current developments.
- Recognize market potential for rail as a viable mode of tourism transportation.

Rail transportation can be generally divided into freight and passenger transportation, although mixed forms are also utilized; a goods train utilizes wagons for the carriage of cargo, while a passenger train is composed of carriages or coaches for the transportation of people. From a tourism perspective, train travel has been viewed as a form of either 'inter-destination' or 'intra-destination' passenger transportation (Duval, 2007, p. 99). Inter-destination rail transport encompasses tourists travelling between destinations, at the international, inter-regional, or even intra-regional level, while intra-destination rail transport refers to transportation within a destination or attraction. However, a third form of rail transportation applicable to tourism is the train tour or vacation, in which the means of transportation is part of the attraction. These trips can range from independent or custom rail vacations, escorted rail tours, to luxurious all-inclusive journeys. Furthermore, the growing interest in heritage tourism experiences has also spurred a renewed interest in scenic train tours and heritage railway experiences.

DEFINITIONS

As illustrated in Fig. 6.1, there are many different types of rail passenger transportation serving a variety of functions, from long distance international or intercity travel, to local urban

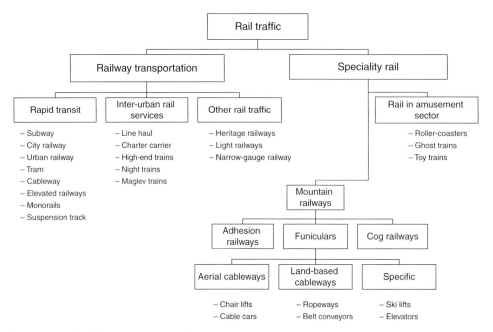

Fig. 6.1. Rail traffic system. From Gross, 2011.

transit services. However, with respect to tourism, high-speed rail, rapid transit, light rail and speciality rail are of particular interest and will therefore be highlighted here. When we think of rail transportation we automatically think of trains: vehicles that operate on tracks, gliding either above or below the tracks, suspended above or below a magnetic field, or even guided by cables. The majority of trains are guided along the track on steel wheels, some utilize rubber tyres on concrete, while a few utilize magnetic technology (Kepper, 2010). Therefore, before we examine the definitions of varying forms of rail transportation, let us first define what is meant by train.

According to the *Glossary of Transport Statistics* (2009) compiled by the International Transport Forum (ITF), Eurostat and the United Nations Economic Commission for Europe (UNECE), a train is:

> One or more railway vehicles hauled by one or more locomotives or railcars, or one railcar travelling alone, running under a given number or specific designation from an initial fixed point to a terminal fixed point. A light engine, i.e. a locomotive travelling on its own, is not considered to be a train (p. 25).

Comparatively, the Federal Transit Administration (part of the US Department of Transportation) publishes a National Transit Database Glossary, in which a train is defined as:

> One or more passenger cars (including locomotives) coupled together and propelled by self-contained motor equipment. Also known as a *consist* which may be any one of the following:
>
> • A locomotive and one or more passenger cars as in the commuter rail (CR) mode, or
> • One or more heavy rail (HR) or light rail (LR) vehicles, or
> • One vehicle only, if appropriate to that mode (e.g. cable car (CC)).
>
> (p. 86)

Hence, trains move either under their own power (tractive vehicles such as locomotives) or are hauled by another vehicle (coaches, railcar trailers and wagons). There are three types of locomotives: electric, diesel and steam. Steam was the dominant form of propulsion until the early 20th century, when it was replaced by diesel and electric power (Kepper, 2010). Although there are still a few steam locomotives in use, they are mainly used as tourist or educational attractions (see speciality trains later in this chapter). Defining rail transportation is not an easy task, as terminology often differs between Europe and North America. Therefore, definitions from both a European and North American perspective are offered here with a few examples.

Focus box

- An electric locomotive primarily derives its current from overhead wires or conductor rails. However, they often have an engine (diesel or other) to supply current to the electric motor in the event that electric current cannot be obtained from the usual source.
- Diesel locomotives use a diesel engine as the main source of power, irrespective of the type of transmission.
- Steam locomotives utilize steam as their source of power, whether cylinder or turbine driven, irrespective of the type of fuel used.

From ITF, 2009.

High-speed rail

According to the International Union of Railways, there is no single standard definition of high-speed rail. However, the European Union (Directive 96/48) provides a very broad definition encompassing many high-speed systems, including infrastructure, trains and their compatibility. In essence, high-speed trains are designed to travel at a speed between 250 and 300 km/h on special lines, or around 200 km/h on existing older but upgraded lines (UIC, 2010a). The US Department of Transportation's definition distinguishes between two types of high-speed rail:

- High-speed rail – Express. Frequent, express service between major population centers 200–600 miles apart, with few intermediate stops. Top speeds of at least 150 mph on completely grade-separated, dedicated rights-of way (with the possible exception of some shared track in terminal areas). Intended to relieve air and highway capacity constraints.
- High-speed rail – Regional. Relatively frequent service between major and moderate population centers 100–500 miles apart, with some intermediate stops. Top speeds of 110–150 mph, grade-separated, with some dedicated and some shared track (using positive train control technology).

(Lee, 2009)

Examples of high-speed rail in Europe include the French *Train à Grande Vitesse* (TGV), Germany's InterCity Express (ICE), the *Alta Velocidad Española* (AVE) in Spain, the Eurostar, offering service between the UK, France and Belgium, and the Thalys trains, which link major cities in France, Belgium, Germany and the Netherlands. In the USA, Amtrak's Acela Express is a high-speed train that operates between Washington, New York and Boston; however, due to ageing infrastructure and the lack of a separate, dedicated track, the train has severe speed limitations and is not truly comparable to the European high-speed train services.

Rapid transit

An urban electric transport system characterized by high speed, capacity and frequency, which is totally independent from other traffic running along an unimpeded right of way (International Association of Public Transport). Examples include the New York City subway (Fig. 6.2), the London Underground, the Paris Metro, and the German U-Bahn system. The Transportation Research Board (TRB, a division of the National Research Council) bases its definitions on the *Glossary of Transport Statistics* (2009) and defines rapid transit as:

> a transit system that uses steel wheeled passenger rail cars operating singly or in trains on fixed steel rails in exclusive rights of way in underground tunnels, on elevated structures, in open cuts, or at surface level with very few, if any, grade crossings (at which rail traffic has the right of way) using a third rail power source or overhead catenary and that generally serves one contiguous urban area. Sometimes referred to as Metro.

In the *Public Transportation Fact Book* (APTA, 2011) published by the American Public Transportation Association (APTA), rapid transit is defined under the term 'heavy rail' as:

> a mode of transit service (also called metro, subway, rapid transit, or rapid rail) operating on an electric railway with the capacity for a heavy volume of traffic. It is characterized by high speed and rapid acceleration passenger rail cars operating singly or in multi-car trains on fixed rails; separate rights-of-way from which all other vehicular and foot traffic are excluded; sophisticated signalling, and high platform loading.

(APTA, 2011, p. 37)

Fig. 6.2. MTA subway in New York City. © Luisa Wolter.

The corresponding definition in the *Glossary of Transport Statistics* (2009, p. 10) compiled by the International Transport Forum (ITF), Eurostat and the United Nations Economic Commission for Europe (UNECE) can be found under metro line/subway and is as follows: 'an electric rail line mainly for urban transport with the capacity for heavy volumes of traffic involving very frequent train movements. Metro lines are also characterised by closely spaced stations, normally with around 1,000 m between the stations.'

Light rail

Light rail transit is also mainly an electric form of transportation, but in comparison to rapid transit, it travels at lower speeds and is designed for lower traffic volumes. According to the International Association of Public Transport, light rail transit (LRT) can be developed in stages, from a tramway to a rapid transit system, and operates partially on its own right-of-way. A good example of light rail is the German Stadtbahn system. The TRB defines light rail as 'an urban transportation system that uses electrically powered lightweight rail cars operating singly or in short trains on fixed duo-rail guideways; may be grade separated, and loads passengers from low-to medium-height platforms' (*Transportation Research Board*, 2014).

Similarly, in its *Public Transportation Fact Book* (APTA, 2011), APTA defines light rail as:

> a mode of transit service (also called streetcar, tramway, or trolley) operating passenger rail cars singly (or in short, usually two-car or three- car, trains) on fixed rails in right-of-way that is often separated from other traffic for part or much of the way. Light rail vehicles are typically driven electrically with power being drawn from an overhead electric line via a trolley or a pantograph; driven by an operator on board the vehicle; and may have either high platform loading or low level boarding using steps.
>
> (APTA, 2011, p. 39)

In the *Glossary of Transport Statistics* (2009, p. 10), light rail is defined simply as 'a rail line mainly for urban transport of passengers often electrified. Stations/halts are generally less than 1,200 m apart.' However, a comparison to rapid transit is also provided which explains that it is:

> more lightly constructed, is designed for lower traffic volumes and usually travels at lower speeds. Normally the power is drawn from an overhead electric line via a trolley or a pantograph. It is sometimes difficult to make a precise distinction between light rail and trams; trams are generally not separated from road traffic, whereas light rail may be separated from other systems.
>
> (*Glossary of Transport Statistics*, 2009, p. 10)

Trams can be categorized as a sub-category of light rail, although they differ from railways as most systems utilize both segregated and street-running sections, i.e. mixed with road traffic. In the *Glossary of Transport Statistics* (2009, p. 11), a tramline is defined as 'a railway mainly installed on and well integrated into the urban road system. The tramcars are powered either electrically or by diesel engine, particularly for special rail borne road vehicles.'

Some systems are in fact both light rail and tramways, such as the Manchester Metrolink and the Croydon Tramlink in the UK.

Speciality

Monorail

Currently monorails tend to be used mainly in airports (e.g. Düsseldorf International Airport, Germany; Tampa International Airport, Florida, USA; Newark International, New Jersey, USA), theme parks (Disney World, Orlando, Florida, USA; Alton Towers, UK; Mirabilandia Ravenna-Savio, Italy) and zoos (Chester Zoo, England; Ueno Zoo, Tokyo, Japan), although urban monorail transit systems exist in Japan (Tokyo-Haneda and Shonan) and one in Germany (Wuppertal Schwebebahn). A monorail has been defined by Vuchic (2007, p. 579) as a 'guided transit mode riding on or suspended from a single rail, beam or tube; vehicles usually operate in trains'. Similarly, APTA (2011, p. 39) defines a monorail as 'an electric railway of guided transit vehicles operating singly or in multi-car trains. The vehicles are suspended from or straddle a guideway formed by a single beam, rail, or tube'.

Cable-propelled

There are several types of cable-propelled forms of transit, including aerial tramways, funiculars, gondolas and cable cars, all of which are popular forms of tourist transportation as well as being attractions in and of themselves. There are two basic distinctions, those that operate in the air, and those that run on or under-ground. While there are further differentiations within these two groups, they are often rather mechanical and difficult for laymen to detect with the naked eye; therefore we have included examples of each to try and help make the differences a little clearer.

Aerial tramway

As the name implies, aerial tramways operate in the air and are defined by APTA (2011, p. 38) as an 'electric system of aerial cables with suspended powerless passenger vehicles. The vehicles are propelled by separate cables attached to the vehicle suspension system and powered by engines or motors at a central location not on board the vehicle'. Similarly, Vuchic (2007, p. 575) describes them as a 'passenger transportation mode consisting of cabins suspended on a stationary cable and towed by a moving, usually closed-loop cable, used to overcome steep gradients, deep valleys, or bodies of water'. The Sandia Peak Aerial Tramway located on the eastern edge of Albuquerque in New Mexico, USA, is one of the most popular tourist attractions in Central New Mexico due to the spectacular views.

Funicular or inclined plane

A funicular or inclined plane is another sub-group of cable-propelled transit; much like the cable car it operates:

over exclusive right-of-way on steep grades (slopes) with powerless vehicles propelled by moving cables attached to the vehicles and powered by engines or motors at a central location not on board the vehicle. The special tramway type of vehicles has passenger seats that remain horizontal while the undercarriage (truck) is angled parallel to the slope.

(APTA, 2011, p. 39)

Traditionally they operate using the principle of gravity and hence Vuchic (2007, p. 578) included the idea of counterbalance in his definition:

> a passenger transportation mode consisting of a pair of rail vehicles (or short trains) permanently attached to two ends of the same cable, counterbalancing each other. May have a single track with a turnout or a double track. Used to overcome steep gradients.

The Great Orme Tramway in Llandudno, Wales is an example of a cable-hauled funicular based on the principle of gravity (although motorized help is provided), and is the only cable-hauled tram still operating on UK public roads.

Gondola

Gondolas operate in the air, that is both the propulsion and support come from steel cables above. This is a popular form of transport in ski resorts, although some gondolas can also be found in relatively flat urban environments such as the Telecabina Lisboa that runs along the Parque das Nacoes in Lisbon, Portugal, or the Kölner Seilbahn, a gondola crossing the river Rhine in Cologne, Germany, which is popular for its stunning views of the city.

Cable car

As the name implies, cable cars (Fig. 6.3) are powered using a cable mechanism. However, unlike a Gondola, they are propelled from below rather than above and are supported by rails on the ground. Vuchic (2007) defined cable cars as a 'rail transit mode with single cars (without motors) propelled by a continuously moving cable located in an underground slot between rails'. Similarly, APTA (2011, p. 38) uses the following definition: 'a railway with individually controlled transit vehicles attached while moving to a moving cable located below the street surface and powered by engines or motors at a central location not on board the vehicle'. San Francisco's historic cable cars are probably one of the most famous cable car systems in the world, although it is surprising how many exist worldwide.

Rack or cog railway

Vuchic (2007, p. 577) defines a cog railway as 'a rail transportation mode with auxiliary or full traction via a geared wheel in the middle of a powered axle, which is engaged with a linear vertical gear (rack) installed along the track centre, providing traction on very steep grades'. The first mountain cog railway was the Mount Washington Cog Railway, in New Hamphire, USA. A popular rack railway for sightseeing tourists travelling in the Rhine River Valley region around Königswinter in Germany is the Drachenfelsbahn.

Fig. 6.3. Cable car in Lisbon. © Katja Wiesner.

Narrow gauge railway

As the name implies, a narrow gauge railway is one that utilizes a narrower track gauge than the standard of 1435 mm. Both the Harzer Schmalspurbahn, in Wernigerode, Germany and the Conway Scenic Railroad, North Conway, New Hampshire, USA are good examples of narrow gauge railways used mainly for tourism.

HISTORICAL DEVELOPMENT OF THE MARKET

Railroads have their historical roots in wagon roads, wooden rails using man or horse power to pull wagons or carts. Examples of such transportation can be found from as early as the 1500s in Germany (Bellis, 2011a) and were used in the mid-1600s in British coal mines (Houk, 2008).

By the late 1700s, iron replaced the wooden rails and wheels and early tramway systems spread throughout Europe, although at this time they were still horse driven. Two inventions in the UK at the turn of the 18th century were critical for the modern railroad: first, the flanged wagon wheel was designed by William Jessup in 1789 (the groove in the wheel allowed for a better hold along the track and was to become the standard for future rail transportation); and second, the advent of the steam engine enabled the development of the first tramway locomotive in 1804 by Richard Trevithick in Wales, with the Englishman George Stephenson following with a steam locomotive engine designed for railways in 1825 (Bellis, 2011a).

The Stockton and Darlington Railroad Company was the first railroad to run regular scheduled services for the transportation of goods and passengers in 1825 (Rühle, 2007). At this time there were only 25 miles of public railroad open in the world, over the next 50 years this would increase to 160,000 miles and would continue to grow exponentially. Similarly, there were only two locomotives available for use on a public railway in 1825, but this increased to 70,000 by the turn of the century (Metcalfe, 2006). Some historians see the opening of the Liverpool to Manchester railway in 1830 as the true beginning of railway passenger transportation, as it was the first substantial railway to rely entirely on steam power and it was the first railway to earn a significant amount of its revenue from the transportation of passengers (Lowson, 1998). According to the Association of American Railroads, the first regularly scheduled steam-powered rail passenger service in the USA began operation in 1830 in South Carolina, and Canada's first public railway soon followed in 1836 between Saint Jean sur Richelieu and La Prairie, Québec. Continental Europe soon followed with both Germany and Belgium opening their first rail routes in 1835, between Nürnberg and Fürth in Germany (Gross, 2011), and between Brussels and Mechelen in Belgium (Immers *et al.*, 2001). Railroads expanded at amazing rates in both Europe and America from 1830 onwards. According to Butler (2007), for example, Britain had only 95 miles of track in 1830, yet in ten years this grew to 1500 miles, and by 1850 to 6600 miles. By 1890, Great Britain had 20,000 miles of track, while Germany had 26,000 miles and the USA had 167,000 miles.

Railroads helped to spread the notion of travel for pleasure in both Europe and North America. For example, the industrial revolution in Great Britain led to more leisure time for workers through mechanization, which, combined with affordable rail travel and the Bank Holiday Act of 1871, meant that leisure trips to British seaside resorts such as Blackpool and Torquay became very popular. The forerunner to such leisure travel was a trip to Liverpool organized by Thomas Cook in the summer of 1845, which turned out to be the first of many, as the Thomas Cook company is still a renowned name within the modern travel industry! Similarly, the American railroad companies played an important part in the development of the US national park system, including setting up hotels in or near the parks so that travellers had a place to stay on their excursions, which in turn was a precursor to modern tourism (see the history of the Northern Pacific Railroad, for example). The invention of the sleeping car also had an important impact on passenger rail transportation; although not the first, George Pullman's design of 1857 offered the first truly comfortable coaches designed for overnight travel (Bellis, 2011a). The golden age of rail transportation began in the mid-19th century, and it was not until the early 20th century that other modes of transport, such as automobiles, buses and planes, began to challenge the railway dominance (Association of American Railroads, 2013). The advent of relatively inexpensive air travel and the widespread availability of the private automobile drew passengers away from railroad travel in the 1950s; despite significant post-Second World War investments and modernization efforts, there is a continued decline in rail market share.

Between the 1960s and 1980s, most nations had brought the railways under various forms of public ownership (Profillidis, 2006). The North American rail operators were not exempt from these developments; in 1967 Canada's two railway companies, Canadian Pacific and Canadian National Railway, wanted to eliminate passenger services completely until the federal government agreed to cover 80% of the two company's losses due to its strong belief in the importance of passenger rail transportation. Ten years later, the federal government created VIA Rail Canada to organize and provide all intercity passenger train services in Canada (VIA Rail Canada, 2011). Similarly, the US passenger rail operations experienced decreasing ridership in the 1960s and several operators burdened by heavy regulation, as well as subsidized competition, had to file for bankruptcy protection by the early 1970s (Association of American Railroads, 2013). In response, the Consolidated Rail Corp. was created from six bankrupt northeastern railroads based on the Railroad Revitalization and Regulatory Reform Act in 1976. The act included regulatory reforms, intended to make the rail regulatory system more responsive to the changing circumstances of the rail industry. Although private freight railroads operated intercity passenger operations in the USA until this point, they did so at a net loss of millions of dollars for many years. In 1970 the Rail Passenger Service Act established the National Railroad Passenger Corporation (Amtrak). More than half of the rail passenger routes operated by the freight railroad companies were eliminated when Amtrak began service on 1 May 1971 (Amtrak, 2012). Today, Amtrak is the sole intercity US passenger rail carrier in the continental USA and the majority of the approximately 22,000 miles over which Amtrak operates are actually owned by the mainly privately held freight railroads. Interestingly, the opposite scenario occurred in Mexico, where the Ferrocarriles Nacionales de Mexico (FNM) operated rail transportation under the supervision of the Ministry of Transportation and Communications until 1995, when the government announced the FNM would be privatized. Most passenger services were eliminated at this time, except for tourist lines such as the Chihuahua al Pacifico (Copper Canyon), the Expreso Maya, and the Tequila Express, for example.

Another important event within the history of rail passenger transport is the emergence of advanced train systems using high-speed technology. In fact, scholars have made the case that high-speed rail has prompted the resurgence of rail travel (Banister and Hall, 1993; Givoni and Banister, 2008). The first high-speed train was developed in Japan (Tokaido line using the Shinkansen high-speed train) and is presently well established in Japan and most of Europe, while the network is being introduced in the Far East and the USA (Givoni, 2006). Although high-speed trains are seen as a viable alternative to air travel for some routes (particularly for trips under 1000 km), it is not clear yet whether high-speed trains can have a positive impact on rail's overall share of passenger transportation at a global level. Nonetheless, the integration between rail and other transport modes will provide opportunities for more sustainable travel in the future.

INSTITUTIONAL FRAMEWORK

The railway system is extremely complicated and requires extensive regulatory frameworks to ensure safe, uninterrupted and cost-effective service. To this end, the coordination of infrastructure providers, service providers, operating systems, safety and communication is of vital importance (Gross, 2011). Rail networks are governed and regulated at many levels; in addition to national laws, there are regional and international agreements that must be observed.

Unfortunately, there is no internationally uniform legal or regulatory framework regarding rail infrastructure or operations (UNECE, 2010). However, some regulatory provisions have been achieved at the regional level. For example, the countries of the European Union have institutional provisions laid out by the Convention concerning International Carriage by Rail (Convention relative aux Transports Internationaux Ferroviaires, also known as COTIF). The first international convention regarding rail transportation was held in Berne, Switzerland as early as 1890, at which time the Central Office for International Carriage by Rail was created. However, this organization was replaced by the Intergovernmental Organization for International Carriage by Rail (OTIF) in 1985 after the original conventions were reformed. Hence, the present institutional provisions are based on COTIF of 1980, and were again amended by the Vilnius Protocol of 1999, entering into force in 2006. COTIF currently comprises seven areas of rail transport law concerning:

- the international carriage of passengers by rail (CIV);
- the international carriage of goods by rail (CIM);
- the international carriage of dangerous goods by rail (RID);
- the use of vehicles in international rail traffic (CUV);
- the contract of use of infrastructure in international rail traffic (CUI);
- the validation of technical standards and the adoption of uniform technical prescriptions applicable to railway material intended to be used in international traffic (APTU);
- the technical admission of railway material used in international traffic (ATMF).

Presently, these regulations apply to 46 member states in Europe, North Africa and the Middle East, and are applicable on railway infrastructure of approximately 250,000 km (OTIF, 2011).

European institutional framework

A common European transport policy was first envisioned in the EU Treaty of Rome of 1957; unfortunately, it was not very clearly formulated at this time and so in 1980, the European Parliament took legal action against the Council of Ministers in the European Court of Justice for not fulfilling its duties in this matter (ECMT, 2002). Having found the Council guilty, actions were then undertaken to establish a common transport policy. The Treaty of Maastricht first introduced the concept of a Trans-European Transport Network (TEN-T). The

> policy aims to provide the infrastructure needed for the internal market to function smoothly and for the objectives of the Lisbon Agenda, with special emphasis on economic growth and employment. It also promotes accessibility and territorial cohesion. It facilitates every EU citizen's right to move freely within the territory of the member states, integrating environmental protection requirements with a view to promoting sustainable development (COM 2009, 1).
>
> (Martin, 2011)

Upon the examination of current European railway legislation, it becomes apparent that the policies are guided by a desire to develop a strong and competitive rail transport industry. Furthermore, the European Commission proposed a white paper to develop a transportation system capable of shifting the balance between modes of transport, which includes the revitalization of rail (COM, 2001). More specifically, the links between different modes of transport should be strengthened to overcome technical barriers that slow down rail traffic between countries. To help regain lost passenger and freight traffic back to trains, the Transport White Paper 'European transport policy for 2010: time to decide' (COM, 2001) proposed:

- making rail transportation more competitive in terms of punctuality, reliability and speed;
- ensuring the continuity of traffic across borders;
- creating trans-European rail freight networks;
- improving the interoperability of trains between different national networks and systems; improving the capacity of rail infrastructure throughout the EU (European Commission, 2010d).

Hence, three railway packages were created which focused on opening the rail transport market to competition, improving the interoperability and safety of national networks and developing rail transport infrastructure (European Commission, 2010b).

According to the British Office of Rail Regulation, the goal of the first railway package adopted by the European Commission in 2001 was the creation of a general framework for the development of European railways. In order to open the railway market and enable rail operations according to commercial principles (and hence facilitate greater competition with other modes of transport), part of the general framework for the development of European railways included the separation of rail infrastructure management and train operating activities. While states have implemented this separation in different ways, it generally provides non-discriminatory access to rail infrastructure allowing new companies to enter the railway markets and offer new and better services (ECMT, 2002).

The aim of the second railway package adopted in 2004 was the creation of a legally and technically integrated European railway area. Although the interoperability of European rail has become a major goal, it has not been without difficulties. Technical integration between infrastructure and rolling stock requires significant cross-border coordination. Several problems exist due to technical differences between national railway systems, such as differences in structure and track gauges, electrical power supply systems, signalling, braking and information technology systems (ECMT, 2002). Moreover, in 2010 there were more than 20 different train control systems within Europe, and trains could have 'up to seven different expensive, bulky monitoring systems to make sure they can operate safely as they travel between countries' (European Commission, 2010d). The European Railway Agency is currently the driving force in creating policies that combat the interoperability problems in order to attain a fully integrated European railway area.

Focus box

How does interoperability affect tourism?

'Fully integrated (and rational) ticketing systems, time-tabling and vehicle tracking would go a long way toward improving customer satisfaction. As a recent example, during the Icelandic volcano eruptions, some railway operators failed to impress many stranded passengers who needed to find their way home by travelling across several national rail systems. These passengers faced information, ticketing and availability frustrations. It is not yet possible to go to any station, check the times and buy a one-way ticket to any European destination. Such a vision is a challenge that research is gradually making a reality. Rolling out the common signalling system (ERTMS) throughout Europe and achieving a safer interoperable rail network will go a long way to supporting cross-border travel and making rail a more attractive option for long distance transport.'

From European Commission, 2010b.

Finally, the aim of the third railway package adopted in 2007 was to open up international passenger services within the European Union, to regulate passenger rights and to address the certification of train crews. Open access rights (including cabotage) were introduced for international passenger rail service, meaning that operators could transport passengers between any rail stations along international routes, even within the same state. Furthermore, a European train-driver licence was created ensuring the attainment of basic requirements pertaining to education and practical skills as well as physical and mental health (European Commission, 2010b). The strengthening of passenger rights includes the guaranteed provision of certain quality standards, including 'non-discrimination of handicapped travellers or persons with reduced mobility, liability in case of accidents, and availability of train tickets and personal security of passengers in stations' (European Commission, 2010b).

North American institutional framework

The Land Transportation Standards Subcommittee (LTSS) was created under the North American Free Trade Agreement (NAFTA) to address the compatibility of operational standards regarding land transportation between the USA, Canada and Mexico. According to the US Federal Railroad Administration (2012), the group's mission was to increase the compatibility of technical and safety regulations, focusing particularly on the improvement of safety, efficiency and quality in the delivery of North American rail services. The group published a report in 1995, which concluded that the US, Canadian and Mexican rail regulations relating to railroad equipment, rail infrastructure, safety regulations and operating practices were essentially compatible. Cross-border rail transportation issues between the NAFTA countries are presently addressed by the LTSS and the Transportation Consultative Group (Federal Railroad Administration, 2011).

Several institutions and organizations are involved in the railroad governance of the USA, Canada and Mexico respectively. These include federal departments and agencies, provinces or states, railway companies and labour unions. In Canada, the railway regulatory framework encompasses legislation, regulations, rules and standards both at the federal and provincial level. More specifically, there are 34 Canadian railways regulated by federal law as they have either interprovincial or international (Canada–US) operations, while provincial governments regulate those that operate entirely within a single province. Table 6.1 gives an overview of the Canadian Railway Safety Act. In Fig. 6.4 a selection of the most relevant enactments pursuant to the Act are illustrated. While Transport Canada has the overall responsibility for the Canadian transportation system, several directorates share the responsibilities regarding rail transportation. For example, the Rail Safety Directorate is responsible for railway safety, while the Rail Policy Branch provides ongoing policy advice and administers the VIA Rail subsidy. The Transportation Safety Board of Canada is an independent body that conducts accident investigations and inquiries under federal jurisdiction, making safety recommendations, and regularly reports accident and incident statistics. The Canadian Transportation Agency has regulatory power in economic matters such as licensing, cost appointment, and competitive access, while environmental concerns, such as the prevention of pollution or environmental incidents, are regulated by Environment Canada (although environmental response, clean up and remediation fall under provincial and municipal jurisdictions).

In the USA, the federal government is the main regulatory authority for rail transportation; state laws regulating rail operations must be consistent with, and are secondary to, federal laws. Hence, the Department of Transportation has the overall responsibility for the US transportation system, within which the Federal Railroad Administration (FRA) promotes and enforces rail safety regulations[1]. An overview of the FRA organization and its various departments can be seen in Fig. 6.5. Economic regulations fall within the jurisdiction of the Surface

Table 6.1. Canadian Railway Safety Act. (From Transport Canada, 2001.)

Railway Safety Act

1989 (amendments in 1999)	An Act to ensure the safe operation of railways and to amend certain other Acts in consequence thereof. The objectives of this Act are to: (a) promote and provide for the safety of the public and personnel, and the protection of property and the environment, in the operation of railways; (b) encourage the collaboration and participation of interested parties in improving railway safety; (c) recognize the responsibility of railway companies in ensuring the safety of their operations; and (d) facilitate a modern, flexible and efficient regulatory scheme that will ensure the continuing enhancement of railway safety.

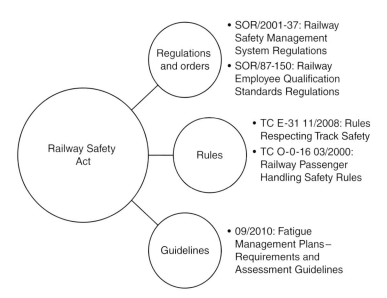

Fig. 6.4. Canadian railway safety legislation. Compiled by the author.

Transportation Board, and the Environmental Protection Agency ensures adherence to environmental regulations.

ASSOCIATIONS

A brief overview of some of the international organizations is given here, in addition to which most countries of course also have national associations. For tourism suppliers, organizations such as railway museum associations and tourist train associations are also of interest.

Union International de Chemin de Fer (UIC)

Founded in 1922, the original focus of the International Union of Railways was the standardization and improvement of both constructional and operational conditions at the international level. Today, the UIC is a global non-profit organization whose general mission is the promotion of rail transport. Furthermore, it facilitates the sharing of best practices among members; supports members in their efforts to develop new business and new areas of activity; proposes new ways to improve technical and environmental performance; promotes interoperability and creates new world standards for railways (including common standards with other transport modes); and develops centres of competence (such as high-speed, safety, security, e-Business, etc.) (UIC, 2010a). The key roles are illustrated in Fig. 6.6. The UIC has approximately 200 members spanning five continents; members consist of railway companies, infrastructure managers, railway or combined transport operators, rolling stock and traction companies, and service providers (such as rail catering and sleeping cars). The UIC has many partner organizations within intergovernmental organizations, international financial institutions,

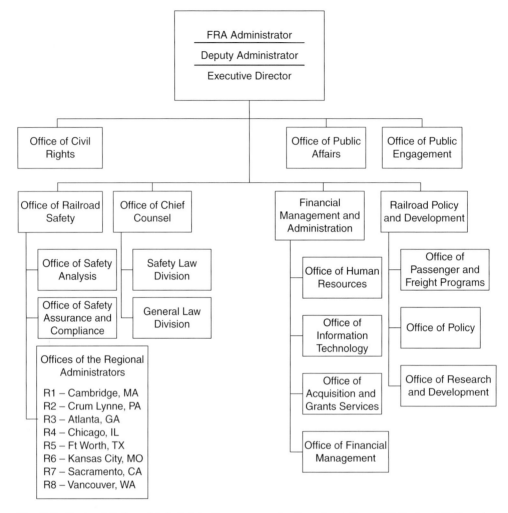

Fig. 6.5. Federal Railroad Administration – organization chart. From US Federal Railroad Administration, 2013.

standardization bodies, trade associations, the railway industry and contractors, and other railway associations. Furthermore, the UIC has had consultative status to the United Nations (ECOSOC) since 1949.

European Railway Agency (ERA)

The European Union established the ERA in 2004 based on regulation EC881. The agency was fully operational by 2006 and provides EU member states and the Commission with technical assistance through the development and implementation of technical specifications regarding railway safety and interoperability. There are five operational units: railway safety, interoperability, European rail traffic management system (ERTMS), economic evaluation and cross acceptance. An administrative board composed of a representative from each member

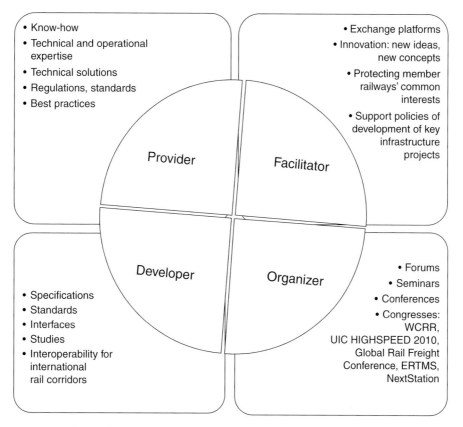

Fig. 6.6. Key roles of the UIC. From UIC, 2010.

state and four representatives of the European Commission supervises the work of the ERA. Although they do not have voting rights, six industry professionals also sit on the administrative board in an advisory capacity[2].

Rail Forum Europe (RFE)

RFE is an international non-profit association composed of members of the European Parliament who aim to liaise between EU decision makers and members of the rail industry. They facilitate cooperation with scientific, technical, economic, industrial and professional groups and organizations whose activities affect rail transportation.

Union des Industries Ferroviaires Européennes (UNIFE)

The Association of the European Rail Industry is the amalgamation of three French associations in 1991: the Association Internationale des Constructeurs de Matériel Roulant (AICMR), the Association des Fabricants Européens d'Equipements Ferroviaires (AFEDEF), and the Constructeurs Européens des Locomotives Thermiques et Electriques (CELTE). UNIFE represents European companies responsible for the design, manufacture, maintenance and refurbishment of rail transport systems, subsystems and related equipment. National railway industry associ-ations are also represented as associated members. Its main role is the representation of members' interests at the EU and international level, and to pro-actively develop an environment in which UNIFE members can provide competitive railway systems for increasing rail traffic.

The Association of American Railroads (AAR)

Based in Washington, DC, AAR is a North American association serving the rail industry of the USA, Canada and Mexico. Although there is a heavy focus on freight services, Amtrak is also a member. The association promotes the interests of the rail industry and works with elected officials and leaders in Washington, DC to set new rail standards and improve the safety and productivity of rail transportation.

DEMAND AND SUPPLY

Demand

In 2010, the members of UIC represented a transport volume of 2.7 billion pkm (UIC, 2010b). Overall, passenger rail transport has shown a 3.5% increase in worldwide pkm, due mainly to the Asian market, particularly by India which saw an 8% increase (UIC, 2011). As illustrated in Fig. 6.7, Asia and Oceania represent the highest percentage of pkm worldwide, followed by Europe, Russia, Africa and finally the USA and Canada. Although the railway infrastructure of the EU27 and the USA is extremely comparable with networks of 212.9 and 202.0 thou-sand km respectively; the EU reported 410.5 billion railway pkm in 2008, compared to 37.2 billion pkm in the USA. Statistics for tram and metro usage are similar, with 89.2 billion pkm in the EU compared with 21.1 billion pkm in the USA (Eurostat, 2011).

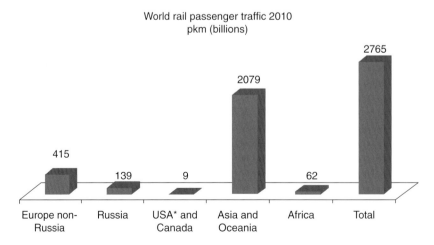

Fig. 6.7. World rail passenger traffic 2010. *USA only 2009 data – 2010 available in September 2011. From UIC, 2011.

The rail share of the total passenger transport market within the EU has remained relatively stable at around 6% since 2000 (Dionori *et al.*, 2011). Interestingly, based on the EC statistics regarding the performance of passenger transport, between 2000 and 2009 the EU15 saw an increase of almost 14% in the transport of passenger rail. More specifically, Denmark, the UK and Belgium experienced the most rapid growth in rail passenger traffic during this period with 41.9%, 36.4% and 35.7% growth respectively. In fact, according to the British National Travel Survey (2010), rail travel accounted for 9% of all distances travelled in 2010 by UK households. More specifically, the average number of trips and the distance travelled by surface rail had increased by 61% and 58% respectively since 1995. Conversely, the EU12 member states saw a decrease in patronage of almost 34%, with Latvia (89.5%), Romania (48.7%) and Lithuania (41.6%) experiencing the largest fall in rail passenger traffic. This was largely due to increased automobile ownership in the 'new' member states, which limited the demand for rail services (European Commission, 2010d).

Some of the increase in rail transport within the EU was driven at least partly by the development of the high-speed sector, which increased from 58.8 to 104.1 thousand million pkm between 2000 and 2009. In fact, the UNWTO (2008) reported that arrivals by train increased approximately 1.4% yearly between 1990 and 2006 due to the extension of high-speed train services. According to Givoni (2006), high-speed trains increase route capacity and reduce travel time, which in turn can lead to increased demand and changes in transport modal shares: increase in high-speed train ridership at the expense of air travel, car usage and conventional train ridership. Interestingly, after the introduction of the TGV high-speed train service between Paris and Lyon, there was a traffic generation effect of 37%. Moreover, 24% of air traffic was diverted to the new line, as well as 8% of car and bus traffic. Martin (2011) also noted that the high-speed line between Brussels and Paris has virtually replaced all air travel with a travel time of under 1.5 h. Givoni (2006) noted a similar effect on the AVE service between Madrid and Seville, with a total traffic increase of 35%, and a 27% diversion from air travel, as well as 8% from car and bus travel. Although operational differences between countries still lead to passengers experiencing inconveniences such as ticketing and timing frustrations, the European railway is being revitalized, and high-speed trains constitute an important part of the process.

Although rail constituted 4% of global international arrivals in 2006, this figure decreased to a mere 2% in 2012 (UNWTO, 2013). However, based on annual data published by the German National Tourist Board, the percentage of Europeans using rail for international trips has remained fairly constant at around 7% since 2004. The preference for train travel increased slightly to 12% for domestic vacations among Europeans (Eurostat, 2010b). In fact, Eurostat reported that 'the high share of domestic tourism in combination with the extended network of long distance high speed trains, made railway transport the second most important mode of transport for French tourists (13%)' (Eurostat, 2010b, p. 36). The Polish reported the highest share of trains as the main mode of transport for long holiday trips with 18%, while Irish, Greek, Portuguese and Slovenian tourists chose the train for only 2% of their long holiday trips. Overall, Europeans reached their vacation destination by train in 9% of cases for vacation trips of four nights or more in 2008 (Eurostat, 2010b).

Based on a pan-European study conducted by the Boston Consulting Group in 2009, 'passengers expect travel to be safe, clean, convenient, punctual, fast, and good value for money' (Boston Consulting Group, 2009, p. 2). If these conditions are met, then operators can expect to keep their existing customers and attract new ones. The study found that airlines satisfied these requirements to a greater extent than railway operators, although some of the top-league railways were managing to compete effectively. Furthermore, consumers perceived booking air travel to be more straightforward, easier to navigate and generally easier to plan than rail travel. However, travellers perceived railways to be more environmentally friendly and a more 'leisurely, comfortable, and sociable experience than either planes or automobiles' (Boston Consulting Group, 2009, p. 2). The authors felt that the relative dissatisfaction with rail travel, compared with flying, was due to the lack of competition between rail providers. The current lack of customer segmentation or service differentiation among rail operators was compared to the state of the airline industry before deregulation and the advent of LCCs. The study concluded that rail operators must look beyond 'smooth operations' and focus on travellers' needs, utilizing market segmentation strategies to cater to differentiated groups. Moreover, working with other companies to provide seamless door-to-door services could give transportation operators the needed competitive advantage; due to the centrality of most railway stations within cities, as well as less restrictive security measures, railways are well positioned to take advantage of such strategies. Hence, rail companies could improve their competitive position by learning from leading airlines' and rail providers' best practices and focus more on customer demands rather than merely on production (Boston Consulting Group, 2009).

Supply

Trying to pinpoint the exact number of rail operators worldwide is a difficult task; however, within Europe there are at least 600 (derived from VDB, 2010). Based on total revenue figures, the five biggest European rail operators in 2011 were SNCF, DB Bahn, Ferrovie dello Stato (FS), Schweizerische Bundesbahn (SBB) and Nederlandse Spoorwegen (NS) + Abellio (DB AG, 2013). An overview of worldwide track infrastructure broken down by continents is given in Table 6.2, as well as a more detailed overview of the European infrastructure. It should be noted that North America has a track infrastructure of 275,000 km, Russia covers 87,000 km, followed by China with about 75,000 km and India with 63,000 km. Other states with a large track network are Australia (38,550 km), Argentina (32,000 km), South Africa (21,000 km) and Mexico (18,000 km) (CIA, 2013).

As can be seen in Table 6.3, there are 50 high-speed lines currently in operation in Europe, 19 are under construction and a further 42 are planned for the near future (UIC, 2012). This translates to 6914 km of high-speed lines, or sections of lines, in which trains currently operate at speeds over 250 km/h; 2936 km are under construction and 8384 km are planned. The evolution of high-speed rail in Europe is illustrated in Fig. 6.8.

The USA currently has one high-speed line operating along the North East Corridor between Boston and New York although another line is planned between Los Angeles and

Table 6.2. Worldwide and European track infrastructure (in km). (From UIC, 2009; VDB, 2011, p. 8; VDB, 2012, p. 8; EUROSTAT, 2013b.)

	2004	2005	2006	2007	2008	2009	2010
Africa	56,099	57,517	57,779	58,582	52,482	52,299	50,275
Americas	391,720	389,199	386,945	381,884	386,773	383,079	375,774
Asia and Oceania	213,309	215,632	216,851	215,492	221,827	224,151	224,205
Europe (Turkey and Russia included)	349,695	352,364	360,169	356,058	349,000	353,747	370,700
Worldwide (estimated)	1,010,723	1,014,712	1,012,744	1,012,016	1,010,082	1,013,276	1,020,954

Europe (in km)

Country	Railway system 2011	Country	Railway system 2011
Belgium	6,436 (2009)	Austria	8,334 (2007)
Bulgaria	5,661	Poland	2,801 (2002)
Czech Republic	15,666 (2010)	Portugal	2,793
Denmark	3,181 (1998)	Romania	20,129
Germany	41,876	Slovenia	2,177
Estonia	2,164	Slovakia	3,624
Ireland	1,889 (2008)	Finland	8,885
Greece	3,062 (2008)	Sweden	15,497 (2010)
France	51,217 (2009)	UK	31,324 (2010)
Italy	24,240	Croatia	4,101
Latvia	2,202	Hungary	9,208 (2009)
Lithuania	2,184	Norway	4,191
Luxembourg	275 (2009)	Former Yugoslav Republic of Macedonia	925
Netherlands	2,811 (2003)	Turkey	11,488 (2010)

Table 6.3. High-speed lines in the world. (Adapted from UIC, 2012.)

Country	Number of high-speed lines in operation	Number of high-speed lines under construction	Number of planned high-speed lines
Belgium	4	–	–
France	9	4	14
Germany	11	3	5
Italy	9	–	2
Netherlands	1	–	–
Poland	–	–	2
Portugal	–	–	6
Russia	–	–	1
Spain	13	10	10
Sweden	–	–	1
Switzerland	1	2	–
UK	2	–	1
Total Europe	**50**	**19**	**42**
China	19	11	13
Taiwan-China	1	–	–
India	–	–	1
Japan	15	3	3
Saudi Arabia	–	–	1
Turkey	2	2	4
Total Asia	**37**	**16**	**22**
Morocco	–	1	1
Brazil	–	–	1
USA	1	–	1
Total worldwide	**88**	**36**	**67**

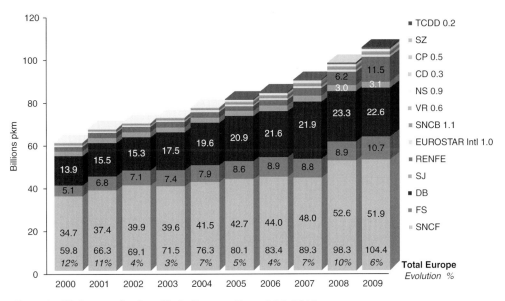

Fig. 6.8. High-speed rail traffic in Europe. From UIC, 2010c.

Sacramento. Furthermore, President Obama has proposed a long-term strategy to build an efficient, high-speed passenger rail network of 100–600-mile (160–965-km) intercity corridors as part of a modernized transportation system for the USA. The Passenger Rail Investment and Improvement Act of 2008 (PRIIA) is the legislation that established competitive grant programmes to fund high-speed and intercity-rail capital improvements, while the American Recovery and Reinvestment Act of 2009 contained further 'jump start' appropriations (US Department of Transportation, 2009b). Interestingly, Canada has no high-speed lines although several routes, such as Toronto–Montreal, Montreal–Boston–New York, Vancouver–Seattle, and Calgary–Edmonton, have been discussed.

According to the International Association of Public Transport website (as of October 2011), there are some 400 light rail systems in operation worldwide, with some 60 more in construction and well above 200 planned. Europe is the densest LRT continent with 170 systems in operation and nearly 100 more in construction or planning, while North America has 30 systems in operation and 10 in construction; Toronto's legacy streetcar system in Canada, and Portland's Metropolitan Area Express (MAX) in the USA are examples of such systems in North America. Light rail systems are well established in Europe; Germany, for example, has ten light rail systems as well as 56 tramways. The Light Rail Transit Association endeavours to keep an up-to-date index of light rail systems worldwide; a brief overview can be seen in Table 6.4. Furthermore, based on Table 6.4, it can be seen that there are 55 metro systems in Europe and 22 in North America.

Table 6.4. Light rail systems worldwide. (Adapted from LRTA, 2013.)

Country	Metros	Light rail	Tramways	Light railways	Heritage tram
Austria	1	2	6	4	1
Belgium	1	–	5	–	1
Bulgaria	1	–	2	–	–
Croatia	–	–	2	–	–
Czech Republic	1	–	7	–	–
Denmark	1	–	–	–	–
Estonia	–	–	1	–	–
Finland	1	–	1	–	–
France	7	4	19	6	–
Germany	4	10	56	3	1
Greece	1	–	1	–	–
Hungary	1	1	4	–	–
Ireland	–	–	1	–	–
Italy	6	3	11	10	–
Latvia	–	–	3	–	–
Netherlands	2	2	3	–	1
Norway	1	–	3	–	1
Poland	1	1	14	–	–
Romania	1	–	13	–	–
Russia	6	2	64	–	–
Serbia	–	–	1	–	–
Slovakia	–	–	3	2	–
Spain	9	4	12	8	2
Sweden	1	1	4	2	1

(Continued)

Table 6.4. Continued.

Country	Metros	Light rail	Tramways	Light railways	Heritage tram
Switzerland	1	2	10	38	
Turkey	2	5	7	–	4
UK	2	3	9	3	4
Ukraine	3	1	23	–	–
Total Europe	**55**	**40**	**285**	**76**	**16**
Canada	4	3	2	–	4
Mexico	2	2	1	–	
USA	18	27	7	–	20
Total North America	**24**	**32**	**10**	**–**	**24**

As highlighted in the definition section, cable-propelled rail systems also play a significant role within tourism transportation either as a form of transportation or as an attraction in and of themselves. As can be expected, cable-propelled systems can be mainly found in mountainous countries such as France, Switzerland, Italy and Austria (see Table 6.5). These systems are an integral part of many tourism products; for example, they provide transportation for skiers during the winter seasons, hikers and mountain bikers during the summer season and provide scenic and enjoyable transportation to several touristic sites.

Luxury trains also constitute an important segment regarding train transportation within tourism. While high-speed trains and intercity services provide the means of transportation between origin and destination, and light rail systems function as transportation within the destination, luxury trains often represent a vacation experience in and of themselves (similar to the idea of a cruise vacation within water based transportation). Hence, the product varies in form from a day trip to vacations that last over two weeks or more in which several destinations are included. Generally though, all luxury trains provide the possibility of accommodation and a washroom. While more limited than their water based counterparts, luxury trains can also offer certain amenities and amusement on board, including standard services such as dining cars and bars, wellness areas, entertainment in the form of national or local informational lectures, musical and dance events and disco evenings, and even laundry services (Gross, 2011). Table 6.6 provides a selection of some of the most well-known luxury trains worldwide.

Table 6.5. Number of funiculars and ropeways in Europe and North America (2006–2008). (From OITAF, 2009.)

Number and form of railway systems	Funicular	Monocable ropeway	Bicable ropeway	Doublecable ropeway	Ski lift	Total
Europe						
Andorra	0	50	2	1	34	87
Austria	22	959	58	7	1030	2076
Bulgaria	0	10	0	0	3	13
Czech Republic	4	65	1	0	0	70
Finland	1	27	0	0	308	336
France	20	1091	48	12	2706	3877
Germany	21	129	34	0	1519	1703
Hungary	1	2	0	0	34	37
Italy	27	981	91	2	1189	2290
Norway	4	68	5	0	715	792
Poland	3	61	2	0	715	792
Portugal	5	6	7	0	5	23
Romania	1	23	8	0	89	121
Slovakia	1	44	1	0	0	46
Slovenia	1	8	4	0	210	223
Spain	13	167	6	0	779	337
Sweden	4	59	3	0	779	845
Switzerland	56	447	352	2	1670	2527
North America						
USA	4	2172	20	1	1090	3287

Table 6.6. A selection of luxury trains worldwide. (Adapted from Gross, 2011.)

Name	Route	Founding year	Company
Europe			
Venice Simplon-Orient-Express	London–Paris–Venice–Prague	1982	Orient Express Hotels Ltd
Northern Belle	UK	2000	Orient Express Hotels Ltd
British Pullman	England	1982	Orient Express Hotels Ltd
Royal Scotsman	Scotland	1985	Orient Express Hotels Ltd
El Transcantabrico	Andalusia	1983	Ferrocarriles de Via Estrecha SA
Majestic Imperator	Austria	1991	Majestic Imperator Train de Luxe Waggon Charter GmbH
Danube Express	Eastern and Central Europe	2008	Danube Express Ltd
Asia			
Eastern & Oriental Express	South East Asia	1993	Orient Express Hotels Ltd
Shangri La Express	Peking–Urumqi/–Lhasa/–Moscow	1985	n/a
Deccan Odyssey	India	2004	Indian Railways & Maharashtra tourism
The Golden Chariot	Southern India	2008	The Karnataka State Tourism Development Corporation & Indian Railways
Palace on Wheels	Rajasthan	1984	Palace on Wheels Inc.

(Continued)

Table 6.6. Continued.

Name	Route	Founding year	Company
Royal Rajasthan on Wheels	Rajasthan	2009	Palace on Wheels Inc.
The Maharaja Express	Dehli–Mumbai	2010	Indian Railway Catering and Tourism Corporation Limited
Golden Eagle	Moscow–Vladivostok	2007	Trans-Siberian Express Group
Grand Trans-Siberian Express	Moscow–Beijing	1999	Trans-Siberian Express Group
Africa			
Rovos Rail	South Africa, Tanzania, Namibia	1989	Rovos Rail Tours Ltd
Blue Train	South Africa	1920s	The Blue Train Company
Desert Express	Namibia	1999	TransNamib
Americas			
American-Orient-Express	USA	1991	GrandLuxe Rail Journeys
Royal Canadian Express	Canada	2000	Mount Stephen Properties Ltd
The California Zephyr	Western USA	1949	Amtrak
Capitol Limited	Chicago–Washington DC	1923	B&O Baltimore & Ohio Capitol Ltd
The Canadian	Canada	1955	Canadian Pacific Railway Limited
Rocky Mountaineer	Canada	1990	Rocky Mountaineer

(*Continued*)

Table 6.6. Continued.

Name	Route	Founding year	Company
Hiram Bingham	Machu Picchu (Peru)	n/a	Venice Simplon-Orient-Express Ltd
Great Brazil Express	Rio de Janeiro–Foz do Iguacu	2008	Serra Verde Express
Australia			
The Ghan	Adelaide–Darwin	2004	Great Southern Rail
The Overland	Melbourne–Adelaide	1887	Great Southern Rail
The Great South Pacific Express	Brisbane–Sydney–Cairns	1999–2003	Queensland Rail
Indian Pacific	Perth–Adelaide–Sydney	1970	Great Southern Rail

NOTES

1. More information pertaining to US railroad legislation can be found under http://www.fra.dot.gov.
2. For more information regarding the ERA, see www.era.europa.eu.

FURTHER READING

Becker, C. and George, B.P. (2011) Rapid rail transit and tourism development in the United States. *Tourism Geographies* 3, 381–397.

Garnett, C. (1993) Impact of the Channel Tunnel on the tourism industry – A sea of change in cross-Channel travel. *Tourism Management* 6, 436–439.

Givoni, M. (2006) Development and impact of the modern high-speed train: a review. *Transport Reviews* 5, 593–611.

Givoni, M. and Banister, D. (2008) Airline and railway integration. *Transport Policy* 13, 386–397.

Groeneveld-Deussen, E. (2007) Low cost carriers and railway – competition or cooperation? Practical examples based on a theoretical approach of competitive strategies. In: Gross, S. and A. Schröder (eds) *Handbook of Low Cost Airlines – Strategies, Business Processes and Market Environment*. Erich Schmidt Verlag, Berlin, Germany, pp. 263–292.

Groupe Eurotunnel (annual edition) *Annual Review*. Paris, France.

Halsall, D.A. (2001) Railway heritage and the tourist gaze: Stoomtram Hoorn-Medemblik. *Journal of Transport Geography* 9, 151–160.

IATA – International Air Transport Association (2003) *Air/Rail Intermodality Study*. London, UK.

Knowles, R.D. (1998) Passenger rail privatization in Great Britain and its implications, especially for urban areas. *Journal of Transport Geography* 6, 117–133.

OITAF (2009) *Ropeways Statistics 2009*. Bozen, Italy.

Prideaux, B. (1999) Tracks to tourism: Queensland Rail joins the tourist industry. *International Journal of Tourism Research* 1, 73–86.

Steer Davies Gleave (2006) Air and rail competition and complementarity – final report. Study prepared for the European Commission DG TREN, Brussels, Belgium.

Su, M.M. and Wall, G. (2009) The Qinghai-Tibet railway and Tibetan tourism: Travelers' perspectives. *Tourism Management* 30, 650–657.

Thompson, L.S. (2003) Changing railway structure and ownership: is anything working? *Transport Reviews* 3, 311–355.

van Goeverden, C.D. (2007) Long distance travel in Europe: the potential of the train. In: Peeters, P.M. (ed.) *Tourism and Climate Change Mitigation. Methods, Greenhouse Gas Reduction and Policies*. Stichting NHTV Breda, The Netherlands.

Trade journals/magazines and scientific organizations

European Railway Review, European Rail Technology Review – International Journal for Railway Engineers, Heritage Railway, International Railway Journal, International Transport Journal, Internationales Verkehrswesen, Japan Railway and Transport Review, Progressive Railroading, Travel and Tourism Research Association (www.ttra.com).

Internet sources

http://epp.eurostat.ec.europa.eu/portal/page/portal/eurostat/home/, www.arema.org,www.bitre. gov.au, www.bahn.de, www.era.europa.eu, www.eurotunnelgroup.com, www.progressiverailroading. com, www.uic.org, http://www.oitaf.org/. http://www.ntdprogram.gov/ntdprogram/Glossaries/pdf/ Glossary2013.pdf, http://trt.trb.org/trt.asp?NN=Aetrd, http://trt.trb.org/trt.asp?NN=Aetrh

chapter 7

Speciality Ground Transportation

LEARNING OBJECTIVES

• Identify and describe different forms and experiences of passenger transportation.
• Assess and evaluate the importance of various recreational transportation forms within the tourism industry.

AUTOMOBILE EXPERIENCES AND COURSES

As learned on p. 69, private car transportation accounts for 74% of total passenger transport activities within the EU27 and about 82% in the USA. However, the automobile experience is not only limited to passenger transportation and car rental. The tourism industry offers a variety of automobile products. A selection of popular products is given below.

Theme parks

Due to its consideration as the birthplace of the automobile from the time of Karl Benz and Nikolaus Otto, it is no wonder that Germany has many car theme parks to offer. One of the most famous is the Autostadt (Car City) in Wolfsburg, Germany. The Autostadt is a visitor attraction adjacent to the Volkswagen factory and features a museum, a customer centre where customers can pick up new cars, research stations, cinemas and guided tours through the enormous factory. Visitors have access to seven pavilions dedicated to the different car manufacturers at Autostadt. Hence, the following brands are represented at the theme park: Volkswagen, Bentley, Škoda, Lamborghini, Audi and SEAT. The theme park attracts about 2 million visitors a year and is not only famous for its focus on automobiles but also for its ultra-modern architecture (Autostadt GmbH, 2012). Another German car theme park is the

BMW World in Munich. Starting 2013, a theme park for vintage cars is planned to be constructed in Cologne, Germany (Nikolaus Otto Park GmbH & Co. KG, 2012). Other car theme parks across Europe can be visited in the UK (Mercedes Benz World in Surrey) and in Italy (Mirafiori Motor Village in Turin).

Racing adventures

Racing and Formula 1 lovers have the opportunity to create their own experiences on different Grand Prix circuits such as the Nurburgring and Hockenheimring in Germany, since the tracks are open for tourist drivers. The experience can take place with the visitor's own car or a rental car. The price varies according to the number of laps; the minimum age of the driver is 21 (Nürburgring Betriebsgesellschaft mbH, 2012). Other European GP circuits are Brands Hatch and Donington Park in the UK, and the Circuito de Jerez and the Valencia Street Circuit in Spain. In the USA, the Indianapolis Motor Speedway is open for Formula 1 fans. Throughout the USA, there are seven NASCAR racetracks that offer a unique driving experience, for example, in Florida, Illinois and Nevada (Racing Adventure, 2012). Visitors can not only race on these tracks but also take part in driving safety training and improve their driving skills. These courses address the basic challenges drivers face on the road and teach the correct action in dangerous situations. Moreover, most circuits also offer museums and guided tours.

World class driving

Driving exotic cars, such as Jaguars, Lamborghinis or Ferraris, either on tracks or on open roads on a guided tour is possible throughout the USA in Florida, Nevada and New York. These luxury tours start at a price of $299 but offer a once-in-a-lifetime experience (World Class Driving, 2012). In Europe, however, the experience includes not only the driving of luxury cars but also enjoying exquisite hotels and spas as well as enjoying breathtaking cities and countryside. High performance sports cars can be raced down the high-speed autobahn and across alpine mountain passes. Suppliers such as Autobahn Adventures offer different driving tours across Europe. In a period of only two weeks, 2200 km can be covered and different sites and locations in four countries can be visited (Autobahn Adventures, 2012).

GoCar

A new form of guided tour is the so-called GoCar. In the USA, the GoCar can be used for sightseeing in San Francisco and San Diego, and in Europe, in cities such as Madrid, Barcelona and Lisbon. The GoCar is a GPS-guided storytelling car that navigates and takes the driver to the best sites of the city. An on-board computer and GPS system replace the traditional guidebook and allow the driver to enjoy the cities at his or her own pace (GoCar Franchise Services, Inc., 2008).

Off-road trekking

The tourism industry offers unconventional products to discover places and make every experience unique. Off-road trekking tours with four wheelers and sport utility vehicles are just another form of automobile experience set apart from mass tourism trips. European suppliers offer tours through the mountain ranges of the Pyrenees and the Alps and along the coastlines in Western and Eastern Europe. In North America, the Rocky Mountains are ideal for such tours.

ANIMALS

Dog sledding

Dog sledding might be one of the most sustainable forms of passenger transportation and nowadays a perfect alternative to ski tourism. Archaeological evidence proves the coexistence of sled dogs and humans for over 4000 years (International Federation of Sleddog Sports Inc., 2012). Especially in arctic areas, sled dogs were used to pull cargo and people through the deep snows and made life easier for people living in these areas. However, dog sledding was not only used for occupational activities but also recreational. In 1886, the first sled dog race occurred at the Winter Carnival in the state of Minnesota in the USA and is still one of the festival's attractions these days (Crego, 2003). The tourism industry adapted the idea of dog sledding and tour operators now offer special winter holiday trips making use of huskies as sled dogs to discover the unique landscapes of Scandinavia, Alaska and Canada. During the 8- or 10-day-long visit, the tourist stays at different lodges and every day a distance of 40 to 60 km is covered by guided dog sledding. Tourists not only experience the white wilderness but also get the chance to see how huskies live, play and train (Huskytrack, 2012).

Donkey taxis

The history of donkeys as draught and pack animals dates back to 2500 BC when the Egyptians started to build their pyramids. The geographical distribution of donkeys spread from Egypt to Mesopotamia, Greece and later to Italy. During the 1st century AD, donkeys were brought to China, India and Mongolia and also to northern Europe. It was not until the 16th century that the Spanish and Portuguese took the first donkeys to North America (Peschke, 2011). Ever since, donkeys have been used as draught animals, especially in agriculture or for accessing remote mountainous regions. In the tourism sector, donkey trekking is becoming more and more popular, mainly for country tourism. Excursions through the countryside and woods on a donkey's back are offered. One may also go trekking on foot, but with a donkey which carries the hiker's food and goods. Donkey trekking is a slow way of travelling, but it enables the tourist to fully enjoy the beautiful views and panoramas of the landscape (National Association for Donkey-Trekking, 2012). Very popular destinations for donkey trekking are the southern European countries, such as Greece (e.g. Lindos in Rhodes), France (in the Pyrenees or on Corsica) or Italy (in Tuscany). In North America, tours on donkeys are very popular in the various national parks, such as the Grand Canyon National Park in Arizona or the Yosemite National Park in California.

Horseback

Horses, as we know them today, started to develop 24 million years ago (Pickeral, 2003). Due to their burliness, horses are even more excellent draught and pack animals than donkeys, and very popular for passenger transportation in different ways. Trail riding, also called horse trekking, today is a major tourist/recreational activity that 'takes place in a wide spectrum of environmental situations and countries' (Buckley, 2004, p. 62). During such guided and mostly cross-country tours, a group of travellers saunters on horseback through nature to principally enjoy the landscape and see its sights. Particularly in Europe and the USA, such tours are widely marketed and often combined with other activities, such as camping and fishing, and related to ecotourism (Kline, 2008). According to the Southern Research Station of the United States Department of Agriculture Forest Service (USDA Forest Service, 2004), over 7% of the US population participated in horseback riding on trails in 2004, which accounted for about 15.2 million people. Horse trekking tours are especially prominent among the activities in the US and Canadian national parks (Kline, 2008).

In Europe, trail riding can be combined with discovering castles in Italy, beaches in Spain or the extensive hilly landscape in Ireland. The type of accommodation varies according to the area's state. Trails that lead through areas that are inaccessible to vehicles are mostly used for camping tours, and the group may carry its own equipment. In areas with established local populations, the travellers 'may stay in local accommodation, which may range from simple huts or tents to luxurious lodges, guesthouses or private estancias' (Buckley, 2006, p. 309). Another way of discovering the landscape by horse and which mainly relates to agritourism is staying at a dude ranch. In the 1880s, dude ranches arose in the west of the USA. At that time, the American West, which provided magnificent unspoiled scenery, was attractive to many wealthy foreigners for hunting trips and sightseeing excursions. A famous early 'dude' was Theodore Roosevelt. After the First World War the popularity of dude ranches increased enormously, and it was during the decade of the 1920s that the dude ranch business really boomed. Dude ranches became the main tourist attraction in the Rocky Mountain area at that time, since the industrial revolution was transforming the American East Coast, polluting and scarring the countryside and destroying wildlife. Cowboy movies also attracted Europeans who wanted to experience the intoxicating freedom of the frontier and enjoy the magnificent scenery of the Western world (Bales, 2002). Nowadays, dude ranches are a long-established tradition and continue to be a vacation destination. Travellers get to know the local life and learn horse riding. According to the Dude Ranchers Association (2012), a trade association for promoting and standardizing dude ranches in North America, the second most important activity is the 'art of relaxation' that every traveller will learn to appreciate while spending time in the countryside. However, dude ranches do exist now in Europe as well, especially in Spain, France, Portugal, Italy, Germany and Croatia.

Horses are not only popular for passenger transportation in the countryside, but also in urban areas in the form of carriage rides, four-wheeled horse-drawn passenger vehicles, which are one of the oldest means of transportation within one destination or between several destinations

Fig. 7.1. Carriage ride – Harz Mountains, Germany. © Michael Lück.

(Gross, 2011; Fig. 7.1). Due to protests by several animal welfare activists, there are a couple of regulations for companies offering carriage rides. For instance in Berlin, Germany or Vienna, Austria, horses may only have a working time of 9 h and two breaks of 30 min have to be taken. In Germany, the coachman has to be at least 18 years old and be in possession of a driving licence (Senatsverwaltung für Gesundheit, Umwelt und Verbraucherschutz, 2009). Horse-drawn carriage rides are very popular in big cities, such as in New York City's Central Park or in the downtown area of Bruges in Belgium.

CYCLES

According to the South Australian Commission (2005, p. 3, as cited by Weed and Bull, 2009), cycle tourism visits are 'considered to be for the purpose of holidays, recreation, pleasure or sport; and to include either overnight stays, or day trips to other tourism regions during which the visitor either engages in active cycling, or is a spectator at a cycling event'. In recent years, the cycle has become more important as a means of transportation. Destinations have started to promote their mountain bike regions and the construction of cycle routes is still increasing (Dreyer *et al.*, 2012). Several factors are responsible for the growth of cycle tourism around the world (One Street, 2012):

- the bike is more and more recognized as a vehicle which is good for the health;
- tourists realize the enjoyment of slow and contemplative travel;
- accommodation vendors recognize the profit potential of single-night guests;
- plenty of maps and route programmes have been launched;
- cycling athletes are choosing to travel by bike to attractive places where they can train.

With the increasing demand for good cycling infrastructure, high quality equipment and suitable accommodation, the tourism industry has adapted since sustainability gained in importance and the touristic cycling market is on the rise.

EuroVelo is a sustainable project of the European Cyclists' Federation (ECF) that promotes and coordinates the creation and operation of a complete European cycle route network. The EuroVelo network comprises 14 long-distance cycle routes with a total length of about 70,000 km (45,000 km is already in place). The network enables the tourist to cross the whole European continent by bike. Every 30 km on the routes there is somewhere to stop for food and drink, every 50 km cyclists can find various types of accommodation and every 150 km public transport is available (European Cyclists' Federation, 2012).

The American counterpart, Adventure Cycling Association, represents cyclists' interests in the USA and supports the construction and maintenance of the US Bicycle Route System, which is about 66,000 km long and 'links together rural roads to create low-traffic bike routes through some of the nation's most scenic and historically significant terrain' (Adventure Cycling Association, 2012). Both networks allow cyclists to take either a roundtrip or do a trip with different stages since accommodation is available.

However, tourists do not always have to take their own bikes with them. Especially in big cities bike rental has become very popular. Tourists can either discover the city on their own or take part in a guided bike tour. In 2008, un Cotxe Menys (one car less), one of the biggest suppliers in Barcelona, Spain, had about 15,000 bookings of such tours. Other European suppliers are Berlin on Bike in Germany or Paris à Velo c'est Sympa in France. Tours like 'Bike the Big Apple' or 'Bike the Bridge' even invite tourists to go on a discovery tour by bike in metropolises such as New York City or San Francisco (Dreyer *et al.*, 2012). In the last few years, however, rentals of e-bikes and pedelecs have been on the rise. Electric bicycles (e-bikes) have electric motors to power the vehicle and can travel at up to 45 km/h. In contrast, the electric power of pedal electric cycles (pedelecs) only assists human power rather than replacing it. Hence, a pedelec does not move without pedaling. Its maximum velocity is 25 km/h (Allgemeiner Deutscher Fahrrad-Club eV, 2012). To support the use of bicycles, e-bikes and pedelecs, many cities offer car-free days. Every year, New York City offers the event 'Summer Streets'. On three consecutive Saturdays in the summer, the streets are opened for sustainable forms of transportation to provide healthy recreation (The City of New York, 2012). Other countries offering car-free days are Germany and Switzerland; in the capital of France the event is called 'Paris Plage'.

SEGWAYS

The American company Segway Inc. introduced the segway personal transporter, also known as the human transporter, for the first time in 2001. The segway is a self-balancing battery-powered personal transportation device with two wheels that can go at speeds up to 20 km/h. Computers and motors in the base of the device keep the segway upright when powered on with balancing enabled. A user controls the segway by shifting his or her body weight forward and backward on the platform. The segway detects, as it balances, the change in its centre of mass, and first establishes and then maintains a corresponding speed, forward or backward. Detecting the weight shift is enabled by gyroscopic sensors and fluid based levelling sensors. By pressing the handlebar to the left or right, the user can turn the vehicle. Best performance of segways is ensured on adequate pavements and ramps (Segway Inc., 2008). In tourism, segways have become popular for guided tours in big cities throughout Europe and North America. However, the vehicle is also qualified for tours through the mountains, for instance in Tyrol, Austria. Segways are also used as a means of transportation at trade fairs, in theme parks and on golf courses (Segway Inc., 2013). The use of the human transporter on public streets is allowed in most countries, but often with restrictions. In Denmark, Switzerland and Germany, segways can be used on public roads and pavements but have to be equipped with lighting, reflectors, brakes and a licence plate (Motion GmbH, 2007). Germany even introduced a new class of vehicle for the segway and classified it as an electronic mobility aid. The driver must hold at least an M type (moped) licence and have procured vehicle insurance when renting (Bundesministerium für Verkehr, Bau und Stadtentwicklung, 2009). Throughout the USA, segways are also used for guided tours in cities, mostly on cycle lanes and designated trails to prevent accidents (Governors Highway Safety Association, 2012). However, in Canada segways cannot be driven on public roads and are limited to use by people older than 14 years with disability, door-to-door delivery personnel of the Canada Post and police officers. Segways are not considered as a means of transportation for tourist activities in Canada (Ontario Ministry of Transportation, 2011).

RECREATIONAL VEHICLES

The Recreation Vehicle Industry Association (2012a) describes a recreation vehicle (RV) as 'a motorized or towable vehicle that combines transportation and temporary living quarters for travel, recreation and camping. RVs do not include mobile homes, off-road vehicles, snowmobiles or conversion vehicles.' According to Timothy and Teye (2009), RVs include caravans, motor homes and camper vans, with each one of these having a broad range of types and subcategories. In general, the RV family can be distinguished between towable and motorized RVs. Towable RVs are 'designed to be towed by family car, van or pickup truck' (Recreation Vehicle Industry Association, 2012b) and are also called caravans. The traveller can unhitch the RV and leave it at the campsite while exploring in the car. A motorized RV (Fig. 7.2), in contrast, is a self-propelled vehicle and its living quarters are accessible from the driver's area in one convenient unit. Motor homes and campervans belong to this group of RVs. The difference between these two is in their length and comfort. Motor homes are larger and intended to be more comfortable than campervans (Campervan Adventures, 2011). Table 7.1 indicates the characteristics of the three main types of RV.

The beginning of RV tourism cannot be precisely determined, although the idea of utilizing a vehicle for travelling and living quarters is certainly not new. First mention of such use dates back to 1500 BC by the Asian Hittites culture, while other sources also identify such use by

Fig. 7.2. RV in Monument Valley, Arizona, USA. © Michael Lück.

Table 7.1. Types of recreational vehicle. (Adapted from Campervan Adventures, 2011; Discovery Motorhomes, 2012.)

Type of RV	Characteristics
Motor home	• motor vehicle built on a truck or bus chassis • self-contained living quarters, divided from the cab • sleeping space, ablution and kitchen facilities
Campervan	• van equipped as a self-contained travelling home • smaller than a motor home • no divide between cab and living quarters • only basic facilities for cooking, washing and sleeping
Caravan	• mobile home or trailer • towed behind a road vehicle • fully equipped with household accessories • sleeping quarters, ablution and cooking facilities

the Romans. Modern RV tourism within Europe and North America dates back to the early 20th century (Kubisch, 1998). This time represented an experimental stage as most RVs were custom-made vehicles built by travel enthusiasts. After the Second World War, the production of RVs in series began, and travelling in recreational vehicles became a major trend in tourism. Initially, caravanning was considered as a low-priced vacation but since the 1980s, due to the construction of motor homes and campervans, it is generally viewed as a holiday of high investment and comparable to a vacation at a hotel (Widmann, 2006). Travellers going on RV vacation are most of all looking for relaxation, nature experience, independence, flexibility and individuality. However, caravanning is related to experiencing community and meeting like-minded people when staying at a camping ground (Widmann, 2006; Bues *et al.*, 2008).

In Europe, according to a study by the Caravanning Industry Association (CIVD, 2010), especially travellers older than 40 years are interested in RV vacation. Younger people are also interested in this kind of travelling; however, due to their lower income, they are renting RVs rather than possessing their own vehicle (see Table 7.2).

In Fig. 7.3 the results of a study from 2008 show that Canadian caravan users are younger families while motor home and campervan users are older with smaller families or empty nesters (The Praxis Group/Alberta Tourism, Parks and Recreation, 2008).

Figure 7.4, showing newly registered vehicles in 2010, indicates the popularity of RVs in North America and Europe. About 8.5 million US households own a recreational vehicle (Timothy and Teye, 2009). Especially in the European countries Germany, UK and France, RVs are very popular, as Table 7.3 illustrates. At the beginning of 2012 about 5.46 million recreational vehicles were in use throughout Europe (European Caravan Federation, 2012a).

Table 7.2. Age and income groups of RV travellers in Europe. (Adapted from CIVD, 2010.)

	Population	Owners of caravans	Owners of motor RVs	Interested in caravan rental	Interested in RV rental
Age					
14–29 years	20%	15%	15%	32%	29%
30–39 years	17%	14%	17%	24%	25%
40–49 years	18%	27%	23%	20%	24%
50–59 years	14%	20%	24%	14%	12%
Older than 60 years	31%	25%	22%	11%	11%
Income					
Up to €1499	30%	21%	15%	26%	23%
€1500–€2499	42%	41%	45%	45%	39%
€2500–€3499	19%	27%	28%	20%	25%
More than €3500	10%	11%	12%	9%	13%

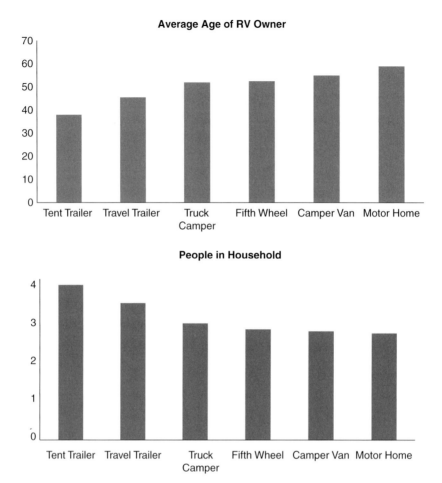

Fig. 7.3. Demographic profiles of RV owners in Canada in 2008. From The Praxis Group/ Alberta Tourism, Parks and Recreation, 2008.

Approximately 465 million overnight stays per year can be registered in total, and average expenditures per day and capita are estimated to account for €33. Consequently, recreational vehicle vacation has a gross turnover of €15.33 billion per year (DWIF, 2007).

North American preferred destinations for RV vacations are the mild and sunny states, such as Florida, Texas, New Mexico and California but also rural areas in the deserts of Arizona (Timothy and Teye, 2009). In Europe, the top five destinations are Germany, France, Italy, Scandinavia and Spain (Obier and Peters, 2003).

Fédération Internationale de Camping et de Caravanning (FICC) is the only association that represents the interests of RV travellers worldwide. 'FICC was originally established in 1933, for the mutual benefit of a number of European camping clubs. Today, it represents 56 member Clubs and Federations in 32 different countries on four continents' (Fédération Internationale de Camping et de Caravanning, 2012).

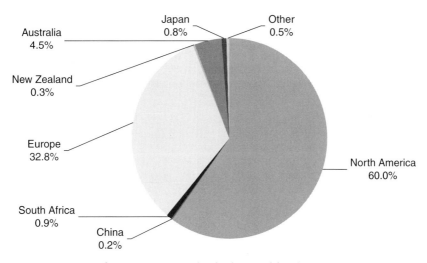

Fig. 7.4. Registrations of new recreational vehicles worldwide in 2010. From CIVD, 2011.

There are several European associations, such as the European Federation of Camping Site Organisations and Holiday Park Associations (EFCO&HPA) and the European Caravan Federation (ECF). The objective of the ECF, the umbrella organization of the European Caravanning Industry, is to 'represent the interests of all organisations commercially involved in the caravanning business, particularly manufacturers, and to promote the leisure experience caravanning in all its forms' (European Caravan Federation, 2012b). In the USA, the Recreation Vehicle Industry Association (RVIA) is in charge for representing RV manufacturers and suppliers; in Canada it is the Canadian Recreational Vehicle Association (Canadian Recreational Vehicle Association, 2012; Recreation Vehicle Industry Association, 2012c).

RICKSHAWS

Rickshaws have their origin in Asia, where they were invented during the 19th century. Nowadays, rickshaws are getting more and more popular as a mode of passenger transportation in major cities, most of all in Europe. There are three different types: a runner-pulled, a cycle and an auto rickshaw. A runner pulled rickshaw is, as the name suggests, a two-wheeled passenger cart pulled by a human runner, which seats one or two persons (Root, 2003). Due to the required physical load of the workers to move the cart, runner-pulled rickshaws have been replaced by cycle and motorized rickshaws. Cycle rickshaws, also known by a variety of other names, such as bike taxi, velotaxi, pedicab, cyclo or trishaw (Miller *et al.*, 2010), are propelled only by muscle power, though very often there is an electric assist that allows a maximum speed of 14 km/h, and the auto type is equipped with an electronic motor. Auto-rickshaws are also called three-wheeler, tricycle, mototaxi or baby taxi and can reach speeds up to 25 km/h (Veloform GmbH, 2012a). There are several rickshaw manufacturers worldwide. An example of an international company is Veloform GmbH from Germany, which was founded

Table 7.3. Registrations of new recreational vehicles in Europe in 2012. (From European Caravan Federation, 2013.)

Country	Touring caravans			Motor caravans			Leisure vehicles total		
	2011	2012	change %	2011	2012	change %	2011	2012	change %
Austria	781	865	+10.8	846	1,025	+21.2	1,627	1,890	+16.2
Belgium	1,167	1,026	+0.1	2,789	2,647	−5.1	3,956	3,673	−7.2
Denmark	3,090[a]	2,680[a]	−13.3	150[a]	140[a]	−6.7	3,240	2,820	−13.0
Finland	1,055	918	−13.0	1,650	1,398	−15.3	2,705	2,316	−14.4
France	10,451	9,063	−13.3	19,307	17,786	−7.9	29,758	26,849	−9.8
Germany	17,324	17,638	+1.8	21,791	24,062	+10.4	39,115	41,700	+6.6
Italy	1,698	1,425	−16.1	7,016	4,681	−33.3	8,714	6,106	−29.9
Netherlands	8,814	7,527	−14.6	1,420	1,295	−8.8	10,234	8,822	−13.8
Norway	3,350	3,169	−5.4	2,445	2,609	+6.7	5,795	5,778	−0.3
Portugal	159	131	−17.6	168	103	−38.7	327	234	−28.4
Slovenia	168	142	−15.5	151	143	−5.3	319	285	−10.7
Spain	2,004	1,432	−28.5	1,774[a]	1,377	−22.4	3,590	2,809	−25.6
Sweden	4,207	3,449	−18.0	3,735	3,598	+3.7	7,942	7,047	−11.3
Switzerland	1,761	1,766	+0.3	2,656	3,060	+15.2	4,417	4,826	+9.3
UK	23,342	20,403	−12.6	7,265	7,734	+6.5	30,607	28,137	−8.1
Others	1,641[a]	1,481	−9.8	1,831[a]	1,821	−0.5	3,472	3,302	−4.9
Total	81,012	73,115	−9.7	74,994	73,479	−2.0	156,006	146,594	−6.0

[a]Estimates

in 1997 and started with only 30 vehicles in Berlin. Today, the company has a large network in 52 countries on all five continents and has about 1800 vehicles in 120 establishments in service. Rickshaw drivers work mostly between 10 am and 8 pm from April to October but some suppliers try to prolong the season to include Christmas time to make some extra profit. The majority of the drivers are between 20 and 40 years old and 50% of them are attending university (Veloform GmbH, 2012b). In the UK and Germany, for instance, rickshaws need to be licensed and meet safety and insurance regulations (Veloform GmbH, 2012a). In contrast, in the USA regulations vary in every city. In Tampa, Florida, there is only a city-required permit but in San Francisco, California, pedicabs need a permit issued by the chief of police as well as a plate, an identification card, an operator's badge and insurance (City and County of San Francisco, 2009). In Las Vegas, however, pedicabs are prohibited on the famous Strip as well as in some parts of Canada's resort town Whistler in British Columbia (Las Vegas Review Journal, 2004).

WALKING

Since the beginning of the human race, walking is the oldest form of covering a distance. In the past, it served a specific purpose. However, due to several motivations, such as relaxation, peace and quiet, there are various forms of walking nowadays (Leder, 2004). In the tourism sector, the three main types are hiking, trekking and backpacking.

Hiking

Although there are many books and articles available, there is no generally accepted definition for the term hiking. Within the academic literature, hiking is described rather than defined. According to Dreyer *et al.* (2010), hiking refers to the voluntary and purposeful locomotion by foot in nature. The movement results from the hiker's own power, wherein at least one foot stays on the ground and no special equipment is required. In hiking, the journey is more important than the destination. The Romantic era during the 19th century proclaimed the strong sense of nature and at that time, hiking became a preferred activity (Krüger, 2010).

While hiking is popular among all age groups, it is most popular among the slightly older population. For example, the average age of hikers in Germany is 47 years (Deutscher Wanderverband, 2010). Motivations for hiking are, among others, the physical activity, spending time with family and friends, relaxation, the enjoyment of nature and landscapes and education (Brämer and Gruber, 2005). The majority (about 76%) of hikers make use of a passenger car to get to the destination where they go hiking (Hallerbach, 2010).

12% of all US-Americans (older than six years) go hiking; that accounts for 34.5 million participants (see Fig. 7.5). In Germany, however, hiking is a lot more popular. About 60% of the German population goes hiking, which is a total of about 35.4 million (Deutscher Wanderverband, 2010).

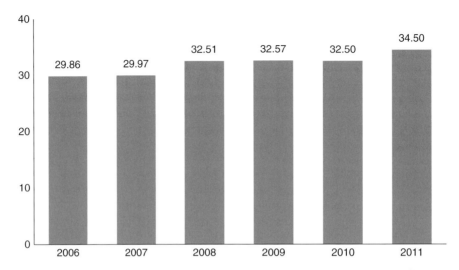

Fig. 7.5. Number of participants in hiking in the USA from 2006 to 2011 (in millions). From The Outdoor Foundation, 2012a.

In Europe, there are several trails and routes for hiking. One network of 11 long-distance footpaths that traverse Europe is the 'European long-distance paths' that were designated by the European Ramblers' Association (ERA). The ERA's objective is the protection of the countryside, environment and European cultural heritage (European Ramblers' Association, 2012). In North America, there are more than 1200 trails that range from less than 2 km to 780 km in length (National Recreation Trails, 2012). The Trans Canada Trail will be the world's longest network of trails when completed and will stretch over 23,000 km from the Atlantic to the Pacific to the Arctic Oceans, linking 1000 communities in Canada (Trans Canada Trail, 2012).

It is obvious that hiking concentrates not only on nature but also on culture, sustainability and sports. Figure 7.6 illustrates the overall importance of hiking in tourism and shows its linkage with other forms of tourism.

Trekking

Trekking is similar to hiking; however, it is more challenging than hiking as the paths mostly traverse remote and undeveloped regions. Therefore, hiking is often combined with camping for an overnight stay in backcountry wilderness. The traveller carries his supplies and equipment in a backpack. Trekking has its focus on the intensive outdoor experience off the beaten track. Moreover, the sporting activity is of high importance. Hence, trekking is a form of adventure holiday and usually comprises the walking of ascents and descents for 5 to 6 h or 9 to 14 km a day with a guide. Due to the missing comfort of accommodation and the high physical activity, trekking is more popular among younger travellers (Beedie, 2003). Therefore, the European mountains are preferred destinations for trekking, such as Mont Blanc between France and Italy, the Pyrenees, the Sierra Nevada in Spain, the mountains

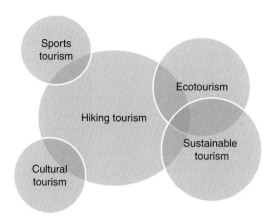

Fig. 7.6. Hiking tourism and its linkage with other forms. Compiled by the author.

of Corsica, the Alps in Germany, Italy, Austria and Slovenia or the Tatra Mountains in Poland and Slovakia. In the USA, the number one destinations for trekking are the Grand Canyon and the Rocky Mountains. Other examples include the great walks in Australia and New Zealand (see www.greatwalksofaustralia.com.au and www.doc.govt.nz/parks-and-recreation/tracks-and-walks/great-walks, for example).

Backpacking

Backpacking is a low-cost form of independent (international) travel. Backpackers make use of rucksacks or other baggage that can be easily carried for long distances or long periods of time. Typical for this form of travelling is the usage of public transportation, preference for budget accommodation such as hostels and high interest in meeting the locals and other travellers and experiencing the visited destination. Compared with conventional vacations, a backpacking holiday is much longer and very often it comprises a few weeks. It is typically associated with young adults, who generally have fewer obligations and thus more time to travel, concurrently having less money at their disposal for hotels or private vehicles (Hannam and Ateljevic, 2008). In the 20th century, backpacking originated in Europe and started to become popular. The hippies are said to be the pioneers of backpacking when they travelled from Europe to India (on the famous Hippie Trail) in the 1960s. It was not until 1990 that the term 'backpacker' appeared in academic literature and was introduced by Pearce. Unfortunately, as yet there has been little attention paid to the research of those travelling in Europe, as Europe is more considered as a source of outbound backpack travellers and not as a destination per se (Hannam and Ateljevic, 2008). Europeans prefer travelling to more exotic locations such as South East Asia or Australia.

In North America, backpacking is less popular than in Europe. In 2011, there were only about 1 million backpackers, aged between 18 and 24 years (see Fig. 7.7).

Sight jogging

Sight jogging, also called sight running or tourist jogging, is a modern alternative for sight-seeing tours in the 21st century. As the name implies, the sights of a destination are discovered while jogging. There are special tour operators offering guided jogging tours through the major cities of Europe (such as Barcelona, Rome, Copenhagen and Budapest) and the USA. This form of sightseeing allows the tourist to combine cultural and sporting activities (Sightjogging Barcelona, 2012).

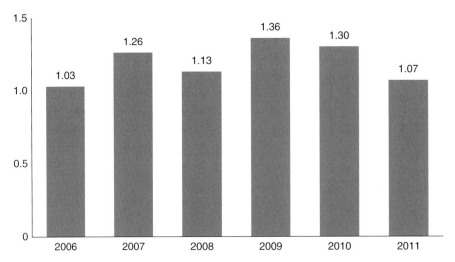

Fig. 7.7. Number of young adults (18–24 years) backpacking in the USA from 2006 to 2011 (in millions). From The Outdoor Foundation, 2012b.

FURTHER READING

Beedie, P. (2003) Adventure tourism. In: Hudson, S. (ed.) *Sport and Adventure Tourism*. Haworth Hospitality Press, Binghampton, New York, pp. 203–240.

Beedie, P. and Huson, S. (2003) Emergence of mountain-based adventure tourism. *Annals of Tourism Research* 30, 625–643.

Dreyer, A., Menzel, A. and Endreß, M. (2010) *Wandertourismus. Kundengruppen, Destinationsmarketing, Gesundheitsaspekte*. Oldenbourg, Munich, Germany.

Faulks, P., Ritchie, B. and Fulker, M. (2007) *Cycle Tourism in Australia: An Investigation into its Size and Scope*. CRC for Sustainable Tourism Pty Ltd. Available at: www.crctourism.com.au/wms/upload/Resources/bookshop/Faulks_AustnCycleTourism.pdf

Gallagher, R. (1992) *The Rickshaws of Bangladesh*. University Press, Dhaka, Bangladesh.

Gross, S. (2011) *Tourismus und Verkehr – Grundlagen, Marktanalyse und Strategien von Verkehrsunternehmen*. Oldenbourg, Munich, Germany.

Gyimóthy, S. and Mykletun, R.J. (2004) Play in adventure tourism. The case of Arctic trekking. *Annals of Tourism Research* 31, 855–878.

Lamont, M. (2010) *Cycle Tourism in Australia: Exploring the Whole Tourism System*. LAP LAMBERT Academic Publishing, Saarbrücken, Germany.

Lumma, K. and Gross, S. (2010) Natur- und Aktivtourismus in deutschen Mittelgebirgsregionen – Produktinnovationen für das Destinationsmanagement. In: Kagermeier, A. and Willms, J. (eds) *Tourism Development in Low Mountain Ranges*. Verlag Metagis-Systems, Mannheim, Germany, pp. 115–134.

Miller, F., Vandome, A. and McBrewster, J. (2010) *Cycle Rickshaw*. VDM Publishing House, Saarbrücken, Germany.

Sacareau, I. (2009) Changes in environmental policy and mountain tourism in Nepal. *Revue de géographie alpine/Journal of Alpine Research* 97. Available at: http://rga.revues.org/1031.

Standeven, J. and de Knop, P. (1999) *Sport Tourism*. Human Kinetics, Champaign, Illinois.

Swarbrooke, J., Beard, C., Leckie, S. and Pomfret, G. (2003) *Adventure Tourism. The New Frontier*. Butterworth-Heinemann, Burlington, Vermont.

Wheeler, T. (1998) *Chasing Rickshaws*. Lonely Planet Publications, Melbourne, Australia.

Internet sources

www.adac.de, www.campingcardinternational.com, www.cycletourism.com, www.civd.de, www.dwif.de, http://www.med.govt.nz/about-us/pdf-library/tourism-publications/Cycle%20Tourism%20Profile%20-123KB%20PDF.pdf, www.segway.com, www.segwayhtpolo.com, http://www.sustainable-tourismonline.com, http://satic.com.au/images/uploads/industry_resources/cycle_tourism_strategy.pdf.

Part 3

Water Based Transportation

There are two kinds of water based transportation: marine and freshwater, where the latter refers to lakes and canals. A second major distinction can be made between freight and passenger transportation; while some freight vessels can accommodate a limited number of passengers with their own cabins, their transportation is secondary to the transportation of cargo. From a tourism perspective, the transportation of passengers is of primary interest and will be explored in this section.

The International Maritime Organization (IMO) is a specialized agency within the United Nations responsible for maritime affairs. The IMO defines a passenger ship as a ship which carries more than twelve passengers but does not make a distinction between the different types of vessels. However, there are two main categories of passenger vessels: commercial passenger vessels and recreational boats.

Within commercial passenger vessels, a further distinction can be made between cruise ships and passenger lines or ferries. While both operate in the capacity of commercial water based transportation, cruise ships focus on the leisure experience while passenger lines and ferries have a more utilitarian function. Although recreational boats such as charter boats, including houseboats and yachts, can be utilized for passenger transportation, as the name implies, they are generally used for personal pleasure rather than large-scale passenger transportation. Each mode of water based passenger transportation plays a role within the tourism industry and hence will be examined separately in Chapters 8 and 9.

Focus box

- While the Institute of Shipping Economics and Logistics (ISL) estimated that more than three out of four ships operate in regional passenger transportation, their tonnage share in the total passenger fleet reached only 9% in 2010.
- Cruise shipping accounts for the majority of passenger tonnage, which increased by an average of 6% per year between 2006 and 2010 due to an increase in ever-larger cruise vessels.
- The world passenger fleet grew an average of 4% annually when measured in gross register tonnage (total internal volume of a vessel), but only 1.1% if measured in number of ships, further demonstrating the increase in overall ship size being ordered.
- As a comparison, the cargo passenger fleet grew an average of only 2.2% yearly during the same period.

From ISL, 2010.

chapter 8

Cruise Ships

LEARNING OBJECTIVES

- Describe the modern cruise as a product, understand its origins and be able to identify important characteristics for definitional purposes.
- Identify and describe the major international associations involved in the regulation of marine safety and environment.
- Critically assess the demand and supply sides of the cruise industry, in order to understand the overall market.

DEFINITIONS

Ocean or maritime cruises dominate the market although cruising can also take place along coastlines and rivers and on lakes. There are a myriad of different products offered, ranging from very small ships catering to highly specialized niche markets, to extremely large ships catering to the mass tourism market. However, no matter what type of cruise, the essence of modern cruising is to provide a holiday experience rather than point-to-point transportation (Goeldner and Ritchie, 2011). In his book, *Liners to the Sun*, ship historian and avid cruiser Maxtone-Graham commented that Atlantic crossings of the past were merely a part of the journey, inevitably too short, and filled with a sense of purpose, while cruising is languorous and the 'cruise's raison d'être is the sea voyage itself' (Maxtone-Graham, 2000, p. 6). The cruise may consist of several ports of call, yet it is often characterized as a mobile resort rather than a mode of transportation (Dowling, 2006; UNWTO, 2010a). It is important to remember that the cruise product is a complex package consisting of transportation, accommodation, and leisure facilities on board, as well as the itinerary of destinations to be visited.

Cruise ship

According to the *Glossary of Transport Statistics* (2009, p. 114) compiled by the International Transport Forum (ITF), Eurostat (the European Union's statistical office) and the United Nations Economic Commission for Europe (UNECE), a cruise ship is 'a passenger ship intended to provide passengers with a full tourist experience. All passengers have cabins. Facilities for entertainment aboard are included'. For the purposes of collecting data on the cruise industry within the European Union, Eurostat excludes normal ferry services (even if some passengers treat the service as a cruise), cargo carrying vessels (even if they are able to carry a limited number of passengers with their own cabins), and ships intended solely for day excursions (*Glossary of Transport Statistics*, 2009).

A cruise or cruising

The USA based *Cruise Industry News* defines cruising as 'ocean travel for the purpose of leisure (as opposed to transportation) on a ship that typically holds 100 or more passengers and lasts a minimum of three days, during which passengers live on the ship' (O. Mathisen, 2011, personal communication). Alternatively, cruise tourism is defined by the UNWTO (2010a, p. 190) as

> sea voyages made by national and foreign travellers on large recreational vessels called cruise ships, with defined and regular routes, calling at different ports in the countries visited and consuming services within the vessels as well as the products services and tourist attractions offered by each destination.

While there is no official internationally accepted definition of cruising, various definitions of a cruise can be found within the academic literature. Gibson (2006, p. 14) presents one of the simplest definitions: 'a vacation involving a voyage by sea, on a lake, or on a river'. While this definition is applicable to a cruise, it does not sufficiently convey the important distinction between travelling for the purpose of reaching a destination as opposed to travelling for the experience itself. Dowling (2006, p. 3) utilizes the definition found within the *Collins English Dictionary*, which adds the important element of passenger motivation as well as eluding to a voyage of some length: 'to make a trip by sea in a liner for pleasure, usually calling at a number of ports'. This definition gives a clearer understanding of the concept that it is the voyage itself that constitutes the holiday. As previously mentioned, Dowling also further expands on the definition by characterizing the cruise ship as a floating hotel, or mobile resort, which transports passengers from place to place. Morgan and Power (2011) further include elements such as destination(s), length, and type of itinerary in their definition:

> A cruise trip is a passage of time spent on board a cruise ship and at a cruise destination. A trip can last for two nights (a short cruise), 2 weeks (an average cruise) or up to several months (a world cruise). A cruise voyage can be a round trip with several en-route stops (e.g. a Mediterranean cruise starting in and finishing in Southampton); a fly cruise (e.g. flying from London to Barbados, then sailing around the Caribbean and returning to London by air from Barbados); or a fly cruise that involves flying to one destination and sailing to another or vice versa (e.g. flying out to New York and sailing back to Southampton).
> (Morgan and Power, 2011, p. 277)

Mancini (2004) also offers a concise definition, but more importantly goes on to delimit the definition and add experiential elements:

> A cruise is a vacation trip by ship. … this definition excludes travelling by water for purely business purpose (e.g. cargo ships), sailing one's own small pleasure craft, or travel on a vessel for primarily transportational purposes (e.g. a short ferry ride). A cruise is primarily a leisure vacation experience, with the ship's staff doing all the work. Some cruise ships also transport cargo, and all of them carry people from place to place. But at the core of cruising – from the perspective of the traveller – is the desire to relax, to get away from it all, to experience, to learn, to be pampered, and to have fun.
>
> (Mancini, 2004, p. 3)

While there is no clear-cut definition of cruising recognized within the academic literature, the main aspects found within most definitions include:

- a vacation on board a ship, calling at several ports;
- transportation is secondary to the overall experience;
- the ship as a floating resort.

Therefore, we propose an encompassing definition of cruising as follows. Cruises are a holiday on board a ship, where several destinations are visited along a specific route. The overall experience is of primary importance with the transportation itself playing only a secondary role. Moreover, as the ship provides accommodation and comprehensive leisure and entertainment components, the voyage itself becomes part of the destination.

HISTORICAL DEVELOPMENT OF THE MARKET

Transatlantic voyages on ocean liners between Europe and America during the early 19th century represent the first luxurious form of commercial marine passenger transportation. Until the 18th century, passenger transportation on merchant vessels was an expensive, uncomfortable, and often risky endeavour reserved for the rich and those on special missions. In fact, ocean-going vessels were primarily utilized for the transportation of cargo until the early 19th century; however, with the advent of steam power around this time, a new era of passenger travel began. The travel time for transatlantic voyages on ocean liners between Europe and America was drastically reduced, and by 1838 the steamship *Sirius* crossed the Atlantic in only 18 days and 10 h, compared to early transatlantic crossings by sail, which could take anywhere from 70 to 100 days or more (Schüssler, 2005).

Furthermore, the transition from wooden sailing ships to steel steam ships enabled much larger and more luxurious vessels to be built; coupled with the mass migration of people from Europe to America between the 1880s and 1920s, the shipping companies soon realized that there was much money to be made in the transportation of people. For example, Mancini (2004) documents that transporting immigrants was the major purpose of ocean liners of the time, with the ships being divided into two or three classes with perhaps 100 wealthy passengers travelling in the luxurious and elegant first class, 100 in the more modest second class, and as many as 2000 in the very austere third class. Sometimes third-class passengers were not only expected to provide their own food and drink, but also left to their own devices regarding sleeping arrangements, having to find any available space within the hold (Morgan and Power, 2011). However, as the transportation of passengers from point A to point B was the underlying reason for these transatlantic voyages, they are regarded as passenger lines rather than cruises.

Accounts regarding the origins of the modern cruise industry vary. However, many feel that the Peninsular and Oriental Steam Navigation Company (P&O) were the true pioneers of modern cruising (Gross, 2011 and sources therein), even though their original venture was a mail carrier service between London and the Iberian Peninsula. One of the co-founders, a Scotsman named Arthur Anderson, had the vision to offer cruises around the Shetland Isles, to the Faroes and Iceland, and back again, placing a newspaper advertisement for such a trip in 1835. While it was a dummy advertisement in the first edition of his Shetland Journal publication and never actually took place, an idea was born (P&O Cruises, 2012). It was not until 1844 that the P&O liner *Ceylon* was converted into a cruise ship for the purpose of pleasure trips. Around this time, other shipping companies also began to undertake pleasure trips to the Norwegian fjords or the Mediterranean; the German Hamburg-Amerikanische Packetfahrt-Aktien-Gesellschaft (HAPAG), for example, utilized their liners for pleasure trips to the warmer Mediterranean as an alternative source of income during the slower winter months (Schüssler, 2005). According to Dickinson and Vladimir (2008), the first American cruise probably took place in 1867 on a paddle-wheel steamer named *Quaker City*. The six-month voyage started in New York and included destinations such as Bermuda, Gibraltar, France, Spain, Italy, Greece, Turkey, Lebanon and Israel (Rasmussen, 2007). Interestingly, the trip is rather well-documented, as Mark Twain was one of the passengers (Rasmussen, 2007; Dickinson and Vladimir, 2008).

These early examples of pleasure cruises were carried out on vessels that were not designated purely for such trips; rather they exemplify early forms of product diversification within maritime transportation. The first ship specifically designed and built for cruising was the *Prinzessin Victoria Luise* which was taken into service in 1900 by the German Hamburg-Amerika Line according to Schüssler (2005), while Morgan and Power (2011) document the first official cruise taking place on a luxurious ship specifically built for leisurely travel between various ports as taking place in 1922. Although slightly varying accounts can be found within the literature, it is clear that modern-day cruising has its origins in the mid-19th century (Schüssler, 2005; Dickinson and Vladimir, 2008; Morgan and Power, 2011).

While the First and Second World Wars had a detrimental impact on the cruising industry, the period between the turn of the 20th century and the Second World War is often viewed as the golden age of cruising (Gross, 2011). During this era, there was great competition between the shipping companies to attract immigrants and tourists alike. Luxurious ships became representative status symbols for nations such as Great Britain (e.g. White Star Line's *Titanic* and

Cunard-White Star's *Queen Mary* and *Queen Elizabeth*), France (e.g. Compagnie Generale Transatlantique's *Ile-de-France* and *Normandie*), Germany (e.g. Hapag-Lloyd's *Augusta Victoria* and Norddeutscher Lloyd's *Bremen*), and Italy (e.g. Italia Flotte Riunite's *Conti di Savoia* and *Rex*). Size and luxury were not the only factors driving the competition; speed was also an imperative to take part in the great North Atlantic race. The two points on either side of the Atlantic between which the race was run were Bishop Rock Lighthouse off the Scilly Isles and the Ambrose Light off New York harbour. A ship had to beat previous records in both eastward and westward directions in the same voyage in order to win the coveted Blue Riband (an actual trophy as well as a pennant to be flown by the winner) (Clifford, 2012). The first ship to be awarded the Blue Riband was the British vessel *Great Western* in 1838, while the *Mauretania* held the trophy for almost 23 years, for an Atlantic crossing in 1907 that took only 4 days and 22 h (Schüssler, 2005). The company holding the record was guaranteed not only great prestige, but also a significant increase in bookings. Governments were also keen in sharing the prestige and often subsidized ships due to the enormous costs associated with the operation of such vessels. For example, the SS *United States* was virtually owned by the US government and intended for use as a fast government personnel carrier, the seaborne equivalent of *Air Force One* (Clifford, 2012).

Focus box

The competition between the British and Germans was fierce in the North Atlantic race between the late 19th and early 20th century. The British held the Blue Riband from 1892 to 1898 and the German shipping company Norddeutscher Lloyd (NDL) gave everything to compete with Cunard's ships *Campania* and *Lucania*, and in 1897 the vessel *Kaiser Wilhelm der Grosse* won the Blue Riband for Germany.

However, at what price did this competition take place?

- The *Kaiser Wilhelm der Grosse* burned 1 ton of coal/h for every knot of speed – at a service speed of 22 knots the fuel supply that had to be carried and consumed was enormous. Later advances in oil burning boilers helped, but they were still not enough to make a fast ship profitable.
- On an eastward voyage, the *Queen Elizabeth* burned 1039 tons of fuel oil daily, and when one considers the trip took 4 days, the consumption was obviously enormous.

From Clifford, 2012.

According to Hobson (1993), over a million people undertook the transatlantic voyage on an ocean liner in 1957; however, with the advent of commercial jet services, more people crossed the Atlantic by plane than by ship in 1958. Over the next 20 years, many passenger line operators repositioned their vessels as cruise ships. Most of the new cruise ships built during this period carried between 750 and 1200 passengers and generally catered to the luxury market.

Since the 1980s, the cruise segment of leisure travel has grown more than any other tourism sector, mainly due to a major expansion of the product palette, and to its repositioning to new market segments.

Based on the new target markets, the cruise product underwent significant changes in terms of ship size, facilities, services offered on board, and length of cruise. In fact, current product packages offer an attractive and extremely viable alternative to the mass-market holiday resorts. The cruise lines modernized their ships, offering such things as expanded pool areas, spa and fitness areas, casinos, discos, movie theatres, libraries and Las Vegas style entertainment as well as bars and all-inclusive dining. Not to be dismissed is the impact of the TV series *The Love Boat* in the late 1970s, which attracted a worldwide audience, and not only was a public relations wonder for Princess Cruise Lines (who made two of their ships available for filming), but also popularized cruising as a fun and affordable mass-market vacation (Dickinson and Vladimir, 1997). Currently, there is a cruise for just about everyone, ranging from budget cruises with fewer amenities to luxury-branded cruises (Duval, 2007).

INSTITUTIONAL FRAMEWORK

Maritime governance is a difficult subject as activities are subject to jurisdictions at international, national, regional and local levels. Due to the international nature of marine environments, delineations of responsibility are not always clear-cut, which also makes enforcement of regulations a difficult issue. From the 17th century until the mid-20th century, the 'principle of the freedom of the seas' governed unrestricted access to the high seas and to waters outside of national territories, defined as a three-mile zone. However, the principle was challenged by several nations that tried to extend their national territory beyond the three-mile zone in order to protect lucrative fish stocks or exploit natural resources. For example, in 1945, the USA extended their jurisdiction zone to the continental shelf and other nations soon followed suit extending their own zones as far as 200 miles (Gross, 2011 and sources therein). Competing demand for the oceans' resources (including fish, oil, gas, minerals, etc.) and increasing marine pollution were some of the issues fuelling national rivalries and an increasing need for an internationally regulated use and management of the marine environment.

International Maritime Organization (IMO)

In 1948, the United Nations adopted a convention establishing an international body dedicated purely to maritime matters: the International Maritime Organization (IMO) headquartered in London, UK. In 1958, the first of three United Nations Conferences on the Law of the Sea took place in Geneva, Switzerland. However, it was not until the third conference convened in New York in 1973 that a comprehensive treaty for the oceans was undertaken, leading to the adoption of the United Nations Convention on the Law of the Sea (UNCLOS III) in 1982 (The United Nations Convention on the Law of the Sea, 1998). The treaty actually went into effect on 16 November 1994 after ratification by 60 nations. Interestingly, although the USA participated in the drafting of UNCLOS, and President Clinton signed the treaty after a clause regarding deep-sea mining was removed, it has yet to be ratified by the Senate. Nevertheless, the USA is in voluntary compliance with the provisions of the treaty and is included as one of the 152 representatives from major maritime nations within the IMO (Global Solutions, 2011).

The treaty established navigational rights, territorial sea limits, economic jurisdiction, legal status of resources on the seabed beyond the limits of national jurisdiction, passage of ships through narrow straits, conservation and management of living marine resources, protection of the marine environment, a marine research regime and a binding procedure for settlement of disputes between states (The United Nations Convention on the Law of the Sea, 1998).

Several zones of international rights were established as part of the UNCLOS III treaty (see Fig. 8.1):

- territorial water – a 12-mile zone from the coastal baseline in which coastal states are free to set laws, regulate use and claim natural resources;
- contiguous zone – a 12-mile zone beyond the territorial waters in which pollution, taxation, customs and immigration laws may be enforced;
- exclusive economic zone – a 200-mile zone from the coastal baseline in which the coastal nation has exclusive right to the natural resources.

The internal waters and the territorial waters belong to the national territory of a nation, and hence the state has absolute sovereignty within these zones. In contiguous zones, nations may exercise necessary controls to prevent infringement of their customs, fiscal, immigration, or

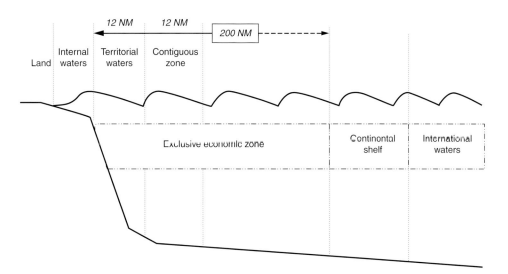

Fig. 8.1. UNCLOS maritime zones. Adapted from The United Nations Convention on the Law of the Sea, 1998.

sanitary laws and regulations within their territory, and they may also punish any infringements committed. However, based on UNCLOS III all countries retain some freedoms of the high sea; for example, foreign vessels have the right to innocent passage (freedom of navigation) and nations are permitted to lay submarine cables and pipelines through these zones (Federal Register, 1999).

Since 1960, the IMO has driven the adoption of more than 50 conventions and protocols and more than 1000 codes and recommendations covering all aspects of maritime transport (European Commission, 2011a). At the international level, the IMO focuses on safety, the environment and security, while the International Labour Organization (ILO) focuses on issues affecting maritime labour. However, regional bodies such as the European Union (EU), the North American Free Trade Agreement (NAFTA), and the Association of South East Asian Nations (ASEAN) also influence and affect regional policy through individual interpretations and refinements of international regulations for application to their own member states (SKEMA, 2010). A selection of international conventions regarding marine protection is illustrated in Fig. 8.2.

There are several important international institutions that help to oversee and regulate maritime affairs. Some of the most influential are the IMO, the International Maritime Bureau (IMB), and the International Association of Classification Societies (IACS), which are briefly highlighted in Table 8.1.

Regional: North America

As previously mentioned, the North American Free Trade agreement (NAFTA) signed by Canada, the USA and Mexico affects maritime policies within the North American region. However, each country coordinates and carries responsibility for their maritime policies. For example, Canada's maritime regulations are based on the Canada Shipping Act of 2001. The maritime governance structure of the USA will be briefly explored for illustrative

UN conventions on maritime law

Global, international agreements	Regional, international agreements
OILPOL	UNEP Regional Seas Programme
Intervention agreements	Mediterranean (BARCON)
London Convention	Gulf Region (Kuwait Convention)
MARPOL 73/78	East Africa (Nairobi Convention)
Montreal Protocol	Southeast Pacific (Lima Convention)
SOLAS	Red Sea/Gulf of Aden (Jeddah Convention)
Anti-fouling Convention	Caribbean (Catagena Convention)
Ballast water Convention	South Pacific (Noumea Convention)
	Northeast Atlantic/North Sea (OSPAR)
	Baltic Sea (HELCOM)
	Scandinavia (Stockholm Convention)

Fig. 8.2. Selection of international agreements on marine protection. From Gross, 2010.

Table 8.1. Main global institutions. (Adapted from IACS, 2011; IMB, 2011; IMO, 2011.)

	International Maritime Organization (IMO)	International Maritime Bureau (IMB)	International Association of Classification Societies (IACS)
Affiliation	Specialized agency of the United Nations	Specialized division of the international Chamber of Commerce	Consisting of the 13 largest classification societies[a]
Year of foundation	1958	1981 as a non-profit organization	1968 as a non-governmental organization
Main purpose	Development of international conventions, codes and recommendations regarding marine safety and pollution	Fight against maritime crime and malpractice in close conjunction with the IMO	Setting technical and engineering standards for the design, construction and life-cycle maintenance of ships
Area of operations	International Convention for the Safety of Life at Sea (SOLAS); International Convention for the Prevention of Pollution from Ships (MARPOL); International Convention on Standards of Training, Certification and Watchkeeping for Seafarers (STCW)	Memorandum of understanding with World Customs Organization; Observer status with Interpol; Maintaining round-the-clock watch on the world's shipping lanes, reports pirate attacks to local law enforcement, and issues warnings regarding piracy hotspots	Consultancy status with the IMO; Observer status which develops and applies rules

[a]Members are: American Bureau of Shipping (ABS), Bureau Veritas (BV), China Classification Society (CCS), Croatian Register of Shipping (CRS), Det Norske Veritas (DNV), Germanischer Lloyd (GL), Indian Register of Shipping (IRS), Korean Register of Shipping (KR), Lloyd's Register (LR), Nippon Kaiji Kyokai (NK/Class NK), Polish Register of Shipping (PRS), Registro Italiano Navale (RINA), Russian Maritime Register of Shipping (RS).

purposes; however, it is an extremely complex subject matter and references for more detailed information will be provided at the end of the chapter.

Within the United States, there is no single agency responsible for maritime affairs. In fact, 11 cabinet-level departments and four independent agencies share responsibility for ocean and coastal policy and management (US Commission on Ocean Policy, 2004).

A Commission on Ocean Policy was established in 2000, and presented a final report in 2004 recommending a new National Ocean Policy Framework, which proposed a new holistic structure for the coordination of ocean activities at a Federal Level, including a National Ocean Council (NOC) within the Executive Office of the President. On 19 July 2010, President Obama signed an executive order establishing a 'National Policy for the Stewardship of the Ocean, our Coasts, and the Great Lakes', which created such an interagency NOC to strengthen ocean governance and coordination (Federal Register, 2012). How this will actually affect the governance structure is yet to be seen. Currently, however, the cruise ship operations within US waters fall under the jurisdiction of several federal agencies. According to a report prepared by the Congressional Research Service (CRS) in 2008, the US Coast Guard and the Environmental Protection Agency (EPA) share the main regulatory and standard-setting responsibilities, while the Department of Justice prosecutes violations of federal laws. However, the Department of State represents the USA at meetings of the IMO and international treaty negotiations while also carrying the responsibility of pursuing foreign-flag violations. Other federal agencies also have limited responsibilities; for example, the National Oceanic and Atmospheric Administration (NOAA, Department of Commerce) reports the effects of marine debris in conjunction with the Coast Guard and the EPA. In some cases, individual states and localities also enact their own laws and regulations and therefore carry some responsibilities as well. For example, cruise ship pollution became a significant problem for the state of Alaska and they enacted their own law extending some of the federal standards regarding the discharge of treated sewage and grey water (CRS, 2008). Other individual states which are actively working towards their own state level ocean management plan include California, Florida, Hawaii, Maine, New York, New Jersey and Massachusetts (Joint Ocean Commission Initiative, 2006). Detailed information regarding US maritime laws can be found in the *Compilation of Maritime Laws* published each year by the Maritime Administration, part of the US Department of Transportation.

Regional: Europe

The United Nations Convention on the Law of the Sea coordinates maritime affairs at the global level, while there are also regional sea conventions within Europe, as follows.

- Convention for the Protection of the Marine Environment of the North-East Atlantic (1992, further to earlier versions of 1972 and 1974) (OSPAR). Based on the previous Oslo and Paris Conventions, the mission of OSPAR is 'to conserve marine ecosystems and safeguard human health ... by preventing and eliminating pollution; by protecting the marine environment from adverse effects of human activities; and by contributing to the sustainable use of the area' (European Commission, 2011b). The 15 governments cooperating under the agreement are Belgium, Denmark, Finland, France, Germany, Iceland, Ireland, Luxembourg, the Netherlands, Norway, Portugal, Spain, Sweden, Switzerland and the UK.

- Convention on the Protection of Marine Environment in the Baltic Sea Area (1992, further to the earlier version of 1974), the Helsinki Convention (HELCOM). The Helsinki Commission is the governing body for an intergovernmental co-operation between Denmark, Estonia, the European Community, Finland, Germany, Latvia, Lithuania, Poland, Russia and Sweden to protect the marine environment of the Baltic Sea.
- Convention for the Protection of the Marine Environment and the Coastal Region of the Mediterranean (1995, further to the earlier version of 1976), the Barcelona Convention. There are currently 22 contracting parties to the Barcelona Convention: Albania, Algeria, Bosnia and Herzegovina, Croatia, Cyprus, Egypt, the European Community, France, Greece, Israel, Italy, Lebanon, Libya, Malta, Monaco, Montenegro, Morocco, Slovenia, Spain, Syria, Tunisia and Turkey.
- Convention for the Protection of the Black Sea (1992), the Bucharest Convention. The Black Sea Commission implements the convention and the contracting parties include Bulgaria, Georgia, Romania, Russian Federation, Turkey and Ukraine.

While there are global and regional conventions and treaties, the governments of individual European member states coordinate and carry the responsibilities for maritime activities individually within their territories. Hence, the European Community and its member states are parties to more than 100 multilateral agreements relating to maritime affairs (European Commission, 2010a).

However, in 2006 the importance of an integrated maritime policy within the European Union was recognized. Hence, in 2007 the European Commission put forth an action plan in the form of a 'Blue Paper' which advocated 'the need for the development and implementation of integrated, coherent, and joined-up decision-making in relation to the oceans, seas, coastal regions and maritime sectors' (European Commission, 2010b). The objectives were endorsed by the General Affairs Council in November 2009 and since then, continued work has been undertaken to further develop and implement the objectives. More specifically, in September 2011, the European Commission proposed to continue financial support to the EU's integrated Maritime Policy until 2013.

According to the *Maritime Facts and Figures*, published by the European Commission's Maritime Affairs (European Commission, 2010a), there are six agencies at the European level dealing with matters related to the seas.

- FRONTEX (the European agency for the management of operational cooperation at the external borders of the member states)
- European Defence Agency

- European Space Agency
- European Maritime Safety Agency
- Community Fisheries Control Agency
- European Environment Agency

Furthermore, within the European Commission, seven Commissioners from different policy areas direct a common task force to look at the oceans and seas in an integrated fashion. More specifically, the task force consists of the Commissioner for the Environment, Commissioner for Science and Research, Commissioner for Transport, Commissioner for Regional Policy, Commissioner for Fisheries and Maritime Affairs, Commissioner for Enterprise and Industry, and Commissioner for Energy. Although we have seen that there are institutions working on an encompassing maritime policy at the international level, the implementation, compliance and enforcement of those rules and regulations is difficult.

Passenger rights

Recent European consumer protection laws came into effect in December 2012, which have increased passengers' rights when travelling by maritime and inland waterway transport. The European Parliament and Council established Regulation EU No. 1177/2010, which applies to all cross-channel ferries. Excursions, sightseeing tours or boats with capacities limited to 12 passengers or under three operational crew members are not affected by this regulation, nor are ferries that travel less than 500 m.

The purpose of the regulation is to:

- offer free assistance to disabled persons when notification has been made at least 48 hours before boarding and hence prevent refusal of boarding;
- provide passengers rights in case of cancellation or delay. More specifically, passengers suffering significant delays will be entitled to compensation of 25% of the ticket price, increasing to 50% for long delays. If delays mean a passenger has to spend the night in a hotel, the ferry operator will have to pay for hotel and meals (up to €80 per night, for a maximum of three nights). In case of cancellation, the new law gives passengers the right to be re-routed at the earliest opportunity and at no extra cost, or receive a full refund;
- ensure minimum rules regarding the provision of information for passengers before and during their journey, as well as general information about their rights in terminals, in ports and on the carrier ships (European Union, 2010).

Hence, the new regulations give passengers the same opportunities and passenger rights when travelling by water as they have in the rail and aviation sectors across the EU.

Issues of ownership and accountability

Shipping governance is complicated by issues of vessel registration and nationality, as there is no true link between vessel ownership and the flag a vessel flies (International Transport Workers' Federation, 2012). The registration of a ship allocates the ship to a specific state, granting the right to fly that state's national flag (Gibson, 2006). Moreover, the vessels are then subject to the laws of their flag nation, and enforcement of international regulations relies primarily on the exercise of their jurisdiction, irrespective of where the ship is sailing. This is particularly pertinent as Weaver and Duval (2008, p. 121) note, 'cruise lines have developed an acute understanding of the crucial differences that exist between legal jurisdictions'. As countries have varying regulations regarding ship construction, crewing and ownership requirements to flag a vessel, the flag state can have a serious influence not only regarding legal matters but also operational costs and the living and working conditions of crewmembers. Each flag state is in principle required to ensure the adherence to international regulations for all of the vessels in its register. Unfortunately, however, this is not always the case. The largest flag states or registers are Panama, Liberia and the Marshall Islands, which are all open registers (SKEMA, 2010), essentially offering 'flags of convenience'. According to the International Transport Workers' Federation, a flag of convenience is defined as follows: 'Where the beneficial ownership and control of a vessel is found to lie elsewhere than the country of the flag the vessel is flying, the vessel is considered as sailing under a flag of convenience' (ITWF, 2012).

Besides registration by non-citizens, the Rochdale Report of 1970 also lists the following qualities of flags of convenience: easy registry access and unrestricted transfer from the registry; minimal to non-existent taxes; registry country is small, and tonnage charges generally have large effects on national income; ships are free to use non-national labour; and most importantly, 'the country of registry has neither the power nor the administrative framework to effectively impose domestic or international regulations; nor does it wish to exert control over the companies' (Shaughnessy and Tobin, 2003–2004). By flying a flag of convenience, the operators often gain advantages such as the less restrictive regulations mentioned previously, as well as a greatly reduced risk of penalty for violations against international regulations. Ships can essentially operate under a lack of regulations due to the virtual absence of regulatory enforcement by the flag nation. Furthermore, labour costs can make up a substantial portion of operating expenses; if operators choose to register their vessel under a flag of convenience they can often immensely reduce those costs due to the lack of restrictive labour laws within those countries. Hence there has been much criticism of the often exploitative working conditions, workloads and welfare provisions within the cruise industry (Hobson, 1993; Weaver and Duval, 2008).

As an indication of the prevalence of the use of such flags of convenience, the US Department of Transportation reports that 95% of passenger ships operating in US waters are foreign flagged (US Coast Guard Roles and Missions, 2011). This is probably due to the fact that

> crewing, ship construction and ownership requirements to flag a vessel in the United States are among the most restrictive of the maritime nations. Current manning regulations for US-flag vessels engaged in coastwise trade mandate that all officers and pilots and 75% of other onboard personnel be US citizens or residents. In addition, US flag vessels engaged in coastwise trade must be owned by US citizens and constructed in US ship yards.
>
> (CLIA, 2011a)

Carnival Corporation & plc is a global cruise company and has the largest market share within the cruise industry (Gross, 2011). Carnival is registered in Panama (Duval, 2007) although it has corporate headquarters in the USA and England (Miami, Florida and London, respectively). One of their major brands is Carnival Cruise Lines (headquartered in Miami, Florida), and according to Tré (2011), of Carnival Cruise Lines' 21 vessels, six are registered in the Bahamas, and 17 in Panama. Similarly, Royal Caribbean Cruises Ltd (the world's second largest cruise company) list their global headquarters as Miami, Florida, yet the company is registered in Liberia (UNWTO, 2010a). Furthermore, its main brand, Royal Caribbean International, has 22 ships that are under the Bahamian flag (currently the most popular flag for cruise ships), while four of its other brands are registered under the Maltese flag (Tré, 2011). As can be seen from these two examples, the use of flags of convenience is a regular phenomenon of the industry.

ASSOCIATIONS

Besides governmental regulatory bodies, there are also numerous industry associations within the cruise industry that participate in the regulatory and policy development process. Largely, however, they represent the interests of operators and play a role in the promotion of the industry. Within the USA and Canada, the Cruise Line International Association (CLIA) and the Florida-Caribbean Cruise Association (FCCA) are the principal cruise line associations, while the European Cruise Council (ECC) is the main association in Europe.

Cruise Line International Association (CLIA)

Founded in 1975, CLIA is a non-profit organization and is North America's largest cruise industry organization in terms of cruise line, industry supplier and travel agency membership according to their website. Today the organization represents 26 of the major cruise lines (representing over 97% of the cruise capacity marketed in North America) as well as having 16,000 affiliated travel agencies and agent members (CLIA, 2011b). Moreover, CLIA serves as a non-governmental consultative organization to the IMO which can be traced back to the 2006 merger with the International Council of Cruise Lines (ICCL), an organization focused mainly on the regulatory and policy development process of the cruise industry. According to CLIA (2011c) their mission is 'to promote all measures that foster a safe, secure and healthy cruise ship environment, educate, train its travel agent members, and promote and explain the value, desirability and affordability of the cruise vacation experience'. While mainly a promotional and marketing organization, CLIA also offers educational and speciality training courses to its affiliated travel agencies, and conducts extensive market research (important publications include *Cruise Industry Source Book*, *Cruise Industry Overview* and *CLIA Market Research*).

Florida-Caribbean Cruise Association (FCCA)

The FCCA was created as a non-profit trade organization in 1972 and is currently composed of 14 cruise operators active in Floridian, Caribbean and Latin American waters (FCCA,

2010). Similarly to CLIA and ECC, the FCCA seeks to promote the cruising industry while also providing a platform for discussion regarding legislation, tourism development, ports, safety, security and other cruise industry issues. According to their website, they are dedicated to working with 'governments, ports and all private/public sector representatives to maximize cruise passenger, cruise line and cruise line employee spending, as well as enhancing the destination experience and the amount of cruise passengers returning as stay-over visitors' (FCCA, 2010).

North West and Canada Cruise Ship Association (NWCCA)

The NWCCA is a non-profit organization founded in 1986 and represents major cruise lines operating in the Pacific Northwest – British Columbia, Washington State, Alaska and Hawaii – as well as in Atlantic Canada and Quebec (NWCCA, 2011). While working with government agencies in areas regarding safety, security and environmental aspects of the industry, their mission also includes the development of partnerships with destination communities as they aim to provide 'support for the work of local organizations to mitigate industry-related concerns, and to develop local opportunities' (NWCCA, 2011).

European Cruise Council (ECC)

The ECC is a non-profit association representing cruise operators in Europe and has 30 cruise members and 34 associate members. Similarly to their North American counterparts, their main mission is to expand the European cruise market while promoting

> the interests of cruise ship operators within Europe, liaising closely with the EU Institutions: the Commission, the Parliament, the Council of Ministers and their Permanent Representatives as well as with the European Maritime Safety Agency (EMSA). The ECC also looks to protect the interests of its Members through close liaison with other European bodies such as the European Community Ship owners Association (ECSA), the European Sea Ports Association (ESPO) and the European Travel Agents & Tour Operators Association (ECTAA).
>
> (ECC, 2011a)

A selection of other industry associations
- Alska Cruise Association (ACA)
- Atlantic Canada Cruise Association
- Cruise British Columbia
- Cruise Industry Association of British Columbia
- Cruise Newfoundland & Labrador
- Great Lakes Cruising Coalition
- Passenger Shipping Association (PSA)
- St Lawrence Cruise Association
- Verband Deutscher Reeder (VDR)

DEMAND AND SUPPLY

Demand

Although cruising comprises a relatively small sector of the world market for international travel, it has witnessed a tremendous growth since the 1990s. In fact, according to a report by the UNWTO (2010b), the cruise industry is the fastest growing segment within the leisure travel market, experiencing an average annual passenger growth rate of approximately 7.5% since the 1980s. More specifically, demand multiplied by 50% during the period from 1989 to 1996 and increased by a further 50% every two years between 2000 and 2004. Hence, for the period between 1989 and 2004, total demand increased by an astonishing 325% (UNWTO, 2010a). Moreover, a CLIA *Cruise Market Overview* (CLIA, 2013a) reported that 225 million passengers took a cruise between 1980 and 2012; of those, 67% were generated in the past ten years, while an astounding 39% were generated in the past five years alone. Furthermore, CLIA continues to see great potential for continued growth based on the current modest market penetration within the USA (24%), as well as continued strong interest in cruising, as over 50 million Americans expressed interest in cruising within the next three years (CLIA, 2012). Continued growth is also expected at the global level based on international demand figures presented by the European Cruise Council and projections from Cruise Market Watch (see Fig. 8.3).

As can also be seen in Fig. 8.3, North America is currently the largest source market within the cruise sector with the USA and Canada representing more than two-thirds of the world demand (UNWTO, 2010a). However, based on double-digit growth of the European market

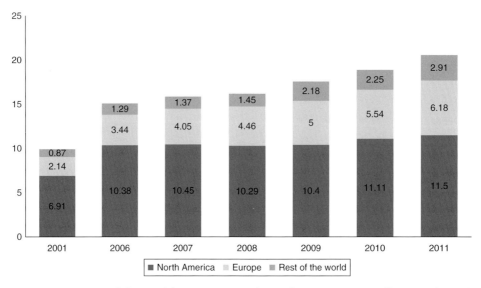

Fig. 8.3. International demand for cruises (numbers of passengers in millions). Adapted from G.P. Wild Ltd, 2012.

between 2007 and 2010, the Passenger Shipping Association (2011) predicted that with such continued future growth rates, Europe could be positioned to overtake North America by 2020. More specifically, in 2010 Europeans represented nearly 30% of all cruise passengers world-wide, compared to 21% ten years earlier (ECC, 2011b). See Table 8.2 for some major highlights of the economic impact of cruise operations in both Europe and North America during 2010.

According to the UNWTO's *Current Situation and Trends* report for Cruise Tourism (UNWTO, 2010a), the main source of outbound cruise tourism in the USA is the New York area, due to the fact that it is the largest centre of consumption in the entire country. The South Atlantic and the Pacific are the second largest source markets based on the effect of base ports on demand: the three largest cruise ports are located in Florida, while the San Francisco and Los Angeles urban areas are base ports for Pacific cruises.

Within Europe the main source market is the United Kingdom, followed by Germany, Italy, and Spain (see Table 8.3). According to the Institute of Shipping Economics and Logistics (2010) and CLIA, the British market doubled in the last nine years and reached an almost 30% share of the European market. Germany also continued its strong growth in second place with just over 1.5 million passengers and a European market share of 25%; while Italy and Spain now have 835,000 and 576,000 passengers respectively.

Interestingly, there are similar trends within all the major generating markets, indicating that the market is still in the initial expansion phase: the average age of cruise passengers is declining and there is a high index of first-time passengers. Although cruising was traditionally seen as a type of tourism for the 'newly weds or nearly dead' (Mancini, 2004, p. 6), the cruise product has become extremely diversified over the last ten years so that current cruises can attract almost

Table 8.2. Economic impacts in Europe and North America in 2011. (Adapted from ECC, 2011b; Business Research and Economic Advisors for CLIA, 2012.)

	Europe	North America
Number of passengers embarking from continental ports	5.2 million	9.8 million
Numbers of residents on cruise vacation	over 5.6 million	approx. 10 million
Main ports of embarkation	Mediterranean, the Baltic and other European regions	Florida (60% of all US cruise embarkations)
Direct spending by cruise lines and their passengers and crew	€15 billion	$18.9 billion
Spending in employee compensation	€9.8 billion	$15.4 billion

Table 8.3. Main source markets in Europe. (From CLIA, 2013b.)

Country	2010 No. of pax (1000s)	2010 Market share (%)	2011 No. of pax (1000s)	2011 Market share (%)	2012 No. of pax (1000s)	2012 Market share (%)	Change from 2010 to 2012 (%)
UK	1622	29	1700	28.0	1701	27.7	+5
Germany	1219	22	1388	22.9	1544	25.2	+27
Italy	889	16	923	15.2	835	13.6	−6
Spain	645	12	703	11.6	576	9.4	−11
France	387	7	441	7.3	481	7.8	+24
Others	805	15	913	15.0	1002	16.3	+24
Total	5567	100	6068	100	6139	100	+10

every demographic group. However, while the clientele is changing, a destination analysis reveals the Caribbean, the Mediterranean, Alaska and the Bahamas remain the most popular cruise destinations (CLIA, 2012). The Mexican Caribbean in particular has been a leading cruise destination with destinations such as Cozumel, Los Cabos, Mazatlán, Port Vallarta, Zihuatanejo and Acapulco being extremely popular (UNWTO, 2010a).

On the demand side, cruise passengers have been profiled and segmented based on demographics, sociographics and psychographics. For example, CLIA identified six main cruise typologies based on socio-demographic profiles of cruise passengers that were profiled in the UNWTO's *Current Situation and Trends* report for Cruise Tourism (UNWTO, 2010a).

- 'Restless baby boomers'. This group includes individuals looking for new travel experiences. They represent 33% of all cruise passengers and 59% of first-timers.
- 'Enthusiastic baby boomers'. Individuals in this segment are already convinced. They are attracted by cruise travel and the variety of activities that go with it. For this group, cruises represent an escape from the routine. They usually travel as families. They count for 20% of all cruise travel and 46% of first-time cruise passengers.
- 'Lovers of luxury'. This group is prepared to spend money on high quality products, which is what most of the specialized cruise lines offer. They account for 14% of all cruise travel and 30% of first-timers.
- 'Demanding consumers'. Individuals in this group are in search of the best price–quality ratio. This segment is the most faithful to holiday cruises. They are very sensitive to promotions and special discounts. They account for 16% of all cruise travel and 20% of first-time passengers.

- 'Explorers'. This group consists of well-informed individuals widely experienced in travel. They are particularly interested in destinations and the areas visited by the cruise. They account for 11% of all cruise travel and 20% of first-time passengers.
- 'Ship aficionados'. This is the segment most advanced in years. Individuals in this group have already been on several cruises and enjoy the cruise ship life, which they consider agreeable and very comfortable. They account for 6% of all cruise travel and 13% of first-timers.

According to a CLIA cruise market profile study[1] (TNS, 2011) the average cruise passenger is 48 years of age with a median household income of $97,000. The majority are college graduates (76%) and married (79%), but only 20% are retired. The cruise vacation typically lasts about a week (7.4 days) and 45% rate their cruising experience as extremely satisfying. While cruisers usually travel with spouses (80%), they continue to be less likely to travel with children than non-cruisers (31% bring their children versus 38% of non-cruiser vacationers). However, segments within cruising reveal that cruisers on 'destination' (40%) and 'contemporary' (36%) lines (which includes Disney) take their children much more often than 'luxury' (24%) or 'premium' (19%) cruisers. As expected, based on higher than average income, cruisers spend almost 25% more on vacation than non-cruisers ($1700 versus $1300), and cruisers on luxury lines and speciality or niche cruises spend the most ($2500 and $2900 respectively). In terms of information sources that influence vacation decision making, cruise passengers find cruise websites to be increasingly influential (38% versus 28% in 2008) while levels of other sources of information remain fairly constant compared to findings from 2008: destination websites (40%), word of mouth referrals (32%), and spouse/travel companion (34%). Interestingly, although 68% of passengers use travel agents to book their cruises, and are extremely/very satisfied with their agents (59%), 48% believe that websites and online travel retailers provide the best prices on cruises.

Supply

There are several possible parties involved in the provision of cruises, including ship owners, shipping companies or ship operators and cruise operators or charters (Gross, 2011). Sometimes these may be one and the same, when the shipping company owns the ship and offers cruises; however, there are also companies which charter all, or part, of a ship from shipping companies or owners in order to offer their own cruises (see Fig. 8.4). For example, some travel companies such as Abercrombie & Kent charter vessels for speciality expedition cruises, such as the Italian-owned MV *Le Boreal* for trips to the Antarctic. Other companies are known for full ship charters geared towards speciality markets, such as Atlantis Events, geared towards gay and lesbian cruises. Furthermore, vessel charters offer an attractive option for the MICE segment (meetings, incentives, conventions and exhibitions), which is becoming an interesting niche market for the cruise industry (Duval, 2007).

The cruise market has been defined by major consolidation in recent years, and currently, worldwide demand is satisfied by a very small number of companies (Dowling, 2006; Duval, 2007; Gross, 2011). More specifically, the 'big three' companies are Carnival Corporation & plc,

Royal Caribbean Cruises and Star Cruises, which together represent almost 80% of the total market share in terms of bed places per day (ISL, 2012). It is predicted that the small but growing Mediterranean Shipping Cruises (MSC) will position itself as a fourth major player in the market as it has experienced rapid growth in the last few years (ISL, 2012). The market share of each company is illustrated in Fig. 8.5.

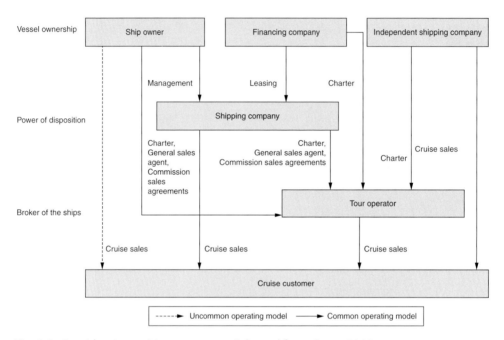

Fig. 8.4. Providers in maritime transport. Adapted from Gross, 2011.

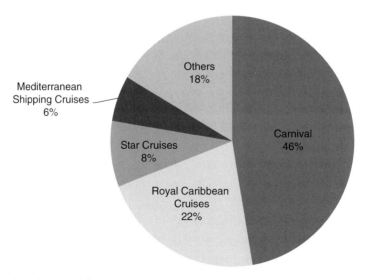

Fig. 8.5. Market shares of the major cruise shipping companies in 2010 (percentage share of berths). From ISL, 2012; ships of 1000 gt and over.

According to Weaver and Duval (2008), this consolidation is the result of large-scale acquisitions based on the desire for product and geographic diversification by the large corporations. For example, Carnival Corporation consists of a diverse collection of brands serving different markets, including Carnival Cruise Lines, Holland America Line, Princess Cruises, The Yachts of Seabourn, AIDA Cruises, Costa Cruises, Cunard Line, Ibero Cruises, Ocean Village, P&O Cruises and P&O Cruises Australia. Despite corporate consolidation, distinct brand identities have been kept. For an overview of the main corporations and their brands see Table 8.4.

Table 8.4. Main corporations and their brands. (Adapted from Carnival Corporation, 2011; MSC, 2011; Royal Caribbean Cruises, 2011; Star Cruises, 2011.)

Corporation	Brands
Carnival Corporation	Carnival Cruise Lines Holland America Line Princess Cruises Seabourn (North America) P&O Cruises (UK) Cunard (UK) AIDA Cruises (Germany) Costa Cruises (Southern Europe) Iberocruceros (Spain) P&O Cruises (Australia)
Mediterranean Shipping Cruises	MSC Divina, MSC Preziosa MSC Magnifica, MSC Splendida MSC Fantasia, MSC Poesia MSC Orchestra, MSC Musica MSC Opera, MSC Lirica MSC Sinfonia, MSC Armonia
Royal Caribbean Cruises	Royal Caribbean International Celebrity Cruises Pullmantur Cruises Azamara Club Cruises
Star Cruises	Star Cruises Norwegian Cruise Line NCL America Orient Lines Cruise Ferries

Cruise ships are generally classified by size (gross tonnage) and passenger capacity (Schüssler, 2005; Ward, 2011). As can be seen in Figs 8.7 and 8.8, the average cruise ship size has dramatically increased over the last ten years in terms of both gross tonnage and passenger capacity.

The size of the ship and cruise-ship capacity ratios impact the type of cruise experience, with mega-ships typically featuring multiple pools, jacuzzis, fitness areas, spas, several dining options and lots of entertainment facilities including casinos, theatres, a variety of nightclubs, etc., while small ships typically do not offer such an abundance of activities and instead focus on a different type of experience (Gibson, 2006). While ships with a capacity of up to 1000 passengers dominated the market until the mid-1990s with a market share of approximately 60%, their present market share has fallen to approximately 20% (Schulz, 2009). Instead, the

Fig. 8.6. *Costa Mediterranea*, Alicante, Spain. © Luisa Wolter.

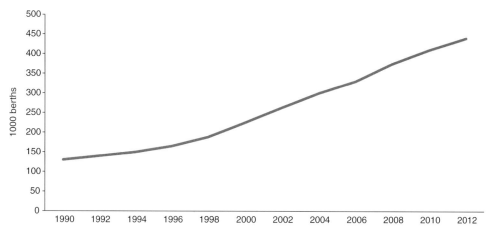

Fig. 8.7. Passenger capacity of world active cruise fleet 1990–2012. From ISL, 2012; ships of 1000 gt and over.

industry is making use of economies of scale and focusing on larger ships. Mega-ships have more than 2000 berths and currently there are 87 ships in this class accounting for 56% of the cabin capacity within the global cruise fleet (ISL, 2010). The largest ships are currently the Oasis-class cruise ships in the Royal Caribbean fleet, including the *Oasis of the Seas* and *Allure of the Seas* which both have a gross tonnage of 225,282 and a capacity of 5400 passengers at double occupancy or 6296 maximum (Royal Caribbean, 2011). Typical vessel sizes and passenger capacities are illustrated in Fig. 8.9.

The space-ratio of a vessel is used as an indicator of comfort as it describes the average amount of space available for each passenger. A space-ratio of under 10 is indicative of an extremely

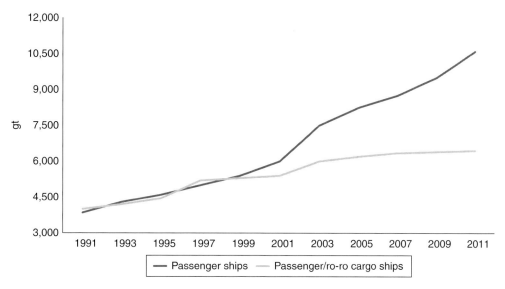

Fig. 8.8. World passenger and cargo passenger fleet: average size development 1991–2012. From ISL, 2012.

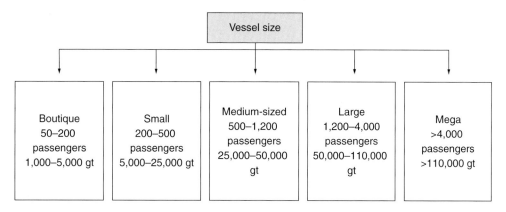

Fig. 8.9. Vessel size and passenger capacities. Based on Gross, 2011 as based on Schüssler, 2005.

cramped environment, while a space-ratio of over 50 is viewed as the absolute ultimate in comfort (Ward, 2011). Similarly, the pax/crew ratio (PCR) is an indicator of service quality as it represents the relationship between number of employees and passengers; the highest possible value is 1:1 which would be represented by a PCR of 1.0.

Cruises have also been classified in a similar manner to the hospitality sector, with classic cruise classification consisting of four broad categories: luxury, premium, contemporary and budget (UNWTO, 2010a). One such widely accepted classification is provided by the independent annual publication *Berlitz Complete Guide to Cruising & Cruise Ships* by Douglas Ward, which classifies cruises in ten categories ranging from five stars plus to one star. Although 20 specific areas are evaluated, the five main areas assessed are the ship, the overall cruise experience, service, cuisine-gastronomy, accommodation and the entertainment programme.

Focus box

Most cruise ships and ferries are built in European shipyards with 71% of all ordered passenger tonnage being placed in Italian, German and French yards in 2010. In fact, the leading shipbuilding country is Italy (in particular, the yards of Fincantieri and Visentini) as a total of 34 passenger ships were ordered in 2010, which corresponded to a market share of 42%.

From ISL, 2010.

CASE STUDY

The parallels between the two disasters of the Titanic and the Costa Concordia are frightening. Almost exactly 100 years after the sinking of the Titanic on 15 April 1912 the catastrophe of the Italian cruise ship took place in the Mediterranean Sea. The disaster of the Titanic is one of the biggest human tragedies in history and one might assume that shipping nowadays is a far safer form of passenger transport than it was back then. Despite all safety improvement endeavours by the maritime industry, significant challenges remain as the recent Costa Concordia disaster demonstrated.

It was at about 9:45pm on 13 January 2012 when the Costa Concordia struck a rock in the Tyrrhenian Sea just off the eastern shore of the Italian island Giglio (one of the seven islands of the Tuscan Archipelago) about 100 km northwest of Rome. The collision caused a 50 m gash on the port (left) side of the Concordia's hull. Parts of the engine room were almost immediately flooded causing a loss of power to the vessel's propulsion and electrical systems. With water flooding in, the ship drifted back to Giglio Island where it grounded just 500 m north of the village of Giglio Porto. Even though the boat gradually began to sink, an order to abandon ship was not issued until over 1 h after the initial impact. Although a regulation by the International Maritime Organization requires total evacuation of all passengers within 30 min of the abandon ship announcement, it took over 6 h for all surviving passengers to be evacuated. Of the 3229 passengers and 1023 crew members known to have been aboard, 32 people lost their lives.

At the time this book was written, the wreck had finally been salvaged (refloated) and the transportation to Genoa for dismantling was forecasted for mid-July (as of June 2014). Moreover, it will cost Costa Crociere, the shipping company, about €400 million and is expected to be the most expensive salvage ever. Interestingly, the Costa Concordia herself was built for €450 million in 2004 and the shipping company offered every passenger compensation of €11,000 for loss of material items and additionally €3000 for travel expenses.

Causes for the Concordia disaster include the failure to comply with the latest safety measures, deviation from the planned route, inadequate safety measures and drills, and the crew members' misunderstandings of commands (perhaps due to language difficulties). Therefore, the most prominent change in maritime law prompted by the Costa Concordia disaster was that all cruise liners must now hold safety drills for passengers before the ship even leaves the dock. Furthermore, Costa Crociere is about to implement a real-time route monitoring system to track every single Costa ship. Language training, especially among multi-national crews, is gaining in importance to provide better service to the passengers, especially in case of emergencies. Moreover, officers are about to have a stronger voice in choosing the route and influencing the captain's decisions. Costa Crociere released its new safety programme in May 2012, which was the first big step to regain customer confidence (Costa Cruise, 2012).

NOTE

1. The study focused on a core target market of US residents over the age of 25, with a minimum household income of $40,000; characteristics that TNS state are met by nearly all cruisers.

FURTHER READING

Central Commission for the Navigation of the Rhine (2012) *Inland Navigation in Europe – Market Observation 2012–2*. Strasbourg, France.
Dervaes, C. (2003) *Selling Cruises*, 2nd edn. Thomson Delmar Learning, Clifton Park, New York.
Douglas, N. and Douglas, N. (2004) *The Cruise Experience*. Pearson Hospitality Press, Frenchs Forest, Australia.
Dowling, R.K. (2006) *Cruise Ship Tourism*. CABI Publishing, Wallingford, UK.
DRV – Deutscher ReiseVerband (annual edition) *Der Kreuzfahrtmarkt Deutschland*. DRV, Berlin, Germany.
Dunlop, G. (2002) The European ferry industry: challenges and changes. *International Journal of Transport Management* 2, 115–116.
Gibson, P. (2012) *Cruise Operations Management,* 2nd edn. Butterworth-Heinemann, Oxford, UK.
Gross, S. (2011) *Tourismus und Verkehr – Grundlagen, Marktanalyse und Strategien von Verkehrsunternehmen*. Oldenbourg, Munich, Germany.
Jennings, G. (2007) *Water-based Tourism, Sport, Leisure & Recreation Experiences*. Butterworth-Heinemann, Oxford, UK.
Klein, R.A. (2005) *Cruise Ship Squeeze*. New Society Publishers, Gabriola Island, Canada.

Klein, R.A. (2008) *Paradise Lost at Sea: Rethinking Cruise Vacations*. Fernwood Books, Halifax, Canada.

Linne, M. (2008) *Touristische Ausprägungen des Segelsports*. ITD-Verlag, Hamburg, Germany.

Lück, M. (2008) *The Encyclopedia of Tourism and Recreation in Marine Environments*. CABI Publishing, Wallingford, UK.

Papathanassis, A., Lukovic, T. and Vogel, M. (2012) *Cruise Tourism and Society: A Socio-Economic Perspective*. Springer-Verlag, Heidelberg, Germany.

Prideaux, B. and Cooper, M. (2009) *River Tourism*. CABI Publishing, Wallingford, UK.

Schulz, A. and Auer, J. (2010) *Kreuzfahrten und Schiffsverkehr im Tourismus*. Oldenbourg, Munich, Germany.

Schüssler, O. (2005) *Passagier-Schifffahrt – Ein Handbuch für Reiseverkehrskaufleute in Ausbildung und Praxis*, 2nd edn. DRV Service GmbH, Frankfurt am Main, Germany.

UNWTO (2010a) *Cruise Tourism – Current Situation and Trends*. Madrid, Spain.

Vogel, M., Papathanassis, A. and Wolber, B. (2011) *The Business and Management of Ocean Cruises*. CABI Publishing, Wallingford, UK.

Ward, D. (annual version) *Complete Guide to Cruising & Cruise Ships*. Berlitz, London, UK.

Trade journals/magazines and organizations

An Bord, International Journal of Tourism Research, Journal of Travel Research, Tourism in Marine Environments, Cruise Research Society (www.cruiseresearchsociety.com), International Centre for Cruise Research (www.cruiseresearch.org), International Coastal and Marine Tourism Society (www.coastalmarinetourism.org).

Internet sources

www.charterboat.it, www.cruise-campus.com, www.cruisejunkie.com, www.cruising.org, www.cruisetricks.de, www.cruisemarketwatch.com, www.faehrverband.org, www.freightercruises.com, www.freightertravel.co.nz, www.freightertravel.info, www.hausboot-boerse.de, www.kreuzfahrt-forschung.de, www.lloydslist.com, www.marinelink.com, www.med.govt.nz/sectors-industries/tourism/tourism-research-data, www.mycruisecommunity.co.uk.

chapter 9

Passenger Lines and Ferries

LEARNING OBJECTIVES

- Identify the main characteristics of ferry and passenger lines and be able to differentiate them from the cruise industry.
- Illustrate the international associations, legal framework and history.
- Assess the demand and supply sides of the industry, in order to understand the overall market.

DEFINITIONS

The main purpose of passenger lines and ferries is the transportation of people and goods from one point to another with both tourist and non-tourist use. They constitute a scheduled service, according to a published timetable, or so regular or frequent as to constitute a recognizably systematic series (as defined by the *Glossary of Transport Statistics*, 2009). In the *Glossary of Shipping Terms*, the US Department of Transportation defines a liner as: 'a vessel advertising sailings on a specified trade route on a regular basis. It is not necessary that every named port be called on every voyage' (US Department of Transportation, 2008, p. 64). Ferry systems can provide transport to remote or difficult to reach areas, offer transportation between islands or offer alternative means of transportation mobility within a destination (Duval, 2007). According to the *Glossary of Transport Statistics* compiled by the International Transport Forum (ITF), Eurostat (the European Union's statistical office) and United Nations Economic Commission for Europe (UNECE), a ferry can be defined as 'a ship designed with one or more decks specifically for the carriage of passengers, and where there is either no cabin accommodation for the passengers (un-berthed) or not all of the passengers are accommodated in cabins where cabins are provided' (*Glossary of Transport Statistics*, 2009, p. 113). Alternatively, the American Public Transportation Association defines a ferry boat as:

a transit mode comprising vessels carrying passengers and in some cases vehicles over a body of water, and that are generally steam or diesel-powered. When at least one terminal is within an urbanized area, it is urban ferryboat service. Such service excludes international, rural, rural interstate, island, and urban park ferries (APTA, 2011).

However, as recently lamented by Mathew Chambers, a senior transportation specialist in the US Bureau of Transportation Statistics (BTS), there is no definitional consensus regarding passenger lines and ferries. An excerpt from the BTS Special Report *Making Sense of Passenger Vessel Data* by the US Department of Transportation (2011b) highlights the different legal definitions utilized within US federal agencies (see Table 9.1).

In general, ferries can be distinguished according to the following three types (Schüssler, 2005; Gross, 2011): conventional, fast and cable ferries.

Passenger ferries and ro-pax (roll on/roll off passenger) ferries rank among the conventional type. Generally, passenger ferries' main purpose is the transportation of passengers and their cars. However, freight and trucks are handled as well. Several car decks accommodate between 500 and 3000 passengers and have a capacity for up to 900 passenger cars. Numerous installations on board and different types of accommodation, depending on the route lengths, are offered (such as reclining seats or even suites). Additionally, a variety of restaurants and bars as well as shopping promenades, casinos, conference facilities, gyms and spas can be found on board. On the contrary, ro-pax ferries are vessels built for freight vehicle transport along with passenger accommodation. The upper limit is mostly about 600 passengers; sometimes the capacity may account for only 50 (Schüssler, 2005; Cruise and Ferry Center AG, 2009).

Fast ferries, also high-speed craft, are commercial vessels capable of a service speed in excess of 30 knots (approximately 56 km/h) and with the ability to carry a minimum of 35 passengers and/or commercial cargo. Thereby, high-speed craft are clearly faster than conventional ferries, which have a service speed between 18 and 26 knots (22–48 km/h). Due to their higher velocity, running time is much shorter and therefore fewer installations on board are available. Notwithstanding, small restaurants or kiosks and self-service areas do exist. Accommodation is not available as the running time does not exceed 4 h. Seats, similar to the ones on an aircraft, are available (Schüssler, 2005; Verband der Fährschifffahrt und Fährtouristik eV, 2012).

There are three main categories in the high-speed craft sector:

- catamaran, a twin-hulled boat with usually a deck connecting the hulls and a service speed of 35 knots (65 km/h). It usually has a capacity for 400 to 700 passengers and up to 150 cars (Schüssler, 2005);
- monohull, a boat on which the line of intersection of the water surface and the boat at any operating draft forms a single closed curve with a service speed of 35 knots and a capacity of 650 passengers and 150 cars (Code of Federal Regulations, 2007; Cruise and Ferry Center AG, 2009);
- hydrofoil, a boat with two foil supports on which the boat rises to reduce water drag and travel at a speed of 37 knots to transport 200 passengers (Schüssler, 2005; Vuchic, 2007).

Table 9.1. Definitions of passenger lines and ferries. (Adapted from US Department of Transportation, 2011b.)

Source	Legal Definition or Meaning
Ferry	
46 United States Codes § 2101, available at http://fr-webgate.access.gpo.gov/ cgibin/getdoc.cgi?dbname=browse_ usc&docid=Cite:+46USC2101 as of March 2011.	… a vessel that is used on a regular schedule – a) to provide transportation only between places that are not more than 300 miles apart; b) to transport only • passengers; or • vehicles, or • railroad cars, that are being used, or have been used, in transporting passengers or goods.
US Department of Homeland Security, United States Coast Guard, 46 Code of Federal Regulations 175,400, available at http://edocket.access.gpo.gov/ cfr_2009/octqtr/pdf/46cfr175.400.pdf as of March 2011.	… a vessel that 1) operates in other than ocean or coastwise service; 2) has provisions only for deck passengers or vehicles; or both; 3) operates on a short run on a frequent schedule between two points over the most direct water route; and 4) offers a public service of a type normally attributed to a bridge or tunnel.
US Department of Transportation, Bureau of Transportation Statistic, National Census of Ferry Operators, available at http://www.bts.gov as of March 2011.	… a vessel that sails an itinerant, fixed route as a common carrier of passengers or vehicles. Railroad car float operations are also included.
Ferry boat and terminal	
US Department of Transportation, Federal Highway Administration, Ferry Boat Discretionary Program, available at http://www.fhwa.dot.gov/discretionary/ fbdinfo.cfm as of March 2011.	… whether toll or free, subject to the following conditions: 1) it is not feasible to build a bridge, tunnel, combination thereof, or other normal highway structure in lieu of the use of such ferry. 2) the operation of the ferry shall be on a route classified as a public road within the State and which has not been designated as a route on the Interstate System.

Cable ferries, in contrast, make use of the power of the river and cables connected to both shores to tack across the current. However, there are also powered cable ferries that have an engine or electric motors (Gross, 2011).

HISTORICAL DEVELOPMENT OF THE MARKET

Interestingly, it was the expansion of the railway system that catapulted the development of ferry transportation; upon reaching coastal areas both passengers and goods hitherto transported by rail had to switch to marine transportation (Schüssler, 2005; Schulz, 2009). Hence in the early days it was often railway companies that operated ferry lines; for example, the *Leviathan* transported railway wagons across the Scottish Firth of Forth in 1850, while the first international railway-ferry-line connected Helsingborg, Sweden and Helsingör, Denmark in 1892 (Schulz, 2009). Private ferry lines began to establish themselves in the 1920s and 1930s although it wasn't until the 1950s that the market truly developed due to the increasing use of automobiles and the subsequent development of roll-on roll-off ferries (ro-ro vessels). Initially, automobiles were loaded on railway wagons and then loaded onto ships for transport, or a crane was utilized to load the cars on and off the vessels; the first vessels to enable drivers to drive on to ships themselves were built in the 1930s (Schüssler, 2005; Schulz, 2009). The increasing international freight transportation using trailer trucks, as well as the rise in automobile use as the choice mode of transportation for vacationers, led to the development of larger ships capable of dealing with these changes: the ro-ro ferries. Ro-ro vessels were especially designed to carry wheeled cargo including automobiles, buses, trucks, trailer trucks or even railroad cars using built in ramps for rolling the cargo on and rolling the cargo off. According to the IMO (2011), the flexibility, speed of operation and ability to integrate with other modes of transportation system make the roll-on roll-off ship one of the most successful types of ship operating today.

At the same time, many ferries started to evolve into cruise ferries (for further information on cruise ships, see Chapter 8).

In the 1990s, more focus was put on developing passenger facilities on primarily cargo services, which has led to the use of the ro-pax term (Talley, 2012). One could say that ro-pax vessels were designed as an upgrade of ro-ro vessels to carry wheeled cargo and passengers at the same time.

Hence, the historical development of the ferry industry has undergone a change from the pure passenger ferry (Figs 9.1 and 9.2) on the one side and the pure cargo liner on the other to a complex set of very different technologies. In very different ways, the many passenger and cargo transportation possibilities and aspects were combined. The result is an industry with a very complex structure.

INSTITUTIONAL FRAMEWORK

The institutional framework of passenger lines and ferries is almost the same as for cruise ships. For detailed information, see p. 160.

Fig. 9.1. Passenger ferry in Seattle. © Michael Lück.

Fig. 9.2. Passenger ferry in Venice. © Konstantinos Dafalias / pixelio.de. Available at: http://www.pixelio.de/media/206727 (accessed 16 February 2013).

European institutional framework

In addition to the information stated in Chapter 8, the legal framework regarding passenger lines and ferry operations has to be mentioned. To increase passengers' rights when travelling by maritime and inland waterway transport EU-wide, the European Parliament and Council have formally signed Regulation EU No. 1177/2010. This consumer protection came into force in December 2012.

The regulation should include all cross-channel ferries, but not excursions, sightseeing tours or boats which can only carry up to 12 passengers or have fewer than three operational crew members. All ferries travelling less than 500 m will also be excluded from the ambit of this regulation.

The purpose of the regulation is to:

- prevent refusal of boarding and to offer free assistance to disabled persons when notification has been made at least 48 h before boarding;
- give rights to passengers in case of cancellation or delay. Passengers suffering significant delays will be entitled to compensation of 25% of the ticket price, rising to 50% for long delays. If delays mean a passenger has to spend the night in a hotel, the ferry operator will have to pay for hotel and meals (up to €80 per night, for a maximum of three nights). In case of cancellation, the new law gives the passenger the right to be re-routed at the earliest opportunity and at no extra cost, or given a full refund;
- ensure certain minimum rules on information for all passengers before and during their journey, as well as general information about their rights in terminals, in ports and on the carrier ships (European Union, 2010).

Hence, the new regulation gives passengers the same opportunities to travel by water as they have in the rail and aviation sectors across the EU.

North American institutional framework

In Canada and the USA, ferries share the same regulation framework as cruises. Therefore, Canadian ferries' regulations are based on the Canada Shipping Act of 2001 and in the USA the Coast Guard is the regulatory body (Transport Canada, 2006; US Government Accountability Office, 2010). For further information on the institutional framework, see Chapter 8.

ASSOCIATIONS

The world's principal association for ferry companies is Interferry. In Europe, there are several smaller associations, such as the Verband der Fährschifffahrt und Fährtouristik (VFF) in Germany or the Passenger Shipping Association (PSA) in the UK. However, in North America there are two main associations, the Passenger Vessel Association (PVA) and the Canadian Ferry Operators Association (CFOA), that participate in the regulatory and policy development process.

Interferry

Interferry is the only shipping association that represents all the world's ferry companies. Founded in 1976 as the International Marine Transit Association, it has nowadays 225 members (such as ferry owners and operators, shipbuilders and marine engineers) from 38 countries. Interferry facilitates networking among its members and represents the industry on regulatory matters. While mainly advocating safety regulations for passengers, crew, cargo and ships as well as free and fair competition, Interferry's concern also is the protection of the natural environment. 'To fulfill this role [of regulation] Interferry has attained Consultative Status at the International Maritime Organization and Observer Status at the European Community Shipowners Association' (Interferry, 2012).

Passenger Vessel Association (PVA)

The PVA is a non-profit trade organization founded in 1971 and represents owners and operators of US-flagged passenger vessels of all type as well as manufacturers of maritime-related products and services and other service companies. The PVA 'is principally concerned with regulation that originates at the federal level and that has wide applicability to the industry' (Passenger Vessel Association, 2007).

Canadian Ferry Operators Association (CFOA)

The CFOA, a Canadian group of ferry owners, operators and associated marine companies, was founded and federally incorporated in 1987. It represents 62 members with a total of about 250 individuals.

> The CFOA provides unified collaborative constructive dialogue between industry and Government on issues concerning ferry operations and regulation in Canada, and offers ferry operators and industry a forum for frank, open exchange of information with the aim of providing safe, reliable, cost effective and environmentally responsible passenger vessel management.
>
> (Canadian Ferry Operators Association, 2012a)

Regional: Europe

In Europe, there is no single association representing ferry companies in all EU countries. However, several countries have their own association representing the industry.

A selection of other industry associations

- Asociación Española de Marina Civil (AEMC; Spain)
- Association of Ferry Transport Operators (AFTO; the Netherlands)
- Danish Ship Owners' Association (Denmark)
- Passenger Shipping Association (PSA; UK)
- Swedish Ship Officers' Association (SSOA; Sweden)
- Verband für Fährschifffahrt und Fährtouristik eV (VFF; Germany)

DEMAND AND SUPPLY

Demand

Based on regional level maritime transport statistics published in 2013 by the European Commission's Eurostat (Eurostat, 2013c), by far the largest number of passengers transported by sea (26.9 million) was recorded by the Attiki region in 2011, where the port of Piraeus is the main gateway for passengers to the Greek islands. The second and third highest numbers of passengers transported were in Jadranska Hrvatska, Croatia, and Kent, UK with 13.3 million and 12.8 million passengers respectively. These statistics are rather impressive as they apply strictly to passenger lines and ferries; passengers from cruises are not included. Perhaps it is not surprising that these regions all have seafaring traditions. Figure 9.3 illustrates the numbers of passengers transported in the 13 European locations with the highest numbers of passengers in 2011.

The English Channel, separating southern England from northern France and joining the Atlantic Ocean and the North Sea, also offers a prime example of the use of ferries. In fact, a ferry service between Dover and Calais has been documented in history since Roman times (Page and Connell, 2006), and the routes between Dover, Medway and Ramsgate on the British side, and Calais and Dunkerque on the French side, still enjoy high passenger counts

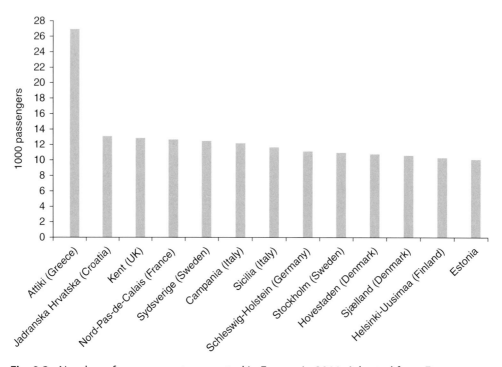

Fig. 9.3. Number of passengers transported in Europe in 2011. Adapted from Eurostat, 2013c.

with approximately 14 million passengers (Eurostat, 2010a). However, although ferry services are still popular, competition between ferry operators and alternative modes of transportation such as low-cost airlines has led many ferry companies to install entertainment facilities including cabins, restaurants, bars, cinemas or casinos as a strategy to attract customers. However, the focus remains utilitarian rather than experiential; in other words, ferries focus on the transportation aspect of the product while trying to offer a consumer-oriented service.

In the EU15 member countries, ferries serve between 5 and 30 million pkm (Peeters, 2004). Depending on the type of vessel used (see Fig. 9.4), the emissions of carbon dioxide (CO_2) average at 0.033 kg/seat kilometre.

However, the amount of ferry transport is obviously declining: for the EU15 countries (excluding Germany), a decline in the number of passengers of about 12% between 1997 and 2001 was registered (Xenellis, 2003). Nevertheless, growth is shown by Italy, Denmark, Finland and the Netherlands. Hence, the total environmental impact of ferries will probably also decline. Attention should be paid to the meaning of this loss of volume. It can be supposed that part of it is being transferred to other modes of transportation (such as LCCs) which have a higher emission of CO_2 and therefore a much higher impact on climate change (Peeters, 2004).

Comparatively, travellers in the USA travelled 628 million pkm in 2008, which accounted for an increase of 32.5% in the last ten years. Table 9.2 shows an overview of travelled pkm in the USA between the years 1999 and 2008. According to the National Census of Ferry Operators, there were more than 82 million passengers carried on vessels in the USA in 2008 (US Government Accountability Office, 2010). Unfortunately there is no data available for the numbers of passengers in Canada and Mexico. However in Canada, the total passenger ferry traffic was estimated at 38.9 million passengers in 2003 (Transport Canada, 2006).

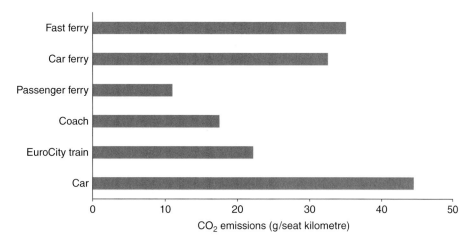

Fig. 9.4. Relative CO_2 emissions of maritime transport, car and rail. Reproduced with permission given by Mr P.M. Peeters from Peeters, 2004.

In contrast to cruise ships, whose main purpose of travel is the enjoyment of the overall offer, facilities and amenities, travellers make use of ferries as gateways. Ferries are used by all age groups and repeat visitors but most of all by families (Tourism Ireland, 2011). The principal reason for using ferries as a mode of transportation is the focus on the destination itself and the discovery of its environs (Wergeland, 2012). However, there is a complexity of demand motives, as shown in Fig. 9.5, based on Maslow's hierarchy of needs in psychology. First, the basic demands (such as security, accessibility and comfort) must be met. The experience itself then is created by the level of service, image and activities offered on board.

Table 9.3 illustrates the world passenger ferry traffic for 2008 and indicates two huge main markets in Europe – Northern Europe and the Baltic, and all of the Mediterranean. In North America the main ferry market is on the Pacific border between the USA and Canada; however, South America has only limited ferry operations. Asia has the world's vastest ferry market (Talley, 2012).

Supply

There are many options for measuring the size of a ferry operator. Criteria such as revenue, lane-metre capacity or passenger capacity of the vessel can be compared. But as this book

Table 9.2. US ferry passenger kilometres. (Adapted from US Department of Transportation, 2013.)

Year	1999	2000	2001	2002	2003	2004	2005	2006	2007	2008	2009	2010
Pkm (millions)	474	480	475	485	570	575	578	579	613	628	587	626

Fig. 9.5. Hierarchy of ferry demands. From Wergeland, 2012.

Table 9.3. Distribution of world ferry traffic in 2008. (Adapted from ShipPax, 2009.)

	Passengers
World traffic volume 2008 (millions)	2052
Regional market shares (%)	
Baltic	10.8
North Sea	4.3
Mediterranean	21.1
Inland lakes/rivers	0.5
America	14.5
Red Sea and Persian Gulf	3.7
Southeast Asia	43.5
Pacific	1.5

focuses on tourism and transport, passenger capacity of vessels is more relevant. Table 9.4 shows the 20 largest ferry operators in Europe in 2008. If revenue had been the reference criteria for the ranking, P&O Ferries would have been number 1.

In the USA, Washington State Ferries is the largest operator with 26 vessels and a passenger capacity of 36,110. The famous NY Waterways is the second largest operator in the USA, offering 16 fast ferries and a passenger capacity of 2631 (Wergeland, 2012). BC Ferries, with a fleet of 35 conventional ferries, has a passenger capacity of 28,148 and is the largest operator in Canada (BC Ferries, 2012). In 2011/2012, there were 133 vessels operating throughout Canada and more than 43 million passengers were transported (Canadian Ferry Operators Association, 2012b). Table 9.5 shows an overview of the operating ferry companies in Canada, including their number of vessels and volume of passenger transportation.

Compared to other industries, the ferry industry is dominated by local, domestic/regional operators (Wergeland, 2012). Stena Line (ranked number 4 in the list below) is the only company that resembles an international profile by offering routes such as the UK and Ireland, or the Netherlands, Germany and Norway, or Sweden and Latvia (Stena Line, 2012). All other operators offer only routes within the same country or region. Thus, it is not quite meaningful to talk about just one passenger ferry market. Also, the diversity of vessels being used for passenger transportation indicates the ferry market as a heterogeneous market. Virtually, each route offered is a market in itself.

Table 9.4. Ranking of European ferry operators by passenger capacity in 2008. (Adapted from ShipPax, 2008.)

Rank	Company	Ferries	High-speed	Ro-pax	Total	Total passenger capacity
1	Tirrenia	16	4	6	26	42,859
2	Istanbul Deniz Otobüsleri (IDO)	10	34		44	29,514
3	Talkink/Silja Line	14		2	16	26,891
4	Stena Line	15	4	13	32	26,511
5	Jadrolinija	23	8		31	20,804
6	Hellenic Seaways	9	20	3	32	20,117
7	P&O Ferries	12	1	15	28	19,746
8	Superfast Ferries/ Blue Star	12			12	19,219
9	Corsica Ferries	10	2		12	19,173
10	MOBY Lines	12			12	17,823
11	Viking Line	8			8	17,583
12	ANEK Lines	10			10	17,445
13	Scandlines	17		6	23	16,748
14	Acciona Trasmediterranea	11	7	10	28	16,736
15	GA Ferries	8	1	1	10	14,985
16	SNCM Ferryterranée	7	1	2	10	14,635
17	Color Line	7			7	14,423
18	Siremar	9	17		26	13,256
19	Brittany Ferries	7	1	1	9	12,028
20	Grandi Navi Veloci (GNV)	8			8	11,516

Table 9.5. Operating companies in Canada in 2011/2012. (Adapted from CFOA, 2012b.)

Operating companies	Number of ships	Passengers
British Columbia Ferry Services Inc.	35	20,200,000
Coastal Transport Ltd	3	212,151
Coast Mountain Bus Co.	3	6,820,000
Govt of British Columbia	16	2,225,000
Govt of Manitoba	8	210,000
Govt of New Brunswick	11	4,748,454
Govt of Newfoundland and Labrador	17	937,000
Govt of North West Territories	5	143,431
Govt of Ontario (Kingston)	7	1,500,887
Groupe CTMA	3	118,516
Marine Atlantic	4	365,786
NFL/Bay	3	481,260
Own Sound – Manitoulin Island Service	1	180,768
Pelee Island Service	2	99,831
Société des traversiers du Québec	13	5,400,000
Totals	133	43,643,084

OTHER FORMS OF WATER BASED TRANSPORTATION

As there are several alternative forms of marine based transportation available, we will briefly highlight some of them in this section although the scope of this book does not allow for a detailed analysis.

Yacht chartering

Yacht chartering ranges from the 'share a yacht' concept (in which the yacht is shared with other guests and an experienced crew), bareboat charters (yacht only for a do-it-yourself skipper), bareboat with skipper and/or crew (depending on size of yacht), to flotilla charters (a bareboat charter travelling as part of a larger flotilla including a lead boat with experienced crew; Zucker and Goericke, 2004).

Houseboat charters

Houseboat charters are somewhat similar to a holiday home for two to 12 passengers and intended for travelling along rivers at a maximum speed of 12 km/h. According to Schulz (2009) houseboats may be classified into the following categories.

- Traditional houseboats: All cabins are at the same level and an additional steering wheel may be installed on the rear deck.
- Sedan boats: The living area and the open rear deck are at the same level.
- Boats with central bridges: The bridge is integrated in the elevated living area and therefore the area is separated into two living areas.
- Boats with sliding roofs: Somewhat similar to boats with central bridges whereupon the roof above the living area/bridge can be opened.
- Boats with elevated rear helmstand: The living area is in the front of the boat, helmstand and an open deck are in the back.
- Flying bridge boats: Two helmstands can be found in the living area as well as on the deck in the middle of the boat.

Kayak and canoe

While kayaks and canoes are classified as recreational vessels and are not utilized for the transportation of passengers, they do constitute a significant tourism recreational activity and are hence very briefly addressed. A kayak is a small light boat that was used by the Eskimos for seal hunting. It is a small and highly manoeuvrable boat and generally accommodates only one person. The oar has a paddle on each side and is used in an alternating manner to stroke through the water. A canoe is similar to a kayak, the difference being that it is open, can accommodate several people if so desired and the oar has only one paddle and the stroke is executed on one side of the vessel (Bhatia, 2006).

Supply and demand

For tourism purposes, with the exception of yachts, the use of all the above-mentioned marine vessels is concentrated mainly on rivers, canals and lakes. As kayaking and canoeing are considered a recreational activity, there is no data available on their use in the tourism industry. However, in the USA there were about 11.8 million participants in kayaking and approximately 9.8 million in canoeing in 2011 (Outdoor Foundation, 2012). One of the most popular kayaking and canoeing destinations in the USA is the Great Calusa Blueway Paddling Trail in southwest Florida's Lee County with a length of 190 miles. While paddling, a great variety of ecosystems and wildlife can be discovered, such as mangrove tunnels and banks of cypress as well as more than a dozen species of wading and water birds and even dolphins (Calusa Blueway, 2013).

In terms of inland waterway transportation, France is one of the most important countries for houseboating in tourism with a water route of 8500 km and an annual turnover of €230 million (Voie navigables en France, 2010). The French houseboat sector comprises 69 suppliers and

1802 boats at 125 bases. The size of the bases is relatively small, as 39% of them have one to 18 boats available but only 8% of the havens house 34 or more boats. Interestingly, there is a high concentration within the sector with only four suppliers (Locaboat, Le Boat, Nicols Yacht and Rive de France) that offer 60% of the boats available. The regions of Languedoc-Roussillon, Bourgogne, Lorraine-Alsace, Pays-de-la-Loire and Franche-Comté are the main destinations for houseboating tourism in France. There were about 149,000 passengers in 2009 (Voie navigables en France, 2010). In Germany, however, houseboating has a high popularity in the northern federal state of Mecklenburg-Vorpommern, where each year more than 200,000 overnight stays can be registered and lead to annual revenues of approximately €20 million (Bundesverband Wassersportwirtschaft, 2006; Tourismusverband Mecklenburg Vorpommern, 2010).

The European leader in the tour-operator market is the houseboat specialist Le Boat. This family brand contains the four brands Crown Blue Line, Connoisseur Cruisers, Emerald Star Line and Sunsail. In total, Le Boat has more than 1000 boats on 40 bases in eight countries on offer. This specialized tour operator is part of TUI Travel PLC (Crown Blue Line GmbH, 2013).

In North America, the most favoured houseboating destinations are British Columbia in Canada with more than 200 houseboating rentals, the Trent–Severn Waterway which links Lake Ontario with Georgian Bay in Lake Huron and the combined Missouri–Mississippi system comprising 6020 km in the USA (Department of Transportation Ports & Waterways Section, 2001; Discover Canadian Outdoor, 2010).

Yacht chartering locations are highly concentrated in the Mediterranean, such as Spain's Costa del Sol, the Balearic Islands, the French coastline, Sardinia, Turkey and Greece. In total, there are about 2000 yachts available in the Mediterranean region (Hudson, 2003). One of the world's leading yacht charter companies is The Moorings, a member of the TUI travel group of companies with more than 650 yachts in its fleet in more than 25 destinations worldwide (TUI Marine, 2013).

Finally, it should be pointed out that boat tourism is a field of research that still has to be investigated as there is only a small amount of information available. The main focus so far has been on recreational and sports activities.

For Further Reading, see Chapter 8.

chapter 10

Future Outlook

This chapter aims to raise an awareness for some of the trends affecting the future of tourism transport. The objective is not to cover all possible trends and developments, but rather to highlight some of the current conditions and ideas that will impact the future of travel and tourism.

Within the framework of environmental analyses (which provide relevant information regarding the general business environment), there are four to six fundamental areas which are usually included: sociological (S), technological (T), economic (E), political (P), environment (E) and legal (L). These environmental analyses are known by various acronyms, including STEP or PEST, STEEP or PESTE, or PESTLE, PESTEL or LEPEST. Based upon the environmental framework, several pertinent trends and their impact on tourism will be further examined (see Fig. 10.1).

DEMOGRAPHIC DEVELOPMENTS

The demographic changes currently experienced particularly by industrialized countries include a changing household structure (growth in single households and a decrease in the traditional family structure) and the development towards an ageing population who are not only more inclined to travel but also have become more discerning travellers based on their past experiences. Furthermore, we can expect changes in travel behaviour with increasing age as there are studies which have shown that increasing physical restrictions after the age of 75 impact behaviour and can lead to a higher need for security or even to travel constraints (Dreyer, 2012). Another aspect is so-called ageless consumption, a concept whereby products are not designed for particular age groups, but rather in which a 'universal design' works for both young and older people (Zukunftsinstitut, 2011, p. 22).

CLIMATIC DEVELOPMENTS/SUSTAINABILITY

As with any human activity, tourism has inevitable impacts on the environments visited. Social inequalities (for example, in terms of education, income and health), economic dependencies (due particularly to increasing globalization) and negative environmental effects (such as the contribution to greenhouse gas emissions from the transportation of tourists) have been observed.

Major environmental problem areas include energy consumption, air pollution (emissions), greenhouse effects and climate change, threats to biodiversity (e.g. species diversity, impacts on flora and fauna), land use and landscape change, generation of waste, water consumption and pollution, as well as noise pollution and effects (Freyer, 2011). Transport (including tourism transportation) was responsible for 22% of worldwide CO_2 emissions in 2010 (see Table 10.1). Interestingly, the top ten emitting countries in 2010 were responsible for two-thirds of global CO_2 emissions, and within the top ten, two countries were responsible for approximately 40% of the emissions (namely China and the USA with 23.8% and 17.7% respectively) (IEA, 2012). However, more sustainable forms of transportation are being developed using current technology by reducing energy consumption and emissions. An example of such developments within the airline industry is given here, although similar developments can be found for other transportation means:

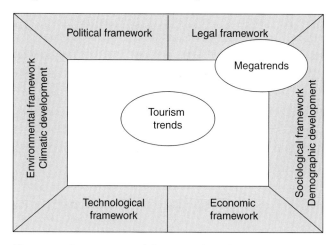

Fig. 10.1. Environmental framework and tourism trends.

Table 10.1. CO_2 emissions by sector in 2010. (From IEA 2012, p. 9.)

Sector	Share
Electricity and heat generation	41%
Transport	22%
Industry	20%
Residential	6%
Other, includes commercial/public services, agriculture/forestry, fishing, energy industries other than electricity and heat generation, and other emissions not specified elsewhere	10%

with the aid of lighter materials it is possible to cut fuel consumption by up to 30 per cent from its present level. [...] In future, nanotechnology will present huge opportunities in the manufacturing of materials. Nanoparticles will make various surfaces extremely resistant to tearing and scratching, give long-lasting protection from corrosion, and improve the aerodynamic attributes of aircraft. [...] Recyclable bio-based materials will be better suited to air transport fuel than in land transport, where enormous amounts would be needed to reduce emissions. [...] It is entirely realistic to assume that at the end of this century, jet fuel (kerosene) will have been replaced with alternative fuels. In the future it will be possible to produce bio-derived fuels much more profitably and in a more environmentally friendly way, for example from bacteria or marine algae. Algae can double its biomass several times per day and it produces at least 15 times more vegetable oil per hectare than rapeseed, palm, soya or jatropha. Algae can be grown in seawater tanks, and no land or fresh water is needed to cultivate it.

(Korhola, 2008, p. 23)

In order to reduce the negative effects of human activities there has been a global call for more sustainable practices, so too within the tourism sector (and particularly for tourism transport). The terms sustainable development and corporate social responsibility (CSR) are prevalent in the current discussions regarding the reduction of negative impacts. The Brundland report defined sustainable development as 'development that meets the needs of the present without compromising the ability of future generations to meet their own needs' (WCED, 1987). While sustainable development is regarded as addressing the social, environmental and economic dimensions holistically at a societal level, CSR focuses on the sustainability at the company level (Freyer, 2011; Lumma et al., 2011). The term CSR originated in the USA during the 1950s and was heavily influenced by Bowen (Bassen et al., 2005). Although early emphasis was placed on social aspects such as welfare and human rights, by the 1980s and 1990s many also considered environmental aspects to be a part of social responsibility (Hansen and Schrader, 2005), which led to an increase in the discussion of the existing sustainability concept at the corporate level.

Further information regarding sustainable tourism and travel as well as concrete measures which can be taken can be found in the Further Reading section at the end of this chapter.

TECHNOLOGY

There are several important technological developments and innovations affecting both transportation means and infrastructure. We have mentioned some of the developments affecting energy consumption and emissions, but of particular significance is the electronic provision of information to the consumer. Companies strive to keep up with the latest technological advancements as web based and mobile technologies (Web 2.0, tablets, smartphones, etc.) create the possibility of almost instantaneous, personalized and interactive communication between companies and individuals. As tourism and transport services are intangible products and services, electronic communication via the internet adds value for the customer by emotionalizing information (through pictures or videos) and companies can update their information and communication very quickly at a relatively low cost. Hence social media has also become very important for the transmission of information, marketing and for digital 'word-of-mouth' recommendations. Regarding the use of mobile phones, specially designed applications (so-called apps) can either simplify the provision of information for tourists/passengers concerning travel planning and management (such as special offers, schedule information, booking, seat reservations and departure/arrival-status queries) or provide completely new services such as mobile check-in options or services such as MyTaxi or Meetup (Bauhuber, 2011). Technology allows companies to focus more on their customers needs and desires and enables the provision of instant, personalized and bookable services, which in turn has influenced consumer behaviour and expectations.

TOURISM MEGATRENDS

Trends are a recurring theme within the academic literature as illustrated by the multitude of studies and articles, including *Tourism Trends for Europe* (European Travel Commission), *Tourism Tomorrow* (European Tourism Research Institute), *ITB World Travel Trends Report* (ITB Berlin) or the *OECD Tourism Trends and Policies* (OECD), yet there is really no common denominator to be found. However, the World Tourism Organization has identified several megatrends, such as (adapted from UNWTO, 2001):

- Globalization–localization: the tourism market is characterized by a trend to globalization (e.g. transnational companies and adaptation of the tourism offer). Simultaneously there is an opposite trend towards localization with authenticity and 'differentiation' of the offer.
- Polarization of tourist tastes: between comfort bases and adventure or education-oriented demand.
- The tourist's 'shrinking world': systematic reduction of boundaries and restrictions (tourism anywhere).
- Electronic technology becoming all powerful: influencing distribution, destination choice and booking behaviour.
- Fast track travel: new technologies (e.g. ticketless travel) and border controls accelerate the travel process.
- Customers will 'call the shots': transformation to a buyers market – the customer may increasingly determine the tourism offer with the help of new technologies (e.g. use of online auctions and internet inspections of destinations, hotels and other facilities).
- Destination as 'fashion accessory': destinations have a life cycle (e.g. changing style destinations).
- Targeted product market development (three Es-oriented): active tourism marketing and product development is indispensable. Focus on one or a combination of Entertainment, Excitement and Education.
- More destinations focus on 'image': customer perceptions will play a more important role.
- Everyone chasing the Asian tourist: immense importance of the Asian market (as outgoing and incoming market).

- Consumer-led campaigns for sustainable tourism: consumers have become more conscious of sustainable development.
- Growing conflict between yearning for travel consumption and the increased sustainable consciousness: manifested in more stringent examination of destinations and their responsible development by travellers.

Besides the identified megatrends there are also more specific tourism trends, which will be highlighted using examples from the arena of tourism travel in Table 10.2.

Table 10.2. Tourism trends with specific travel examples. (From Dreyer, 2009; Zukunftsinstitut, 2011; Dreyer, 2012.)

More comfortable	Convenience – the food industry led the way. Important not only, but especially, for older generations	• Better integration of all travel systems and services including luggage transportation, etc. • E-bikes and rental systems are service offers within the active/sport tourism sector • Biking without luggage (transport of luggage is provided as a service between itinerary stops)
More individual	Individual elements are more important than completely standardized packages	• Building-block and dynamic packages are becoming more important • Hikes and biketours with private guides
Cheaper and spontaneous	Discounted offers increasing; flexible work–life balance is opening new possibilities	• LCCs • Last-minute trips • Online booking is a necessity
Luxurious and exotic	No contradiction, the polarization of offers is increasing	• Luxury trains with accommodation • Luxury cruises • First-class travel and VIP service/lounges
Slower paced/deceleration	Seeking a work–life balance	• Relaxation (rest areas) • Pilgrimages (by bike or on foot) • Slow food/regional cuisine

(Continued)

Table 10.2. Continued.

Health	The goal is unity of body, mind and soul	• Organic food, special allergen-free menus on the plane, train or bus • Healthcare services/programmes
Experience-oriented	Demand for productions and events	• Experiences sought on planes, trains and buses (inflight entertainment, WiFi, etc.) • Themed travel – walks and cycle paths
Shorter and more frequent	Dependent on the economic situation, number of second and third trips increases	• City trips are booming globally, partially due to LCC offers
Safety and security	Especially pertinent for older generations	• Security personnel at train stations • Border security, controls and regulations • Bicycle parking in secure lockers
Climate friendly	Increasing awarenes of climate change	• Electromobility on vacation (sustainable mobility) • CO_2 compensation, such as www.myclimate.org or www.atmosfair.de • 'Green fleets' at car rental companies

FUTURE INNOVATIONS AND VISIONS

The future of tourism mobility will be influenced by innovations within the transport sector. Innovations may include improvements in vehicle types, fuel usage or infrastructure; changes in transport services and policy; or even the introduction of new transport systems. Inter-modal transport is a topic which has received much interest recently, and we are sure to see concrete developments here within the next few years. However, at this point we would like to examine a few interesting vehicle innovations and existing prototypes.

The Dutch company PAL-V Europe NV has developed and tested a 'personal air and land vehicle', a combination of a car and a gyrocopter (see Fig. 10.2). The vehicle already complies with existing regulations in all major markets (allowing it to operate both in road and air traffic) and requires no new infrastructure as it uses existing roads and airstrips. The concept of such

Fig. 10.2. PAL-V.

a personal flying car would mean fast door-to-door mobility for private individuals as well as professionals and organizations. According to the company, the flying range will be between 350 and 500 km (220 and 315 miles), depending on the type, pay load and wind conditions. Driving, a PAL-V will have a range of about 1200 km (750 miles). It runs on petrol like a conventional car and there will also be versions that use biodiesel or bioethanol. It can reach speeds of up to 180 km/h (110 miles/h) both on land and in the air. Apparently it takes off and lands with low speed, is capable of landing almost anywhere, cannot stall and is very easy to control. Some governments are already preparing for increasing traffic with personal air vehicles such as this, determining the infrastructure of 'digital freeways' to provide a safe corridor using GPS technology (www.pal-v.com).

The billionaire entrepeneur Elon Musk (co-founder of PayPal and founder of Tesla Motors and SpaceX) has recently revived the vision regarding a superfast (speed of sound), self-propelling, solar-powered intercity mode of transportation he calls the 'Hyperloop' (see Fig. 10.3). Capsules supported by a cushion of air would be transported at both low and high speeds through a low pressure tube. Each capsule would accommodate up to 28 passengers and travel at speeds up to 746 miles/h (1200 km/h). The Hyperloop is designed to connect cities less than 1000 miles (1610 km) apart. The tubes would be constructed above ground with the solar panels mounted on top.

As previously mentioned, besides new means of transport innovations such as the examples briefly described above, there are many technological innovations being applied to existing means of transport which will affect also the future of tourism mobility. As a brief example of such innovations, a future vision of how customer desires and new safety requirements are being addressed by Finnair is highlighted in Fig. 10.4.

In 2010, the engineers of the European aircraft manufacturer Airbus first unveiled their vision of how an aircraft cabin may look by 2050 and have kept on developing this vision (see Fig. 10.5). Inspired by nature, bionic structures will be utilized for the airplane, oriented along the bone structure of birds. The intelligent cabin structure will be coated by a biopolymer

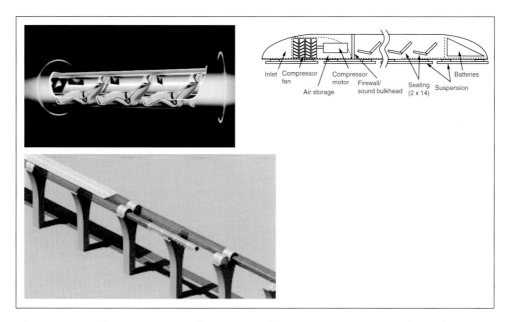

Fig. 10.3. Hyperloop vision. From http://neuerdings.com/2013/08/13/im-hyperloop.

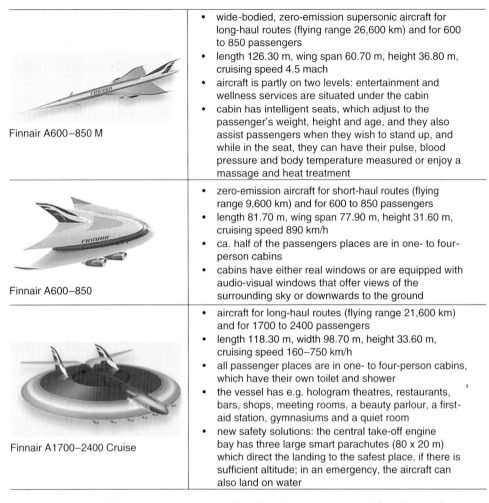

Finnair A600–850 M	• wide-bodied, zero-emission supersonic aircraft for long-haul routes (flying range 26,600 km) and for 600 to 850 passengers • length 126.30 m, wing span 60.70 m, height 36.80 m, cruising speed 4.5 mach • aircraft is partly on two levels: entertainment and wellness services are situated under the cabin • cabin has intelligent seats, which adjust to the passenger's weight, height and age, and they also assist passengers when they wish to stand up, and while in the seat, they can have their pulse, blood pressure and body temperature measured or enjoy a massage and heat treatment
Finnair A600–850	• zero-emission aircraft for short-haul routes (flying range 9,600 km) and for 600 to 850 passengers • length 81.70 m, wing span 77.90 m, height 31.60 m, cruising speed 890 km/h • ca. half of the passengers places are in one- to four-person cabins • cabins have either real windows or are equipped with audio-visual windows that offer views of the surrounding sky or downwards to the ground
Finnair A1700–2400 Cruise	• aircraft for long-haul routes (flying range 21,600 km) and for 1700 to 2400 passengers • length 118.30 m, width 98.70 m, height 33.60 m, cruising speed 160–750 km/h • all passenger places are in one- to four-person cabins, which have their own toilet and shower • the vessel has e.g. hologram theatres, restaurants, bars, shops, meeting rooms, a beauty parlour, a first-aid station, gymnasiums and a quiet room • new safety solutions: the central take-off engine bay has three large smart parachutes (80 x 20 m) which direct the landing to the safest place, if there is sufficient altitude; in an emergency, the aircraft can also land on water

Fig. 10.4. Future visions by Finnair. Note: The electricity is generated for all aircraft by solar panels on the vessel's outer surface, and all materials are 100% recyclable. From Finnair Plc, 2008 illustrated by Kauko Helavuo.

membrane which controls air temperature and can become transparent on demand giving passengers an open air feeling while also eliminating the need for windows. Moreover, views cannot only be seen but also appropriate information provided as to the location and/or sight. Personalized zones will replace the classic airline cabin, in which individual needs such as relaxing, playing games or interacting with others (even holding business meetings with people on the ground) can be offered. Airbus claims that:

> intuitive technology will allow passengers to access all flight, destination and environmental information at the wave of a hand. Pop-up pods will offer more private spaces that can be used for anything from virtual business meetings or lectures to a romantic meal or reading a bedtime story to the kids back home, with global connectivity and holographic projections

Fig. 10.5. Airbus concept cabin. From Airbus, 2013.

adapted to the needs of each user. A virtual shopping wall will project clothes directly on to passengers and the virtual gaming wall will let tennis, baseball and even golf fans get in a bit of practice, while the more adventurous will be able to try out newer options like Airbus Fusion Ball game, which lets you play catch across the skyscrapers of New York or the peaks of the Himalayas!

(Airbus, 2013)

Visions even include morphing materials and fittings and furniture made of self-reliant materials which can clean and repair themselves thanks to innovations inspired by nature. Most impresssively, these future cabins will be fully ecological.

Another futuristic idea comes from the cruising industry: the Freedom Ship project. Presently it merely exists as a design on paper (see Fig. 10.6), and while many question how realistic it may be, much has been speculated about the proposed floating city. This architectural feat would be approximately 4500 feet (approximately 1370 m) long, 750 feet (228 m) wide,

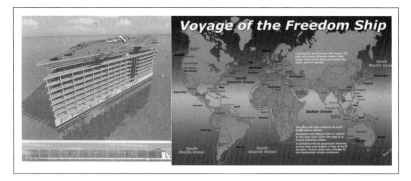

Fig. 10.6. Freedom Ship.

350 feet (106 m) high and would accommodate up to 40,000 full time residents, 30,000 daily visitors, 10,000 nightly hotel guests and 20,000 full time crew (http://freedomship.com). According to some sources the 'city' will include approximately 17,000 homes as well as luxury ocean view apartments and about 4000 businesses. Furthermore, residents will be able to access private jets on the roof top airport or utilize yachts for local excursions. Perhaps it is one man's dream, but who knows, today's dream may be someone's future (Schilling, 2013).

Finally, it should be noted that in the future, tourism on other astronomical objects (especially the Moon and Mars) and within space itself is certainly feasible (see p. 52). Furthermore, there are innovations which will influence or modify tourist mobility and experiences which we cannot even begin to imagine at this point in time. So let's wait and see what the future may bring!

FURTHER READING

Gössling, S. (2010) *Carbon Management in Tourism: Mitigating the Impacts on Climate Change.* Routledge, London, UK.

Gössling, S. and Upham, P. (2009) *Climate Change and Aviation. Issues, Challenges and Solutions.* Earthscan, London, UK.

Reddy, M. V. and Wilkes, K. (2012) *Tourism, Climate Change and Sustainability.* Routledge, Abingdon, UK.

Schott, C. (2010). *Tourism and the Implications of Climate Change: Issues and Actions.* Emerald, Bingley, UK.

Scott, D., Hall, C.M. and Gössling, S. (2012) *Tourism and Climate Change. Impacts, Mitigation and Adaptation.* Routledge, London, UK.

Swarbrooke, J. (1999) *Sustainable Tourism Management.* CABI, Wallingford, UK.

UNWTO – World Tourism Organization/UNEP – United Nations Environment Programme (2008) *Climate Change and Tourism – Responding to Global Challenges.* Madrid, Spain.

Weaver, D. (2012) *Sustainable Tourism.* Butterworth-Heinemann, Oxford, UK.

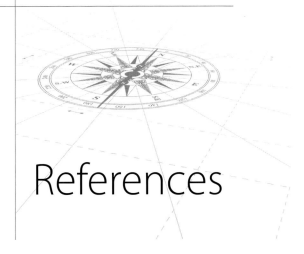

References

6 USC § 1151 (2010) Sec 1151 Definitions. Available at: http://www.gpo.gov/fdsys/pkg/USCODE-2010-title6/pdf/USCODE-2010-title6-chap4-subchapIV-partA-sec1151.pdf (accessed 6 January 2012)

ABA (2010) Economic Impact Report 2009. Available at: http://www.guerrillaeconomics.biz/abafoundation/Abafoundation%20Methodology.pdf (accessed 20 January 2012).

ABA (2012) About Us. Available at: http://www.buses.org/About-Us (accessed 15 January 2012).

ACCRO (2012) About Us. Available at: http://www.accro.org/AboutUs.aspx (accessed 4 October 2012).

ACRA (2012) Mission Statement. Available at: http://www.acraorg.com/about-us/ (accessed 4 October 2012).

ACRISS (2011) Car Classification Code. Available at: http://www.acriss.org/car-codes.asp (accessed 3 October 2012).

Adam, B. (2012) Geschichte der Luftfahrt. Available at: http://www.luftfahrt.net/magazin/geschichte-der-luftfahrt.html (accessed 28 December 2012).

Adventure Cycling Association (2012) Adventure Cycling Network. Available at: http://www.adventurecycling.org/routes/network.cfm (accessed 6 December 2012).

AEA (2012) About Us. Available at: http://www.aea.be/about/ (accessed 22 November 2012).

Airbus (2012) Global Market Forecast. Available at: http://www.airbus.com/company/market/forecast/?eID=dam_frontend_push&docID=27599 (accessed 28 August 2013).

Airbus (2013) The Airbus Concept Cabin. Available at: http://www.airbus.com/innovation/future-by-airbus/concept-planes/the airbus concept cabin/ (accessed 27 August 2013).

AirDialog, LLC d/b/a Linear Air (2013a) Learn more. Available at: http://www.linearair.com/aboutus/faqs.aspx (accessed 13 February 2013).

AirDialog, LLC d/b/a Linear Air (2013b) Additional questions. Available at: http://www.linearair.com/aboutus/morequestions.aspx (accessed 13 February 2013).

Airline Business (2010) *Airline Industry Guide 2010/11*. Reed Business Information, Sutton, UK.

Airlines for America (2012) About. Available at: http://www.airlines.org/Pages/About%20A4A.aspx (accessed 22 November 2012).

Airlines for America (2013) Airline Handbook - Chapter 1. Available at: http://www.airlines.org/Pages/Airline-Handbook-Chapter-1-Brief-History-of-Aviation.aspx (accessed 26 January 2013).

AirPano (2013) All Panoramas. Available at: http://www.airpano.ru/files/Manhattan-New-York-USA/2-2 (accessed 8 April 2013).

Airship Association (2012) About the Airship Association. Available at: http://www.airship-association.org/cms/node/1 (accessed 4 July 2013).

Allgemeiner Deutscher Fahrrad-Club eV (2012) Elektrorad-Typen. Available at: http://www.tour-me.info/ebiketypenunterschiedeunddefinition.php (accessed 6 December 2012).

Alpine Helicopters Inc. (2013) Tourism. Available at: http://www.alpinehelicopter.com/tourism (accessed 7 April 2013).

AM Mindpower Solutions (2010) The US Car Rental Market Outlook. Available at: http://www.ammindpower.com/report.php?A=229 (accessed 5 October 2012).

Amtrak (2012). National Fact Sheet 2012. Available at: http://www.amtrak.com/ccurl/355/968/Amtrak-National-Fact-Sheet-FY2012.pdf (accessed 15 August 2013).

An Ocean Blueprint for the 21st Century (2004) Final Report of the US Commission on Ocean Policy. Available at: http://www.oceancommission.gov (accessed 14 October 2011).

APTA (2011) Public Transportation Fact Book, 62nd edn. Available at: http://www.apta.com/resources/statistics/Documents/FactBook/APTA_2011_Fact_Book.pdf (accessed 30 September 2011).

ARN Online (2012) Auto Rental News – US Car Rental Market 2011. Available at: http://www.autorentalnews.com/fc_resources/editorial/arn-6.pdf (accessed 23 September 2012).

ARN Online (2013) Auto Rental News – US Car Rental Market 2012. Available at: http://www.autorentalnews.com/fileviewer/1650.aspx (accessed 8 February 2013).

Association of American Railroads (2013). Chronology of Railroading in America. Available at: https://www.aar.org/keyissues/Documents/Background-Papers/Chronology-of-RRs-in-America.pdf (accessed 14 April 2013).

Autobahn Adventures (2012) European Driving Tours. Available at: http://www.autobahnadventures.com/european-driving-tours.htm (accessed 2 December 2012).

Autostadt GmbH (2012) About Us. Available at: http://www.autostadt.de/de/ort/ueber-uns/menschen-autos-und-was-sie-bewegt/ (accessed 2 December 2012).

Bales, W. (2002) *American Cowboy* – November/December Issue, Sheridan, Wyoming.

Banister, D. and Hall, P. (1993) The second railway age. *Built Environment* 19, 157–162.

Bassen, A., Jastram, S. and Meyer, K. (2005) Corporate Social Responsibility – eine Begriffserklärung. *Zeitschrift für Wirtschaft- und Unternehmensethik* 6, 231–236. Available at www.zfwu.de/fileadmin/pdf/2_2005/6_2_14_%20Bassen_Jastram_Meyer_Ideenforum.pdf (accessed 26 August 2013).

Bauhuber, F. (2011) Social vs. Search. Wer bringt uns 2015 die Buchungen?, Presentation during the HSMA E-Marketing Day 2011, 14 February 2011 in Munich. Available at: http://www.tourismuszukunft.de/2011/02/social-vs-search-wer-bringt-uns-2015-die-buchungen/ (accessed 27 August 2013).

BC Ferries (2012) About. Available at: http://www.bcferries.com/about/More_Information.html (accessed 17 November 2012).

Becker, H. and Höfling, R. (2000) *100 Jahre Luftschiffe*. Motorbuch Verlag, Stuttgart. Germany.

Becker, O., Goslich, W. and Müller, G. (2006) *Bus- und Gruppenreisen – Marktchancen, Produkte, Erfolgsfaktoren*. Gmeiner Verlag, Meßkirch, Germany.

Beedie, P. (2003) Adventure tourism. In: Hudson, S. (ed.) *Sport and Adventure Tourism*. Haworth Press, New York, pp. 203–239.

Belobaba, P.P. (2009) Overview of airline economics, markets and demand. In: Belobaba, P.P., Odoni, A. and Barnhart, C. (eds) *The Global Airline Industry*. John Wiley & Sons, Chichester, UK, pp. 47–72.

Belobaba, P.P. and Odoni, A. (2009) Introduction and overview. In: Belobaba, P.P., Odoni, A. and Barnhart, C. (eds) *The Global Airline Industry*. John Wiley & Sons, Chichester, UK, pp. 1–17.

Berger, M.L. (2001) *The Automobile in American History and Culture: a Reference Guide*. Greenwood Press, Westport, Connecticut.

Bellis, M. (2011a) The History of Railroad Innovations. Available at: http://inventors.about.com/library/inventors/blrailroad.htm (accessed 18 October 2011).

Bellis, M. (2011b) The History of the Street Car. Available at: http://inventors.about.com/library/inventors/blstreetcars.htm (accessed 18 October 2011).

Bensaude-Vincent, B. and Blondel, C. (2008) *Sciences and Spectacle in the European Enlightenment*. Ashgate Publishing, Hampshire, UK.

Bhatia, A.K. (2006) *The Business of Tourism Concepts and Strategies*. Sterling Publishers, New Delhi, India.

Boeing (2013) Current Market Outlook. Available at: http://www.boeing.com/boeing/commercial/cmo/ (accessed 28 August 2013).

Born, K. (2001) Wie realistisch ist Weltraumtourismus? In: *Integra - Zeitschrift des Instituts für Integrativen Tourismus und Freizeitforschung* 04/2001, pp. 5–9.

Boston Consulting Group (2009) Planes, Trains, and Automobiles. Available at: http://www.bcg.com/documents/file15463.pdf (accessed 27 November 2011).

Boyd, L. (2008) Brief History of Buses and Rental Cars in the US. Available at: http://library.duke.edu/digitalcollections/adaccess/guide/transportation/carandbus/ (accessed 6 January 2012).

Boyd, L. (2013) Brief History of the US Airline Industry. Available at: http://library.duke.edu/digitalcollections/adaccess/guide/transportation/airlines/ (accessed 13 February 2013).

Brämer, R. and Gruber, M. (2005) Profilstudie Wandern '04 – Grenzenlos Wandern, 6/2005. Available at: http://www.wanderforschung.de/files/prostu04lang1251281375.pdf (accessed 15 December 2012).

British Airways (2012a) Explore our past: 1970 – 1979. Available at: http://www.britishairways.com/travel/history-1970-1979/public/en_gb (accessed 27 December 2012).

British Airways (2012b) Fleet Facts. Available at: http://www.britishairways.com/travel/bafleet/public/en_gb (accessed 27 December 2012).

British National Travel Survey (2010) Statistical Release. Available at: https://www.gov.uk/government/uploads/system/uploads/attachment_data/file/8932/nts2010-01.pdf (accessed 25 October 2012).

Buckley, R. (2004) *Environmental Impacts of Ecotourism*. CABI Publishing, Cambridge, Massachusetts.

Buckley, R. (2006) *Adventure Tourism*. CABI Publishing, Cambridge, Massachusetts.

Bues, C., Schwarz, H. and Semper, S. (2008) *Das große Caravan-Handbuch*. Motorbuch-Verlag, Stuttgart, Germany.

BUGC (2013) What is Gliding? Available at: http://www.bugc.moonfruit.com/#/what-is-gliding/4550029053 (accessed 7 April 2013).

Bundesministerium für Verkehr, Bau und Stadtentwicklung (2009) Mobilitätshilfeverordnung. Available at: http://www.thomasknauf.de/ginger/Mobilitaetshilfeverordnung.pdf (accessed 6 December 2012).

Bundesverband Deutscher Leasing Unternehmen eV (2012) Verband – International. Available at: http://bdl.leasingverband.de/verband/international (accessed 4 October 2012).

Bundesverband Wassersportwirtschaft (2006) Hausbootcharter in Deutschland. Available at: http://www.bvww.org/index.php?id=127&uid=98 (accessed 24 February 2013).

Bureau of Transportation Statistics (2012a) Table 1-37: US Air Carrier Aircraft Departures, Enplaned Revenue Passengers, and Enplaned Revenue Tons. Available at: http://www.rita.dot.gov/bts/sites/rita.dot.gov.bts/files/publications/national_transportation_statistics/html/table_01_37.html (accessed 15 February 2013).

Bureau of Transportation Statistics (2012b) Table 1-44: Passengers Boarded at the Top 50 US Airports. Available at: http://www.rita.dot.gov/bts/sites/rita.dot.gov.bts/files/publications/national_transportation_statistics/html/table_01_44.html (accessed 15 February 2013).

Burgdorf, M. (1993) *Autovermietung in Deutschland – Ein Branchenbild mit praktischen Hinweisen*. Verlag Moderne Industrie, Landsberg/Lech, Germany.

Business Research and Economic Advisors for CLIA (2012) The Contribution of the North American Cruise Industry to the US Economy in 2011. Available at: http://www.cruising.org/sites/default/files/pressroom/2011EconomicStudies/EconStudy_Exec_Summary2011.pdf (accessed 8 July 2013).

Butler, C. (2007) Railroads and Their Impact. Available at: http://www.flowofhistory.com/units/eme/17/FC112 (accessed 4 November 2011).

Calusa Blueway (2013) The Great Calusa Blueway Paddling Trail. Available at: http://www.leeparks.org/blueway/ (accessed 10 February 2013).

Campervan Adventures (2011) Campervans and Motorhomes. Available at: http://www.campervan-adventures.com/campervans/campervans-motorhomes/ (accessed 13 December 2012).

Canadian Ferry Operators Association (2012a) Mission Statement. Available at: http://www.cfoa.ca/membership/mission.php (accessed 14 November 2012).

Canadian Ferry Operators Association (2012b) Annual report 2011. Available at: http://www.cfoa.ca/information/reports/2011%20CFOA%20Annual%20Report.pdf (accessed 18 November 2012).

Canadian Recreational Vehicle Association (2012) About. Available at: http://www.crva.ca/association/details-about-the-association/ (accessed 14 December 2012).

CAPA (2011) Oneworld Losing Market Share to SkyTeam, Star Alliance. Global LCC Seats Share Now 23.1%. Available at: http://centreforaviation.com/analysis/oneworld-losing-market-share-to-skyteam-star-alliance-global-lcc-seats-share-now-231-49107 (accessed 15 January 2013).

CAPA (2012a) British Airways. Available at: http://centreforaviation.com/profiles/airlines/british-airways-ba (accessed 27 December 2012).

CAPA (2012b) United Ends 2012 as World's Biggest Airline, Emirates Third. Turkish and Lion Air the Biggest Movers. Available at: http://centreforaviation.com/analysis/united-ends-2012-as-worlds-biggest-airline-emirates-third-turkish-and-lion-air-the-biggest-movers-93047 (accessed 31 December 2012).

CAPA (2012c) Southwest Still World's Biggest LCC, IndiGo the Fastest Growing: Low-cost Carrier Rankings. Available at: http://centreforaviation.com/analysis/southwest-still-worlds-biggest-lcc-indigo-the-fastest-growing-low-cost-carrier-rankings-49110 (accessed 31 December 2012).

Car Rental Show (2012) Overview. Available at: http://www.carrentalshow.com/Page/Overview.aspx (accessed 4 October 2012).

Carnival Corporation (2011) Our Brands. Available at: http://phx.corporate-ir.net/phoenix.zhtml?c=200767&p=irol-products (accessed 15 February 2013).

Carnival Corporation (2012) Investor Relations. Available at: http://phx.corporate-ir.net/phoenix.zhtml?c=140690&p=irol-index (accessed 24 January 2012).

Cento, A. (2009) The Airline Industry – Challenges in the 21st Century. Physica-Verlag, Heidelberg, Germany.

CIA (2013) The World Factbook. Available at: https://www.cia.gov/library/publications/the-world-factbook/rankorder/2121rank.htm (accessed 12 July 2013).

City and County of San Francisco (2009) Article 39 – Pedicabs. Available at: http://austinpedicab.org/wp-content/uploads/2009/04/san-francisco-pedicab-ordinance.rtf (accessed 13 December 2012).

City of New York, The (2012) Summer Streets. Available at: http://www.nyc.gov/html/dot/summer-streets/html/home/home.shtml (accessed 6 December 2012).

CIVD (2010) Soziodemografische Daten. Available at: http://www.civd.de/caravaning/marktzahlen/touristik/soziodemografische-daten/ (accessed 14 December 2012).

CIVD (2011) Freizeitfahrzeuge 2010. Available at: http://www.civd.de/statistik/marktanalyse/weltweiter-markt.html (accessed 2 February 2013).

CLIA (2011a) Maritime Industry Background. Available at: http://www.cruising.org/regulatory/resources/maritime-industry-background (accessed 8 October 2011).

CLIA (2011b) About CLIA. Available at: http://www.cruising.org/regulatory/about-clia (accessed 8 October 2011).

CLIA (2011c) Facts About CLIA. Available at: http://www.cruising.org/regulatory/about-clia/facts-about-clia (accessed 8 October 2011).

CLIA (2012) Cruise Industry Update 2012. Available at: http://www.cruising.org/sites/default/files/pressroom/2012CLIAIndustryUpdate.pdf (accessed 8 July 2013).

CLIA (2013a) North America Cruise Industry Update 2013. Available at: http://www.cruising.org/sites/default/files/pressroom/CruiseIndustryUpdate2013FINAL.pdf (accessed 8 July 2013).

CLIA (2013b) Contribution of Cruise Tourism to the Economies of Europe. Available at: http://www.europeancruisecouncil.com/content/CLIA%20Europe%20Economic%20Impact%20Report%202013%20Edition.pdf (accessed 8 July 2013).

Clifford (2012) The Blue Riband. Available at: http://www.theblueriband.com/thehalestrophy.html (accessed 5 August 2012).

Code of Federal Regulations (2007). Title 46 - Shipping.Intact Stability Standards. Available at: http://www.ecfr.gov/cgi-bin/text-idx?c=ecfr;rgn=div6;vie...de=46%3A7.0.1.1.4.5;idno=46;sid=98a06b

6509d5d0cac41468d8dbbcfd92;view=text;cc=ecfr;node=46%3A7.0.1.3.13.3#46:7.0.1.3.13.3.63.3 (accessed 15 February 2013).

Collins, P. (1992) Benefits of commercial passenger space travel for society. In: Bainum, P., May, G.L., Nagatomo, M. and Ohkami, Y. (eds) Advances in the Astronautical Sciences, International Space Year in the Pacific Basin. Proceedings of 4th ISCOPS, San Diego, California, pp. 41–52.

COM (2001) European Transport Policy for 2010: Time to Decide. Available at: http://ec.europa.eu/transport/themes/strategies/doc/2001_white_paper/lb_com_2001_0370_en.pdf (accessed 20 October 2012).

Condor Flugdienst GmbH (2012a) Our History (1955–2011). Available at: http://www.condor.com/eu/the-company/our-history.jsp (accessed 27 December 2012).

Condor Flugdienst GmbH (2012b) Our Fleet. Available at: http://www.condor.com/eu/the-company/our-fleet.jsp (accessed 27 December 2012).

Conrady, R., Fichert, F. and Sterzenbach, R. (2013) *Luftverkehr – Betriebswirtschaftliches Lehr- und Handbuch*, 5th edn. Oldenbourg, Munich, Germany.

Cooper, C. (2012) *Essentials of Tourism*. Prentice Hall, Upper Saddle River, New Jersey.

Cooper, C., Fletcher, J., Fyall, A., Gilbert, D. and Wanhill, S. (2005) *Tourism – Principles and Practice*, 3rd edn. Pearson Education, Harlow, UK.

COST 349 (2005) European Cooperation in the Field of Scientific and Technical Research, Accessibility of Coaches and Long Distance Buses for People with Reduced Mobility – Final Report. ESF COST Office, Brussels. Available at: http://w3.cost.eu/fileadmin/domain_files/TUD/Action_349/final_report/final_report-349.pdf (accessed 26 October 2011).

Costa Cruise (2012) Update. Available at: http://www.costacruise.com/B2C/EU/Info/concordia_statement.htm (accessed 25 November 2012).

Crego, R. (2003) *Sports and Games of the 18th and 19th Centuries*. Greenwood Press, Westport, Connecticut.

Crouch, G. (2001) The market for space tourism. Early indications. *Journal of Travel Research* 40, 213–219.

Croucher, P. (2004) *FARs in Plain English – Federal Aviation Regulations Translated!* Electrocution Technical, Calgary, Canada.

Crown Blue Line GmbH (2013) Yachtcharter. Available at: http://www.master-yachting.de/informationen/veranstalter.php?aId=29&vId=515 (accessed 15 February 2013).

CRS (2008) CRS Report for Congress. Available at: http://assets.opencrs.com/rpts/RL34384_20080220.pdf (accessed 29 September 2011).

Cruise and Ferry Center AG (2009) Schiffstypen. Available at: http://www.ferrycenter.ch/front_content.php?idart=48 (accessed 21 October 2012).

Cruise Market Watch (2011) Statistics – Growth. Available at: http://www.cruisemarketwatch.com/growth/ (accessed 9 October 2011).

DB AG (2013) Deutsche Bahn Geschäftsbericht 2012. Available at: http://www1.deutschebahn.com/file/3280426/data/2012_duf.pdf (accessed 10 October 2011).

Deilbach, R. and Stump, D. (2009) *Ballonfahrer Romantik: Auf den Spuren des Windes*. Komet Verlag, Cologne, Germany.

Department of Transportation Ports & Waterways Section (2001) River Transportation in Minnesota. Available at: http://www.dot.state.mn.us/ofrw/PDF/2001RiverTransportationMN.pdf (accessed 25 February 2013).

De Syon, G. (2002) *Zeppelin!: Germany and the Airship, 1900–1939*. The Johns Hopkins University Press, Baltimore, Maryland.

Deutsche Zentrale für Tourismus (2011) Incoming-Tourismus Deutschland. Available at: http://www.deutschland-extranet.de/pdf/DZT_Incoming-Tourismus_Deutschland_Edition_2011.pdf (accessed 27 November 2011).

Deutscher Wanderverband (2010) Zukunftsmarkt Wandern. Available at: http://www.wanderverband.de/conpresso/_data/Dokumentation_Grundlagenuntersuchung_Wandern.pdf (accessed 15 December 2012).

Deutsches Museum (2012a) Luftfahrt 1918 – 1945. Available at: http://www.deutsches-museum.de/ausstellungen/verkehr/luftfahrt/luftfahrt-1918-1945/ (accessed 29 December 2012).

Deutsches Museum (2012b) Strahlflugzeuge und Hubschrauber. Available at: http://www.deutsches-museum.de/ausstellungen/verkehr/luftfahrt/strahlflugzeuge/ (accessed 29 December 2012).

Dickinson, B. and Vladimir, A. (1997) *Selling the Sea: An Inside Look at the Cruise Industry*. Wiley, Hoboken, New York.

Dickinson, B. and Vladimir, A. (2008) *Selling the Sea: An Inside Look at the Cruise Industry*, 2nd edn. Wiley, Hoboken, New York.

Dionori, F., Ellis, S. and Crovato P. (2011) Typology and Structure of Regulatory Bodies in the EU Railway Sector. Brussels, Belgium. Available at: http://www.europarl.europa.eu/RegData/etudes/note/join/2011/460038/IPOL-TRAN_NT%282011%29460038%28SUM01%29_EN.pdf (accessed 6 July 2012)

Discover Canadian Outdoor (2010) Houseboating. Available at: http://outdoors.ca/en-CA/Articles/HouseboatingInCanada.aspx (accessed 25 February 2013).

Discovery Motorhomes (2012) Differences. Available at: http://www.discovery-motorhomes.co.nz/differences.php (accessed 13 December 2012).

DLR (2012) Luftverkehrsbericht 2011 – Daten und Kommentierungen des deutschen und weltweiten Luftverkehrs. Available at: http://www.dlr.de/fw/Portaldata/42/Resources/dokumente/pdf/LVB2011.pdf (accessed 4 July 2013).

DLR (2013) Low Cost Monitor 1/2013. Available at: http://www.dlr.de/dlr/Portaldata/1/Resources/documents/2013/Low_Cost_Monitor_I_2013_final.pdf (accessed 4 July 2013).

Doganis, R. (2006) *The Airline Business in the 21st Century*, 2nd edn. Routledge, London, UK.

Dowling, R.K. (2006) *Cruise Ship Tourism*. CABI Publishing, Wallingford, UK.

Dreyer, A. (2009) Tourismus 2025. Quo vadis Urlaub? In: Bastian, H., Dreyer, A. and Gross, S. (eds) *Tourismus 3.0. Fakten und Perspektiven*. ITD-Verlag, Hamburg, Germany, pp. 15–22.

Dreyer, A. (2012) Radtouristische Nachfrage. Entwicklungen in der Freizeit- und Urlaubsgestaltung. In: Dreyer, A., Mühlnickel, R. and Miglbauer, E. (eds) *Radtourismus – Entwicklungen – Potentiale – Perspektiven*. Oldenbourg, Munich, Germany, pp. 9–17.

Dreyer, A., Menzel, A. and Endreß, M. (2010) *Wandertourismus – Kundengruppen, Destinationsmarketing, Gesundheitsaspekte*. Oldenbourg, Munich, Germany.

Dreyer, A., Mühlnickel, R. and Miglbauer, E. (2012) *Radtourismus – Entwicklungen, Potentiale, Perspektiven*. Oldenbourg, Munich, Germany.

Dude Ranchers Association (2012) About. What Am I Going to Do? Available at: http://www.duderanch.org/what-am-i-going-to-do.php (accessed 11 December 2012).

Duval, D. T. (2007) *Tourism and Transport: Modes, Networks and Flows*. Channel View Publications, Clevedon Hall, UK.

DWIF (2007) Economic Impact of Touristic Camping in the ECF-Member States. Available at: http://www.civd.de/fileadmin/civd/images/touristik/dwifTouristikcampingECF_WEST.pdf (accessed 4 July 2013).

ECAC (2012) About Us. Available at: https://www.ecac-ceac.org//about_ecac (accessed 22 November 2012).

ECC (2011a) Home. Available at: http://www.europeancruisecouncil.com/Default.aspx (accessed 11 November 2011).

ECC (2011b) The Cruise Industry - A Leader in Europe's Economic Recovery. Available at: http://ec.europa.eu/competition/consultations/2012_maritime_transport/euc_2_en.pdf (accessed 25 February 2013).

ECMT (2002) Transport and Economic Development, ECMT Round Tables, No. 119, OECD Publishing.

ETC Market Intelligence Group (2011) European Tourism Insight, 2009-2010. Available at: http://www.sete.gr/files/Media/Ebook/2011/111103_ETC_European%20Tourism%20Insights%202009-10.pdf (accessed 30 September 2011).

Europcar Autovermietung GmbH (2008a) Observatory of Lifestyle Trends in Travel and Transports. Available at: http://germany.europcar.de/eci_pdfs/ec_lifestyle_trends_transports.pdf (accessed 9 October 2012).

Europcar Autovermietung GmbH (2008b) Autovermieter und Flughäfen – eine Win-Win-Partnerschaft. Available at: http://www.docstoc.com/docs/9878348/Charts-Aviation-Conference-Philippe-Guyot-Europcar (accessed 5 October 2012).

Europcar Autovermietung GmbH (2012) History of the company. Available at: http://www.europcar.de/EBE/module/render/unsere-geschichte (accessed 29 September 2012).

European Caravan Federation (2012a) Registrations of New Leisure Vehicles. Available at: http://www.e-c-f.com/fileadmin/templates/4825/images/statistics/europazul-6.pdf (accessed 14 December 2012).

European Caravan Federation (2012b) About. Available at: http://www.e-c-f.com/index.php?id=4 (accessed 14 December 2012).

European Caravan Federation (2013) Registrations of New Leisure Vehicles. Available at: http://www.e-c-f.com/fileadmin/templates/4825/images/statistics/europazul-6.pdf (accessed 4 July 2013).

European Commission (2010a) Maritime Facts and Figures. Available at: http://ec.europa.eu/research/press/2007/maritime-briefing/pdf/07-maritime-facts-and-figures_en.pdf (accessed 8 October 2011).

European Commission (2010b) Proposal for a Regulation. Available at: http://www.europarl.europa.eu/meetdocs/2009_2014/documents/pech/am/857/857951/857951en.pdf (accessed 6 November 2011).

European Commission (2010c) Flash-Eurobarometer No. 291. Available at: http://ec.europa.eu/public_opinion/flash/fl_291_en.pdf (accessed 2 February 2012).

European Commision (2010d) On track to a sustainable future. Available at: http://www.gppq.fct.pt/h2020/_docs/brochuras/transportes/On%20track%20to%20a%20sustainable%20future.pdf (accessed 9 February 2013).

European Commission (2011a) Staying Ahead of the Wave. Available at: http://ec.europa.eu/research/transport/pdf/waterborn_web.pdf (accessed 2 October 2011).

European Commission (2011b) Environment – The OSPAR Convention. Available at: http://ec.europa.eu/environment/marine/international-cooperation/regional-sea-conventions/ospar/index_en.htm (accessed 7 October 2011).

European Commission (2012) European Consumer Centres Network – Car Hire: What Are My Rights in Europe? Available at: http://ec.europa.eu/consumers/ecc/consumer_topics/car_rental_en.htm (accessed 30 September 2012).

European Commission's Directorate-General for Transport and Mobility (2012) Road Safety – Vehicle Categories. Available at: http://ec.europa.eu/transport/road_safety/vehicles/categories_en.htm#M (accessed 24 September 2012).

European Cyclists' Federation (2012) EuroVelo. Available at: http://www.ecf.com/projects/eurovelo-2/ (accessed 6 December 2012).

European Ramblers' Association (2012) Foundation. Available at: http://www.era-ewv-ferp.com/index.php?page_id=35 (accessed 15 December 2012).

European Union (1993) Directive 93/13/EEC on Unfair Terms in Consumer Contracts. Available at: http://eur-lex.europa.eu/LexUriServ/LexUriServ.do?uri=CELEX:31993L0013:EN:HTML (accessed 1 October 2012).

European Union (2005) Unfair Commercial Practices Directive 2005/29/EC. Available at: http://eur-lex.europa.eu/LexUriServ/LexUriServ.do?uri=OJ:L:2005:149:0022:0039:EN:PDF (accessed 24 September 2012).

European Union (2009) EEC Regulation No. 1073/2009. Available at: http://eur-lex.europa.eu/LexUriServ/LexUriServ.do?uri=OJ:L:2009:300:0088:0105:EN:PDF (accessed 4 October 2011).

European Union (2010) Regulation EU No. 1177/2010. Available at: http://eur-lex.europa.eu/LexUriServ/LexUriServ.do?uri=OJ:L:2010:334:0017:011:en:PDF (accessed 10 November 2012).

Eurostat (2010a) Maritime Passenger Transport. Available at: http://epp.eurostat.ec.europa.eu/tgm/table.do?tab=table&plugin=1&language=de&pcode=tgs00075 (accessed 16 November 2012).

Eurostat (2010b) Tourism Statistics in the European Statistical System. Available at: http://epp.eurostat.ec.europa.eu/cache/ITY_OFFPUB/KS-RA-10-010/EN/KS-RA-10-010-EN.PDF (accessed 10 November 2011).

Eurostat (2011) EU Transport in Figures. Available at: http://ec.europa.eu/transport/facts-fundings/statistics/doc/2011/pocketbook2011.pdf (accessed 10 November 2011).

Eurostat (2012) EU Transport in Figures. Available at: http://ec.europa.eu/transport/facts-fundings/statistics/doc/2012/pocketbook2012.pdf (accessed 10 July 2013).

Eurostat (2013a) Modal Split of Passenger Transport. Available at: http://epp.eurostat.ec.europa.eu/tgm/refreshTableAction.do;jsessionid=9ea7d07e30db21352447cfcb4057a73f86a325998bf2.e34MbxeSahmMa40LbNiMbxaMbNaQe0?tab=table&plugin=1&pcode=tsdtr210&language=en (accessed July 4 2013).

Eurostat (2013b) Railway Transport – Length of Tracks. Available at: http://appsso.eurostat.ec.europa.eu/nui/show.do?dataset=rail_if_tracks&lang=en (accessed 4 July 2013).

Eurostat (2013c) Personenseeverkehr. Available at: http://epp.eurostat.ec.europa.eu/tgm/table.do?tab=table&plugin=1&language=de&pcode=tgs00075 (accessed 10 July 2013).

Executive Airlines (2013a) Company Overview, Fleet, Helicopters, Yachts, Contact. Available at: http://www.executive-airlines.com/index.htm (accessed 13 February 2013).

Executive Airlines (2013b) Executive Airlines Calalog. Available at: http://www.executive-airlines.com/ExecutiveAirlines_Catalog.pdf (accessed 13 February 2013)

FAA (2006) Flight Instructor. Available at: http://www.faa.gov/training_testing/testing/test_standards/media/faa-s-8081-7b.pdf (accessed 7 April 2013).

FAA (2010) The U.S. Commercial Suborbital Industry. Available at: http://www.faa.gov/about/office_org/headquarters_offices/ast/media/111460.pdf (accessed 8 April 2013).

FAI (2012) Gliding. Available at: http://www.fai.org/gliding/ (accessed 7 April 2013).

FCCA (2010) About the FCCA. Available at: http://www.f-cca.com/ (accessed 16 October 2011).

Federal Ministry of Transport, Building and Urban Development (2012) Amendment of the German Passenger Transportation Act. Available at: http://www.bmvbs.de/SharedDocs/DE/Artikel/IR/novellierung-des-personen-befoerderungs-gesetzes.html (accessed 19 October 2012).

Federal Railroad Administration (2011) Border Issues. Available at: http://www.fra.dot.gov (accessed 10 November 2011).

Federal Railroad Administration (2012) About FRA. Available at: http://www.fra.dot.gov/Page/P0002 (accessed 20 October 2012).

Federal Railroad Administration (2013) Organization Chart. Available at: http://www.fra.dot.gov/Page/P0352 (accessed 6 February 2013).

Federal Register (1999) Presidential Documents, Proclamation 7219, Federal Register, Vol. 64, No. 173. Available at: http://www.gc.noaa.gov/documents/090899-cont_zone_proc_7219_64_48701.pdf (accessed 10 October 2011).

Federal Register (2012) National Ocean Council-National Ocean Policy Draft Implementation Plan. Available at: https://www.federalregister.gov/articles/2012/03/14/2012-6215/national-ocean-council-national-ocean-policy-draft-implementation-plan (accessed 2 April 2012).

Fédération Internationale de Camping et de Caravanning (2012) Organization. Available at: http://ficc.org/txt.php?t=3 (accessed 14 December 2012).

Feigenbaum, E. (2012) Mandated Regulations for Car Rental Companies. Available at: http://smallbusiness.chron.com/mandated-regulations-car-rental-companies-4160.html (accessed 16 January 2012).

Finnair Plc (2008) *Departure 2093 – Five Visions of Future Flying*. Print Libris, Helsinki, Finland.

Flightglobal (2011) Australia and Japan Ink Open Skies Agreement. Available at: http://www.flightglobal.com/news/articles/australia-and-japan-ink-open-skies-agreement-362796/ (accessed 16 January 2013).

FMCSA (2011) About. Available at: http://www.fmcsa.dot.gov/about/aboutus.htm (accessed 20 October 2011).

Freyer, W. (2000) Verkehrliche Wirkungen von Telekommunikation – Wirkungen aus Sicht des Tourismus. In: Freyer, W. (ed.) *Ganzheitlicher Tourismus – Beiträge aus 20 Jahren Tourismusforschung*. FIT-Verlag, Dresden, Germany, pp. 265–277.

Freyer, W. (2011) *Tourismus - Einführung in die Fremdenverkehrsökonomie*, 10th edn. Oldenbourg Verlag, Munich, Germany.

Frost & Sullivan (2010) Strategic Analysis of Carsharing Market in Europe. Available at: http://xa.yimg.com/kq/groups/1088789/1632531212/name/F%26S_M4FA_European+Carsharing_Key+Findings.pdf (accessed 27 September 2012).

FUR (2013) Erste Ausgewählte Ergebnisse der 43. Reiseanalyse zur ITB 2013. Available at: http://www.fur.de/fileadmin/user_upload/RA_2013/ITB/RA2013_ITB_Erste_Ergebnisse_DE.pdf (accessed 28 August 2013).

Futron Corporation (2002) Space Tourism Market Study – Orbital Space Travel & Destinations with Suborbital Space Travel. Available at: http://www1.futron.com/pdf/resource_center/white_papers/SpaceTourismMarketStudy.pdf (accessed 8 April 2013).

G Adventures (2013) Gliding. Available at: http://www.gadventures.com/trips/?q=gliding&ref=navsearch (accessed 7 April 2013).

Gass, S. and Assad, A. (2005) *An Annotated Timeline of Operations Research. An Informal History*. Kluwer Academic Publishers, New York.

Gibson, P. (2006) *Cruise Operations Management*. Elsevier, Oxford, UK.

Gillispie, C. (1983) *The Montgolfier Brothers and the Invention of Aviation, 1783-1784*. Princeton University Press, New Jersey.

Givoni, M. (2006) Development and impact of the modern high-speed train: A review. *Transport Reviews* 26, 593–611.

Givoni, M. and Banister, D. (2008) Airline and railway integration. *Transport Policy* 13, 386–397.

Global Solutions (2011) Fact Sheet. Available at: http://globalsolutions.org/files/public/documents/LOS_Factsheet.pdf (accessed 10 October 2011).

Glossary of Transport Statistics (2009) 4th edn by United Nations Economic Commission for Europe, Transport Forum & Eurostat. Available at: http://epp.eurostat.ec.europa.eu/cache/ITY_OFFPUB/KS-RA-10-028/EN/KS-RA-10-028-EN.PDF (accessed 14 October 2011).

GoCar Franchise Services, Inc. (2008) What is a GoCar? Available at: http://www.gocartours.com/pages/what-is-a-gocar.html (accessed 2 December 2012).

Goehlich, R. A. (2007) Space tourism. In: Conrady, R. & Buck, M. (eds) *Trends and Issues in Global Tourism*. Springer-Verlag, Berlin, Germany, pp. 213–226.

Goeldner, C. and Ritchie, J.R. (2011) *Tourism – Principles, Practices, Philosophies*, 12th edn. Wiley, Hoboken, New York.

Gould, P. (2010) The Horse Bus. Available at: http://www.petergould.co.uk/local_transport_history/generalhistories/general/horsebus.htm (accessed 14 October 2011).

Governors Highway Safety Association (2012) Segway Laws. Available at: http://www.ghsa.org/html/stateinfo/laws/segway_laws.html (accessed 6 December 2012).

G.P. Wild Ltd (2009) Contribution to the Cruise Tourism. Available at: http://www.ashcroftandassociates.com/images/ECC-Report%5B3-LR%5D.pdf (accessed 24 January 2013).

G.P. Wild Ltd (2012) The Cruise Industry. Available at: http://www.ashcroftandassociates.com/downloads/EIR_2012_Report.pdf (accessed 8 July 2013).

Grant, R., Rackliff, L., Reed, S. and Weller, J. (2009) Investigation of the Role of Fatigue in Coach Accidents. Available at: http://ec.europa.eu/transport/road_safety/pdf/2009_06_passenger_transport_by_coach_annexe_d.pdf (accessed 26 November 2011).

Gross, S. (2005) *Mobilitätsmanagement im Tourismus*. FIT-Verlag, Dresden, Germany.

Gross, S. (2011) *Tourismus und Verkehr – Grundlagen, Marktanalyse und Strategien von Verkehrsunternehmen*. Oldenbourg, Munich, Germany.

Gross, S. and Schröder, A. (2007) Basic business model of European low cost airlines – an analysis of typical characteristics. In: Gross, S. and Schröder, A. (eds) *Handbook of Low Cost Airlines – Strategies, Business Processes and Market Environment*. Erich Schmidt Verlag GmbH & Co., Berlin, Germany, pp. 31–50.

Gross, S. and Stengel, N. (2010) *Mietfahrzeuge im Tourismus: Grundlagen, Geschäftsprozesse und Marktanalyse*. Oldenbourg, Munich, Germany.

Gross, S., Lück, M. and Schröder, A. (2013) Low cost carrier – A worldwide phenomenon?! In: Gross, S. and Lück, M. (eds) *The Low Cost Carrier Worldwide*. Ashgate Publishing, Aldershot, UK, pp. 3–15.

Hallerbach, B. (2010) *Zukunftsmarkt Wandern: Erste Ergebnisse der Grundlagenuntersuchung Freizeit- und Urlaubsmarkt Wandern*. Deutscher Wanderverband, Kassel, Germany.

Hannam, K. and Ateljevic, I. (2008) *Backpacker Tourism: Concepts and Profiles*. Channel View Publications, Tonawanda, New York.

Hansen, U. and Schrader, U. (2005) Corporate Social Responsibility als aktuelles Thema der Betriebswirtschaftslehre. Die Betriebswirtschaft 4, 373-395. Available at: http://www.imug.de/pdfs/csr/hp_imug_hansen-_schrader_csr_und_bwl_2005.pdf (accessed 26 August 2013).

Heinze, G.W. and Kill, H.H. (1997) *Freizeit und Mobilität – Neue Lösungen im Freizeitverkehr*. Akademie für Raumforschung und Landesplanung, Hanover, Germany.

Hermann U. and Potgieter, M. (2013) Low cost carrier in Africa. In: Gross, S. & Lück, M. (eds) *The Low Cost Carrier Worldwide*. Ashgate Publishing, Aldershot, UK, pp. 177–197.

Hertz for Car Rental Council of Ireland (2010) Car Rental Fleet Shortages & Tourism in 2010. Available at: http://www.itic.ie/fileadmin/docs/ITIC-Car_Rental_Fleet_Shortage_and_Tourism.pdf (accessed 9 October 2012).

Hertz GmbH (2012) History of the Company. Available at: http://www.hertz.co.nz/rentacar/abouthertz/index.jsp?targetPage=CorporateProfile.jsp&c=aboutHertzHistoryView (accessed 29 September 2012).

Highbeam Business (2012) Industry Report. Available at: http://business.highbeam.com/industry-reports/transportation/bus-charter-service-except-local (accessed 15 January 2012).

Hobson, J.S.P. (1993) Analysis of the US cruise line industry. *Tourism Management* 14, 453–62.

Houk, R. (2008). Railroad History. Available at: http://www.sdrm.org/history/timeline/ (accessed 19 October 2012).

HSH Bank (2005) *Business Jets – Markt, Betreibermodelle, Eigentümer, Markttrends, Gebrauchtmarkt*. HSH Bank, Hamburg/Kiel, Germany.

Hudson, S. (2003). *Sport and Adventure Tourism*. Routledge, London, UK.

Hughes, W. and Lavery, J. (2008) *Critical Thinking*, 5th edn. Broadview Press, Ontario, Canada.

Hung, K. and Petrick, J.F. (2009) How do we get baby boomers and future seniors on motorcoaches? *Tourism Analysis* 14, 665–675.

Huskytrack (2012) Reisehandbuch 2013/2014. Available at: http://www.huskytrack.de/files/reise-handbuch_2013.pdf (accessed 4 December 2012).

Huss, W. and Schenk, W. (1982) *Omnibus-Geschichte – Die Entwicklung bis 1924*. Huss-Verlag, Munich, Gemany.

IACS (2011) IACS Explained. Available at: http://www.iacs.org.uk/explained/default.aspx (accessed 24 November 2011).

IAG (2010) About Us – British Airways Profile. Available at: http://www.iairgroup.com/phoenix.zhtml?c=240949&p=aboutoverview (accessed 27 December 2012).

IATA (2012a) About Us – Our Mission. Available at: http://www.iata.org/about/Pages/mission.aspx (accessed 22 November 2012).

IATA (2012b) History. Available at: https://www.iata.org/about/pages/history.aspx (accessed 22 November 2012).

IBAC (2013) General Information. Available at: http://www.ibac.org/about-ibac/general-information (accessed 18 July 2013).

ICAO (2006) *Convention on International Civil Aviation*, 9th edn. Montreal, Canada.

ICAO (2008) Annual Report of the Council – 2007. Available at: http://www.icao.int/publications/Documents/9898_en.pdf (accessed 20 February 2013).

ICAO (2012a) Annual Report of the Council – 2011. Available at: http://www.icao.int/publications/Documents/9975_en.pdf (accessed 20 February 2013).

ICAO (2012b). Annual Passenger Total Approaches 3 Billion According to ICAO 2012 Air Transport Results. Available at: http://www.icao.int/Newsroom/Pages/annual-passenger-total-approaches-3-billion-accordding-to-ICAO-2012-air-transport-results.aspx (accessed 13 February 2013).

ICAO (2013) Welcome to DAGMAR – ICAO's Database of Aeronautical Agreements and Arrangements. Available at: http://legacy.icao.int/applications/dagmar/main.cfm (accessed 13 February 2013).

IEA (2012) CO2 Emissions From Fuel Combustion – Highlights, Paris. Available at: http://www.iea.org/publications/free-publications/publication/CO2emissionfromfuelcombustionHIGHLIGHTS.pdf (accessed 27 August 2013).

IISC (2011) Orbital Space Tourism Market Revisited. Available at: http://www.iisc.im/news.asp?article=555 (accessed 8 April 2013).

IMB (2011) About Us. Available at: http://www.icc-ccs.org/icc/imb (accessed 24 November 2011).

Immers, L.H., Logghe, S. and Lismont, J. Design methodology for public transport networks. In proceedings of the 8th International Scientific Conference MOBILITA, Bratislava, Slovenia, 2001.

IMO (2011) About IMO. Available at: http://www.imo.org/About/Pages/Default.aspx (accessed 24 November 2011).

Institute of Transport Management, The (2012) Automotive. Available at: http://www.itmworld.com/subcategory_listing.php?iCategoryId=67 (accessed 5 October 2012).

Interferry (2012) About Us. Available at: http://interferry.com/about (accessed 13 November 2012).

International Federation of Sleddog Sports, Inc. (2012) History. Available at: http://sleddogsport.net/index.php?option=com_content&task=view&id=16&Itemid=29 (accessed 4 December 2012).

Irish, M. (2004) *The Auto Pact: Investment, Labour and the WTO*. Kluwer Law International, The Hague, The Netherlands.

IRU (2012) About. Available at: http://www.iru.org/en_history_and_mission (accessed 15 January 2012).

Ishak, S. (2013) Top airline groups by revenue. *Airline Business* 8, 38–41.

ISL (2010) *Shipping Statistics and Market Review*. Volume 54, No. 8. ISL, Bremen, Germany.

ISL (2012) *Shipping Statistics and Market Review*. Volume 56, No. 8. ISL, Bremen, Germany.

ITWF (2012) Flags of Convenience Campaign. Available at: http://www.itfglobal.org/flags-convenience/index.cfm (accessed 7 August 2012).

JAA (2004) Definitions. Available at: http://www.jaa.nl/publications/jars/500969.pdf (accessed 7 April 2013).

Jakhu, R.S., Sgobba, T. and Dempsey, P.S. (2011) *The Need for an Integrated Regulatory Regime for Aviation and Space: ICAO for Space?* Springer-Verlag, Vienna, Austria.

John Dunham & Associates (2012) Motorcoach Census 2011. Available at: http://www.buses.org/files/Foundation/Final_Motorcoach_Census_2011_7-3-2012.pdf (accessed 16 February 2012).

Joint Ocean Commission Initiative (2006) Ocean Policy Reform Nation's Oceans and Coasts Key to Competiveness. Available at: http://www.jointoceancommission.org/news-room/news-releases/2006-02-03_2005_US_Ocean_Policy_Report_Card.pdf (accessed 29 November 2011).

Kepper, U. (2010) Bahnbegriffe. Available at: http://eisenbahnblog.net/informationen/bahnbegriffe/ (accessed 18 September 2010).

Kline, C. (2008) Equestrian Tourism: Current State and Future Trends. Available at: http://www.catalunyaacavall.com/Informes/Equestrian_Tourism-Current_State_and_Future_Trends-Carol_Klein-2008.pdf (accessed 11 December 2012).

Knäusel, H.G. (2002) *Zeppelin – Die Geschichte der Zeppelin-Luftschiffe. Konstrukteure – Technik – Unternehmen*, 2nd edn. Aviatic Verlag, Oberhaching, Germany.

Koch, B. (2010) Aviation strategy and business models. In: Wald, A., Fay, C. and Gleich, R. (eds) *Introduction to Aviation Management*. LIT Verlag, Berlin, Germany, pp. 143–184.

Korhola, A. (2008) Will there be a return to elegance of flying? In: Finnair Plc (ed.) *Departure 2093 – Five Visions of Future Flying*. Print Libris, Helsinki, Finland, pp. 22–24.

Krüger, A. (2010) Historie des Wanderns. In: Dreyer, A., Menzel, A. and Endreß, M. (eds) *Wandertourismus, Kundengruppen, Destinationsmarketing, Gesundheitsaspekte*. Oldenbourg, Munich, Germany.

Krüger, R. and Reise, S. (2005) Beschaffungsvarianten bei Geschäftsflugzeugen. *Internationales Verkehrswesen* 3, 82–86.

Kubisch, U. (1998) *Wohnwagen. Caravan. Geschichte, Technik, Ferienzeit*. Transit Buchverlag, Berlin, Germany.

Las Vegas Review Journal (2004) End of Road of Pedicabs. Available at: http://www.reviewjournal.com/lvrj_home/2004/Mar-03-Wed-2004/news/23348904.html (accessed 13 December 2012).

Leaseurope (2013) Annual Survey. Available at: http://www.leaseurope.org/uploads/documents/stats/European%20Leasing%20Market%202012.pdf (accessed 4 July 2013).

Leder, S. (2004) Wandertourismus. In: Becker, C., Höpfner, H. and Steinecke, A. (eds) *Geographie der Freizeit und des Tourismus – Bilanz und Ausblick*. Oldenbourg, Munich, Germany, pp. 320–330.

Lee, J. (2009) Vision for High-Speed Rail in America. Available at: http://www.whitehouse.gov/blog/09/04/16/a-vision-for-high-speed-rail (accessed 18 October 2011).

Leiper, N. (1990) Tourism Systems: An Interdisciplinary Perspectives. Occasional Paper No. 2, Massey University, Palmerston North, New Zealand.

Leishman, J.G. (2006) *Principles of Helicopter Aerodynamics*. Cambridge University Press, New York.

Lohmann, G. and Duval, D. (2011) *Critical Aspects of the Tourism-Transport Relationship*. Goodfellow Publishers Ltd, Oxford, UK.

Lowson, M. V. (1998) Surface transport history in the UK: analysis and projections. *Proceedings of the ICE - Transport* 129, 14–19. Available at: http://www.ultraprt.com/uploads/Documents/surfac_1.pdf (accessed 1 November 2011).

LRTA (2013) World System List Index. Available at: http://www.lrta.org/world/worldind.html (accessed 13 February 2013).

Luftfahrt-Bundesamt (2013) Number of Listed Balloons in Germany. Available at: http://de.statista.com/statistik/daten/studie/155530/umfrage/anzahl-der-luftschiffe-in-deutschland/ (accessed 7 April 2013).

Lumma, K. and Gross, S. (2009) Ökologische Folgen von Hochseekreuzfahrten. In: Bastian, H., Dreyer, A. and Gross, S. (eds) *Tourismus 3.0 – Fakten und Perspektiven*. ITD-Verlag, Hamburg, Germany, pp. 147–156.

Lumma, K., Kröger, K. and Gross, S. (2011) CSR im Airline-Management – Eine Benchmark-Studie deutscher Fluggesellschaften. In: Boksberger, P. and Schuckert, M. (eds) *Innovationen in Tourismus und Freizeit – Hypes, Trends und Entwicklungen*. Erich Schmidt Verlag, Berlin, Germany, pp. 259–277.

Lumsdon, L. (2006) Factors affecting the design of tourism bus services. *Annals of Tourism Research* 33, 748–766.

Lumsdon, L.M. and Page, S. (2004) *Tourism and Transport – Issues and Agenda for the New Millennium*. Elsevier, London, UK.

Mancini, M. (2004) *Cruising: A Guide to the Cruise Line Industry*. Delmar Learning, Clifton Park, New York.

Marion, F. (2010) *Wonderful Balloon Ascents: The Conquest of the Skies*. Kessinger Publishers, LLC, Whitefish, Massachusetts.

Marlen (2011) Renta de Autos y Seguros en México. Available at: http://www.articuloz.com/alquiler-articulos/renta-de-autos-y-seguros-en-mexico-5214768.html (accessed 3 October 2012).

Martin, J.C. (2011) Transportation changes in Europe. *Transportation Journal* 50, 109–124.

Martinez, H.E. (2008) *Dictionary for Air Travel and Tourism Activities*. iUniverse, Bloomington, Indiana.

Martínez, I. (2013) Balloons. Available at: http://webserver.dmt.upm.es/~isidoro/ot1/Balloons.pdf (accessed 9 April 2013).

Maurer, P. (2006) *Luftverkehrsmanagement – Basiswissen*, 4th edn. Oldenbourg, Munich, Germany.

Maxtone-Graham, J. (2000) *Liners to the Sun*. Sheridan House Inc, Dobbs Ferry, New York.

McKnight, P. (2010) Airline economics. In: Wald, A., Fay, C. and Gleich, R. (eds) *Introduction to Aviation Management*. LIT Verlag, Berlin, Germany, pp. 25–53.

Media.unwto.org, (2014). *Understanding Tourism: Basic Glossary/Wold Tourism Organization UNWTO*. Available at: http://media.unwto.org/en/content/understanding-tourism-basic-glossary (accessed 7 July 2014).

Metcalfe, J. (2006) Stockton & Darlington Railway. Available at: http://www.railcentre.co.uk/RailHistory/Stockton/Stockton.html (accessed 16 October 2012).

Miller, F., Vandome, A. and McBrewster, J. (2010) *Cycle Rickshaw*. VDM Publishing House, Saarbrücken, Germany.

MIT Department of Aeronautics and Astronautics (1997) Theory of Flight. Available at: http://web.mit.edu/16.00/www/aec/flight.html (accessed 08 September 2013)

Mitfahrgelegenheit.de (2012) About Us. Available at: http://www.mitfahrgelegenheit.de/pages/about (accessed 28 September 2012).

Moedebeck, H. (2012) *Die Luftschifffahrt*. DOGMA, Bremen, Germany.

Morgan, P. and Power, L. (2011) Cruise tourism and the cruise industry. In: Robinson, P., Heitmann, S. and Dieke, P. (eds) *Research Themes for Tourism*. CABI Publishing, Oxfordshire, UK.

Morrell, P. (2008) Can long-haul low-cost airlines be successful? *Research in Transportation Economics* 24, 61–67.

Motion Tools GmbH (2007) Le Segway PT i2 est homologué en Suisse! Available at: http://segway.ch/cgi-bin/files/2007.11.19%20Communiqu%C3%A9_Segway%20i2%20homologu%C3%A9_F%20FINAL.pdf (accessed 6 December 2012).

MOVECO GmbH (2013) Homepage. Available at: www.mitfahrzentrale.de (accessed 05 September 2013).

MSC Cruises (2012) Ships. Available at: http://www.msccruises.co.uk/uk_en/Ships/MSC-Divina.aspx (accessed 24 January 2012).

Müller, W. (2005) Entwicklung und Einsatz von Heißluftluftschiff. In: *Jahrbuch der Warsteiner Internationale Montgolfiade*. Warstein, Germany, pp. 16–23.

Nathan Associates Inc. (2008) Motorcoach Census – American Bus Association, Washington DC October 2008. Available at: http://www.buses.org/files/Report08.pdf (accessed 23 November 2011).

National Association for Donkey-Trekking (2012) Who We Are. Available at: http://www.ane-et-rando.com/QuiSommesNous/presentationE.html (accessed 5 December 2012).

National Recreation Trails (2012) Database. Available at: http://www.americantrails.org/NRTDatabase/ (accessed 15 December 2012).

National Transit Database Glossary (2013) US Department of Transportation Federal Transit Administration. Available at: http://www.ntdprogram.gov/ntdprogram/Glossaries/pdf/Glossary2013.Pdf

NBAA (2012) 2012 NBAA Business Aviation Fact Book. Available at: http://www.nbaa.org/business-aviation/fact-book/NBAA-Business-Aviation-Fact-Book-2012.pdf (accessed 30 August 2013).

New Zealand Ministry of Transport (2012) International Air Services Information. Available at: http://www.transport.govt.nz/ourwork/air/internationalairservicesinformation/ (accessed 16 January 2013).

New Zealand Ministry of Transport (2013) Multilateral Agreement on the Liberalization of International Air Transportation. Available at: http://www.maliat.govt.nz/index.php (accessed 16 January 2013).

NHTS (2010) US National Household Travel Survey 2009. Available at: http://nhts.ornl.gov/2009/pub/stt.pdf (accessed 10 February 2012).

Nikolaus Otto Park GmbH & Co. KG (2012) Press Releases. Available at: http://www.otto-park.de/uploads/20121109%20-%20PM-Flughafen-Butz-Leinen.pdf (accessed 2 December 2012).

Ninomiya, J. (2010) Ballooning in the Sky. Available at: www.clusterballoon.org/index.html (accessed 9 April 2013).

Nubert, M. (2010) Aircraft – types, operations and performance. In: Wald, A., Fay, C. and Gleich, R. (eds) *Introduction to Aviation Management*. LIT Verlag, Berlin, Germany, pp. 55–87.

Nürburgring Betriebsgesellschaft mbH (2012) Offers. Available at: http://www.nuerburgring.de/en/angebote/motor-action/car-rentals.html (accessed 2 December 2012).

NWCCA (2011) About the NWCCA. Available at: http://nwcruiseship.org/index.cfm/about/ (accessed 30 November 2011)

Obier, C. and Peters, G. (2003) *Reisemobiltourismus in Deutschland – Eine Empirische Grundlagenstudie*. Vereinigte Motor-Verlage GmbH, Stuttgart, Germany.

O'Connell, J.F. (2009) The Middle East. In: Graham, A., Papatheodorou, A. and Forsyth, P. (eds) *Aviation and Tourism – Implications for Leisure Travel*. Ashgate Publishing, Aldershot, UK, pp. 291–301.

Odoni, A. (2009) The international institutional and regulatory environment. In: Belobaba, P.P., Odoni, A. and Barnhart, C. (eds) *The Global Airline Industry*. John Wiley & Sons, Chichester, UK, pp. 19–46.

OECD (2011) *Trends in the Transport Sector 2011*. OECD Publishing. Available at: http://dx.doi.org/10.1787/trend_transp-2011-en (accessed 13 February 2013).

Office of Travel and Tourism Industries (2012a) 2011 Industry Sector Profile: Rental Car. Available at: http://tinet.ita.doc.gov/outreachpages/download_data_table/2011-rental-car-profile.pdf (accessed 3 October 2012).

Office of Travel and Tourism Industries (2012b) Profile of Overseas Travellers to the United States: 2011 Inbound. Available at: http://tinet.ita.doc.gov/outreachpages/download_data_table/2011_Overseas_Visitor_Profile.pdf (accessed 9 October 2012).

OITAF (2009) *Ropeways Statistics 2009*. Bozen, Italy.

One Street (2012) Cycle Tourism. Available at: http://www.onestreet.org/resources-for-increasing-bicycling/143-cycle-tourism (accessed 6 December 2012).

One World (2013) About One World. Available at: http://www.oneworld.com/general/about-oneworld (accessed 5 July 2013).

Ontario Ministry of Transportation (2011) FAQ Segway. Available at: http://www.mto.gov.on.ca/english/dandv/vehicle/emerging/segway-faq.shtml#a1 (accessed 6 December 2012).

OPM Media GmbH (2009) Homepage. Available at: www.drive2u.de (accessed 28 September 2012).

OTIF (2011) Geschäftsbericht 2011. Available at: http://www.otif.org/fileadmin/user_upload/otif_verlinkte_files/07_veroeff/08_gesch_bericht/RG_2011_d.pdf (accessed 16 June 2013).

Outdoor Foundation, The (2012a), Hiking in the US. Available at: http://www.statista.com/statistics/191240/participants-in-hiking-in-the-us-since-2006/ (accessed 15 December 2012).

Outdoor Foundation, The (2012b), Backpacking in the US. Available at: http://www.statista.com/statistics/190816/young-adult-participation-in-backpacking-in-the-us-since-2006/ (accessed 16 December 2012).

P&O Cruises (2012) History. Available at: http://www.pocruises.com/about-po-cruises/175-years-of-heritage/ (accessed 2 August 2012).

Page, S.J. (2009) *Transport and Tourism – Global Perspectives*, 3rd edn. Prentice Hall, Harlow, UK.

Page, S.J. and Connell, J. (2006) *Tourism: A Modern Synthesis*, 2nd edn. London, UK.

Passenger Shipping Association (2011) UK Cruise Convention: Europe Poised to Overtake North America as Cruise Source Market. Available at: http://www.ttgdigital.com/4675868.article (accessed 25 February 2013).

Passenger Vessel Association (2007) About PVA. Available at: http://www.passengervessel.com/about.aspx (accessed 13 November 2012).

Pearce, P. (1990) *The Backpacker Phenomenon: Preliminary Answers to Basic Questions*. James Cook University, Townsville, Australia.

Peeters, P.M. (2004) European Transport, Tourism and Environment. Available at: http://www.cstt.nl/userdata/documents/appendix_deliverable_1_subject_matter_review_30082004.pdf (accessed 16 November 2012).

Peschke, U. (2011) *Menschen und Tiere weltweit*. Waxmann Verlag GmbH, Münster, Germany.

Pickeral, T. (2003) *Pferde & Ponys*. Parragon, Cologne, Germany.

Pilotfriend (2013) Leonardo Da Vinci's Helical Air Screw. Available at: http://www.pilotfriend.com/photo_albums/helicopters/Leonardo%20Da%20Vinci%27s%20Helical%20Air%20Screw.htm (accessed 7 April 2013).

Pompl, W. (1997) *Touristikmanagement 1 – Beschaffungsmanagement*, 2nd edn. Springer-Verlag, Berlin, Germany.

Pompl, W. (2007) *Luftverkehr: Eine ökonomische und politische Einführung*, 5th edn. Springer-Verlag, Berlin, Heidelberg, Germany.

Praxis Group/Alberta Tourism, Parks and Recreation, The (2008) A Demand Side Perspective. Available at: http://www.tpr.alberta.ca/tourism/docs/RV_Camping_Demand.pdf (accessed 14 December 2012).

Prideaux, B. (2000) The role of the transport system in destination development. *Tourism Management* 21, 53–63.

Profillidis, V.A. (2006) *Railway Management and Engineering*. Ashgate Publishing, Hampshire, UK.

Racing Adventure (2012) Tracks. Available at: http://www.racingadventure.com/tracks/ (accessed 2 December 2012).

Randolph, J. (2003) *Dennis Tito – First Space Tourist*. The Rosen Publishing Group, New York.

Rasmussen, R. K. (2007) *Critical Companion to Mark Twain: A Literary Reference to His Life and Work*. Facts on File, New York.

RDA (2012) Federation. Available at: http://www.rda.de/en/federation.html (accessed 15 January 2012).

RDA (2013) Marktforschungsbericht 2013. Fakten und Trend im Bustourismus. Available at: http://www.rda.de/fileadmin/content/rda/Dateiordner/roter_bus/RDA_Marktforschungsbericht_2013__03.pdf (accessed 28 August 2013).

Recreation Vehicle Industry Association (2012a) RV Types & Prices. Available at: http://www.rvia.org/?ESID=types (accessed 22 September 2012).

Recreation Vehicle Industry Association (2012b) RV Types, Terms & Prices. Available at: http://www.rvia.org/UniPop.cfm?v=2&OID=606&CC=1120 (accessed 13 December 2012).

Recreation Vehicle Industry Association (2012c). About. Available at: http://www.rvia.org/?ESID=about (accessed 14 December 2012).

Research and Markets (2010) Market Entry Strategies and Emerging. Available at: http://www.researchandmarkets.com/reports/2118616/market_entry_strategies_and_emerging.pdf (accessed 9 October 2012).

Reuters (2012) Car Rental Shares Rise After Hertz Boots Bids. Available at: http://www.reuters.com/article/2010/09/13/dollarthrifty-shares-idUSN1321335120100913 (accessed 5 October 2012).

Robinson, P., Lück, M. and Smith, S. (2013) *Tourism*. CABI Publishing, Oxfordshire, UK.

Römer, C. (2010) Die Geschichte des Mietwagens II – von 1920 bis 1945. Available at: http://www.mietwagen-blog.com/blog/die-geschichte-des-mietwagens-ii-von-1920-bis-1945.html (accessed 29 September 2012).

Root, A. (2003) *Delivering sustainable transport*. Pergamon, Oxford, UK.

Roseland, M. (2012) *Toward Sustainable Communities – Solutions for Citizens and Their Governments*, 4th edn. New Society Publishers, Gabriola Island, Canada.

Royal Caribbean (2011) Factsheets. Available at: http://www.royalcaribbeanpresscenter.com/fact-sheets/ (accessed 27 February 2013).

Royal Caribbean Cruises (2012) The Company. Available at: http://www.royalcaribbean.com/aboutus/home.do (accessed 24 January 2012).

Rühle, J. (2007) *Planungssysteme im Schienenpersonenfernverkehr*. Kölner Wissenschaftsverlag, Cologne, Germany.

Sakhdari, F. (2006) *Vermarktung von CarSharing-Konzepten*. dissertation.de, Berlin, Germany.

Scaled Composites (2004) SpaceShipOne Flies Again Within 14 Days – Wins $10M X PRIZE. Available at: http://www.scaled.com/projects/tierone/spaceshipone_flies_again_within_14_days_-_wins_10m_x_prize (accessed 8 April 2013).

Schilling, D.R (2013) $6 Billion Floating City "Freedom" to Dwarf World's Largest Ships Ever Built. Available at: www.industrytap.com/6-billion-floating-city-freedom-to-dwarf-worlds-largest-ships-ever-built/3007 (accessed 5 September 2013)

Schröder, A. and Freyer, W. (2011) Bedeutung von Zusatzeinnahmen bei Airlines – eine geschäftsmodellbasierte Betrachtung. In: Boksberger, P. and Schuckert, M. (eds) *Innovationen in Tourismus und Freizeit – Hypes, Trends und Entwicklungen*. Erich Schmidt Verlag, Berlin, Germany, pp. 245–258.

Schulz, A. (2009) *Verkehrsträger im Tourismus – Luftverkehr, Busverkehr, Straßenverkehr, Schiffsverkehr*. Oldenbourg, Munich, Germany.

Schulz, A., Baumann, S. and Wiedenmann, S. (2010) *Flughafen Management*. Oldenbourg, Munich, Germany.

Schultz-Friese, F. (2011) Jubiläum bei der Deutschen Zeppelin-Reederei: Zehn Jahre Passagierbetrieb mit dem Zeppelin NT. Available at: http://www.bodensee-woche.de/jubilaum-bei-der-deutschen-zeppelin-reederei-zehn-jahre-passagierbetrieb-mit-dem-zeppelin-nt-46734/ (accessed 4 July 2013).

Schüssler, O. (2005) *Passagier-Schifffahrt – Ein Handbuch für Reiseverkehrskaufleute in Ausbildung und Praxis*, 2nd edn. DRV Service GmbH, Frankfurt am Main, Germany.

Segway Inc. (2008) Segway Product. Available at: http://www.segway.com/downloads/pdfs/brochures/2008_Product.pdf (accessed 6 December 2012).

Segway Inc. (2013) Segway Milestones. Available at: http://www.segway.com/about-segway/segway-milestones.php (accessed 28 August 2013).

Senatsverwaltung für Gesundheit, Umwelt und Verbraucherschutz (2009) Berliner Leitlinien für Pferdefuhrwerksbetriebe. Available at: http://www.berlin.de/imperia/md/content/sen-verbraucherschutz/tierschutz/leitlinie_pferdefuhrwerksbetriebe.pdf?start&ts=1240379927&file=leitlinie_pferdefuhrwerksbetriebe.pdf (accessed 11 December 2012).

Seth, P.N. (2006) *Successful Tourism – Tourism Practices*. Sterling Publishers, New Delhi, India.

Shaughnessy, T. and Tobin. E. (2003-04) *Flags of Inconvenience: Freedom and Insecurity on the High Seas*. University of Pennsylvania, Journal of International Law and Policy. Available at: http://www.law.upenn.edu/journals/jil/jilp/articles/1-1_Shaughnessy_Tina.pdf (accessed 14 October 2011).

ShipPax (2008) Ferry market & outlook. In: *ShipPax MARKET 08*.

ShipPax (2009) Ferry market & outlook. In: *ShipPax MARKET 09*.

Sightjogging Barcelona (2012) Press Releases. Available at: http://www.fitforfun.de/sport/laufen/laufstrecken/sightjogging/veranstalter-die-besten-adressen_aid_7899.html (accessed 16 December 2012).

Singh, J. (2010) *Ecotourism*. International Publishing House, New Delhi, India.

Singh, T.V. (2004) *New Horizons in Tourism*. CABI Publishing, Oxfordshire, UK.

Sixt AG (2012) History of the Company. Available at: https://www.sixt.jobs/Geschichte-sm10.php?sel_language=de (accessed 29 September 2012).

SKEMA (2010) Maritime Governance – A Consolidation Study. Available at: http://eskema.eu/default-info.aspx?areaid=6&index=1 (accessed 30 November 2011).

Sky Team (2013) Organization. Available at: https://www.skyteam.com/en/About-us/Organization/ (accessed 5 July 2013).

SkyWest Airlines (2013a) Facts. Available at: http://www.skywest.com/about-skywest-airlines/facts/ (accessed 13 February 2013).

SkyWest Airlines (2013b) History. Available at: http://www.skywest.com/about-skywest-airlines/skywest-history/ (accessed 13 February 2013).

Smart Move Campaign (2013) Available at: http://www.busandcoach.travel/ (accessed 05 September 2013).

Sorensen, J. (2013) The CarTrawler Yearbook of Ancillary Revenues. Available at: http://www.ideaworkscompany.com/wp-content/uploads/2013/09/2013-Ancillary-Revenue-Yearbook.pdf (accessed 11 September 2013).

Southwest Airlines (2012) Southwest Corporate Fact Sheet. Available at: http://www.swamedia.com/channels/Corporate-Fact-Sheet/pages/corporate-fact-sheet (accessed 28 December 2012).

Space Adventures (2013a) Orbital Spaceflights – Our Clients. Available at: http://www.spaceadventures.com/index.cfm?fuseaction=orbital.Clients (accessed 8 April 2013).

Space Adventures (2013b) Orbital Spaceflights – Our Clients. Sarah Brightman. Available at: http://www.spaceadventures.com/index.cfm?fuseaction=orbital.Sarah_Brightman (accessed 8 April 2013).

Space Adventures (2013c) Orbital Spaceflight Program. Available at: http://www.spaceadventures.com/index.cfm?fuseaction=orbital.Orbital (accessed 8 April 2013).

Spaceport America (2012) What is Spaceport America? Available at: http://spaceportamerica.com/ (accessed 8 April 2013).

Star Alliance (2013) Organisation. Available at: http://www.staralliance.com/en/about/organisation/ (accessed 5 July 2013).

Star Cruises (2012) Group Profile. Available at: http://www.genting.com/groupprofile/sc.htm (accessed 24 January 2012).

Statista (2012) European Market Share of Rental Car Companies. Available at: http://de.statista.com/statistik/daten/studie/172602/umfrage/marktanteile-der-autovermieter-in-europa/ (accessed 5 October 2012).

Statistics Canada (2012a) The Canadian Passenger Bus and Urban Transit Industries. Catalogue Vol. 27, no. 1. Available at: http://www.statcan.gc.ca/pub/50-002-x/50-002-x2012001-eng.pdf (accessed 4 July 2013).

Statistics Canada (2012b) Statistics of the Automotive Equipment Rental and Leasing Industry 2008 – 2010. Available at: http://www.statcan.gc.ca/pub/63-242-x/2012001/t001-eng.htm (accessed 6 October 2012).

Statistisches Bundesamt (2013) Anzahl der Personen, die in der Freizeit Sport- oder Segelfliegen, nach Häufigkeit von 2007 bis 2012. Available at: http://de.statista.com/statistik/daten/studie/171156/umfrage/haeufigkeit-von-segelfliegen-oder-sportfliegen-in-der-freizeit/ (accessed 6 April 2013).

Steer Davies Gleave (2009) Study of Passenger Transport by Coach. Available at: http://ec.europa.eu/transport/modes/road/studies/doc/2009_06_passenger_transport_by_coach.pdf (accessed 20 November 2011).

Stena Line (2012) Ferry Routes. Available at: http://www.stenaline.co.uk/ferry/routes/ (accessed 18 November 2012).

Stoyles, P. and Pentland, P. (2006) *The A to Z of Inventions and Inventors. Volume 2: C to F.* Macmillian, Australia.

Straesser, A. (2010) *Das Marketing-Geheimnis für Autovermietungen*. Books on Demand, Norderstedt, Germany.

T2impact/Flight Insight (2008) *The Future of Low Cost Carriers*. London/Sutton, UK.

Talley, W. (2012) *The Blackwell Companion to Maritime Economics*. Blackwell, West Sussex, UK.

Taumoepeau, S. (2013) Low cost carriers in Asia and the Pacific – development and the business structure. In: Gross, S. and Lück, M. (eds) *The Low Cost Carrier Worldwide*. Ashgate Publishing Limited, Aldershot, UK, pp. 113–138.

Timothy, D.J. and Teye, V.B. (2009) *Tourism and the Lodging Sector*. Elsevier Inc, Burlington, Massachusetts.

TNS (2011) CLIA Cruise Market Profile Study. Available at: http://www.cruising.org/sites/default/files/pressroom/Market_Profile_2011.pdf (accessed 8 July 2013).

Tomlinson, K. (2010) Vancouver Car-Rental Customer Warns of Gouging. Available at: http://www.cbc.ca/news/canada/british-columbia/story/2010/02/08/bc-budgetbill.html (accessed 3 October 2012).

Torok, S. and Holper, P. (2008) *Inventing Millions: Creating Wealth, Changing Lives*. Orient Paperbacks, New Delhi, India.

Tourism Ireland (2011) Cruise & Ferry Tourism. Available at: http://www.tourismireland.com/CMSPages/GetFile.aspx?guid=593a7c19-0e5d-48cd-b6a1-3b19e761eb8d (accessed 16 November 2012).

Tourismusverband Mecklenburg Vorpommern (2010) Statistische Daten. Available at: http://www.tmv.de/marktforschung/statistische-daten/ (accessed 23 February 2013).

Trans Canada Trail (2012) Facts About the Trail. Available at: http://tctrail.ca/about-the-trail/facts-about-the-trail (accessed 15 December 2012).

Transit Cooperative Research Program (2005). Car-Sharing: Where and How It Succeeds. Available at: www.tcrponline.org/PDFDocuments/TCRP_RPT_108.pdf (accessed 16 February 2013).

Transport Canada (2001) An Overview: Railway Safety Act. Available at: http://www.tc.gc.ca/media/documents/railsafety/2001overview.pdf (accessed 8 December 2011).

Transport Canada (2006) Ferry Safety. Available at: http://www.tc.gc.ca/eng/mediaroom/backgrounders-b05-m007e-2109.htm (accessed 15 November 2012).

Transportation Research Thesaurus (2014) provided by the Transportation Research Board. Available at: http://trt.trb.org/trt.asp

Tré, M. (2011) The Cruise Examiner. Available at: http://cruise-examiner.blogspot.de/ (accessed 19 November 2011).

TUI Marine (2013). About Us. Available at: http://www.tuimarine.com/aboutus.html (accessed 26 February 2013).

UIC (2010a) Available at: http://www.uic.org/IMG/pdf/_16_pages_avec_bat29-4-2010_2_.pdf (accessed 24 October 2011).

UIC (2010b) Activities Report. Available at: http://www.uic.org/IMG/pdf/_uic-ra-2010a.pdf (accessed 24 October 2011).

UIC (2010c) High Speed Traffic in Europe 2000-2009. Available at: http://www.uic.org/spip.php?article1349 (accessed 5 February 2013).

UIC (2011) Press Release No. 18/2011. Available at: http://www.uic.org/com/IMG/pdf/cp18_uic_stats_2010_en.pdf (accessed 11 November 2011).

UIC (2012) High Speed Lines in the World. Available at: http://www.uic.org/IMG/pdf/20120701_a1_high_speed_lines_in_the_world.pdf (accessed 13 February 2013).

Ultramagic (2013) Hot Air Balloon Baskets. Available at: http://www.ultramagic.com/balloons/hot-air-ballon-Baskets-s34_113.html (accessed 6 April 2013).

UMA (2012) About. Available at: http://www.uma.org/about/ (accessed 15 January 2012).

UNECE (2010) Report of the Working Party on Rail Transport on Its Sixty-fourth Session. Available at: http://www.unece.org/fileadmin/DAM/trans/doc/2011/sc2/ECE-TRANS-SC2-214e.pdf (accessed 12 October 2012).

United Nations Convention on the Law of the Sea, The (1998) Division for Ocean Affairs and the Law of the Sea, Office of Legal Affairs, United Nations. Available at: http://www.un.org/depts/los/convention_agreements/convention_historical_perspective (accessed 16 October 2011).

United Nations (2010) *Tourism Satellite Account: Recommended Methodological Framework 2008*. Department of Economic and Social Affairs, Statistics Division. Available at: http://unstats.un.org/unsd/publication/Seriesf/SeriesF_80rev1e.pdf (accessed 14 October 2013).

UNWTO (2001) *Tourism Vision 2020 – Volume 7: Global Forecasts and Profiles of Market Segments*. Madrid, Spain.

UNWTO (2008) *Tourism Market Trends – Europe*. Madrid, Spain.

UNWTO (2010a) *Cruise Tourism – Current Situation and Trends*. Madrid, Spain.

UNWTO (2010b) *International Recommendations for Tourism Statistics 2008*. New York.

UNWTO (2011) Tourism Highlights. Available at: http://mkt.unwto.org/sites/all/files/docpdf/unwto-highlights11enlr.pdf (accessed 24 September 2011).

UNWTO (2013) Tourism Ministers Call for Higher Policy Coordination Between Tourism and Aviation. Available at: http://media.unwto.org/press-release/2013-11-08/tourism-ministers-call-higher-policy-coordination-between-tourism-and-aviat (accessed 18 November 2013).

US Coast Guard Roles and Missions (2011) US Department of Transportation. Available at: http://www.bts.gov/publications/maritime_trade_and_transportation/2007/html/us_coast_guard.html (accessed 16 October 2011).

US Commission on Ocean Policy (2004) An Ocean Blueprint. Available at: http://www.oceancommission.gov/documents/doc_archive.html (accessed 24 October 2011).

US Consulate General (2012) About Us – Consulate Offices. Available at: http://montreal.usconsulate.gov/about-us/consulate-offices/international-civil-aviation-organization.html (accessed 22 November 2012).

US Department of Commerce (2011) U.S. Travel and Tourism Satellite Accounts for 2007–2010. Available at: http://www.bea.gov/scb/pdf/2011/06%20june/0611_travel.pdf (accessed 26 November 2011).

US Department of Transportation (2001) Balloon Flying Handbook. Available at: http://www.us-ppl.de/pdf/faa/hb/balloon/faa-h-8083-11.pdf (accessed 6 April 2013).

US Department of Transportation (2008) Glossary of Shipping Terms. Available at: http://www.marad.dot.gov/documents/Glossary_final.pdf (accessed 23 February 2013).

US Department of Transportation (2009a). Motorcoach Safety Plan. Available at: http://www.fmcsa.dot.gov/documents/safety-security/MotorcoachSafetyActionPlan_finalreport-508.pdf (accessed 11 February 2012).

US Department of Transportation (2009b). High-Speed Rail Strategic Plan. Available at: www.fra.dot.gov/Elib/Document/1468 (accessed 11 November 2012).

US Department of Transportation (2011a) FMSCA: The Motor Carrier Moratorium, Mexico, and NAFTA. Available at: http://www.fmcsa.dot.gov/intl-programs/whnaftafactsheet.htm (accessed 10 October 2011).

US Department of Transportation (2011b) Special report. Available at: http://www.rita.dot.gov/bts/sites/rita.dot.gov.bts/files/publications/special_reports_and_issue_briefs/special_report/2011_07_11/pdf/entire.pdf (accessed 14 November 2012).

US Department of Transportation (2013) US Passenger Kilometers. Available at: http://www.rita. dot.gov/bts/sites/rita.dot.gov.bts/files/publications/national_transportation_statistics/excel/ table_01_40_m.xls (accessed 08 July 2013).

US General Services Administration (2013) Airline Open Skies Agreements. Available at: http://www. gsa.gov/portal/content/103191 (accessed 16 January 2013).

US Government Accountability Office (2010) Maritime Security – Ferry Security Measures Have Been Implemented. Available at: http://www.gao.gov/products/GAO-11-207 (accessed 15 November 2012).

USDA Forest Service (2004) Participation Rates for Outdoor Activities in 2004. Available at: http:// www.srs.fs.usda.gov/recreation/RECUPDATES/recupdate0804.pdf (accessed 11 December 2012).

VDB (2010) *Die Bahnindustrie in Deutschland – Zahlen und Fakten zum Bahnmarkt und -verkehr – Ausgabe 2010*. Berlin, Germany.

VDB (2011) *Die Bahnindustrie in Deutschland – Zahlen und Fakten zum Bahnmarkt und -verkehr – Ausgabe 2011*. Berlin, Germany.

VDB (2012) *Die Bahnindustrie in Deutschland – Zahlen und Fakten zum Bahnmarkt und -verkehr – Ausgabe 2012*. Berlin, Germany.

Vehicle & Operator Services Agency (2011) Rules on Drivers' Hours and Tachographs. Available at: http:// www.dft.gov.uk/vosa/repository/Rules%20on%20Drivers%20Hours%20and%20Tachographs %20-%20Goods%20Vehicles%20in%20GB%20and%20Europe.pdf (accessed 14 November 2011).

Veloform GmbH (2012a) FAQ. Available at: http://www.veloform.com/data/veloform_faq_ en11121311836.pdf (accessed 13 December 2012).

Veloform GmbH (2012b) Press Release – Hanover Fair. Available at: http://www.veloform.com/data/ pressemitteilung_hannovermesse110519112541.pdf (accessed 13 December 2012).

Verband der Fährschifffahrt und Fährtouristik eV (2012) Schiffstypen. Available at: http://faehrver- band.org/faehre-inside/schiffstypen.html (accessed 22 October 2012).

VIA Rail Canada (2011) About VIA Rail. Available at: http://www.viarail.ca/en/about-via-rail (accessed 20 October 2012).

Virgin Galactic (2013) Booking. Available at: http://www.virgingalactic.com/booking/ (accessed 8 April 2013).

Voies navigable en France (2010). Le tourisme fluvial, un secteur porteur. Available at: http://www.vnf. fr/vnf/img/cms/Tourisme_et_domainehidden/secteur_porteur_201002021126.pdf (accessed 27 February 2013).

Vuchic, V. R. (2007) Frontmatter, in *Urban Transit Systems and Technology*. John Wiley & Sons, Inc., Hoboken, New Jersey.

Wald, A. (2013) Low cost carriers in the Middle East. In Gross, S. and Lück, M. (eds) *The Low Cost Carrier Worldwide*. Ashgate Publishing, Aldershot, UK, pp. 199–213.

Wall, G. and Mathieson, A. (2006) *Tourism: Change, Impacts and Opportunities*. Harlow, UK.

Walsh, M. (2010) The Bus Industry in the United States. Available at: http://eh.net/encyclopedia/ article/walsh.bus.industry.us (accessed 19 October 2011).

Ward, D. (2011) *Berlitz Complete Guide to Cruising & Cruise Ships*, 20th edn. Berlitz Publishing, London, UK.

WCED (1987) Our Common Future. Available at: http://conspect.nl/pdf/Our_Common_Future- Brundtland_Report_1987.pdf (accessed 18 October 2013).

WCED (2013) Our Common Future, Chapter 2: Towards Sustainable Development. Available at: http:// www.un-documents.net/ocf-02.htm#I (accessed 26 August 2013).

WDR – Westdeutscher Rundfunk (2012) Mediathek. Available at: http://www.wdr.de/mediathek/ html/regional/2012/08/20/die-story.xml (accessed 26 November 2012).

Weaver, A. and Duval, D. (2008) International and transnational aspects of the global cruise industry. In: Coles, T. and Hall, M.C. (eds) *International Business and Tourism – Global Issues, Contemporary Interactions*. Abingdon, UK.

Weed, M. and Bull, C. (2009) *Sports Tourism – Participants, Policy and Providers*, 2nd edn. Elsevier, Oxford, UK.

Wensveen, J.G. (2007) *Air Transportation: A Management Perspective*, 6th edn. Ashgate Publishing, Aldershot, UK.

Wergeland, T. (2012) Ferry passenger markets. In: Talley, W. (ed.) *The Blackwell Companion to Maritime Economics*. Blackwell, West Sussex, UK, pp. 161–184.

Whittall, N. (2002) *Paragliding: The Complete Guide*. Airlife Pub, Ramsbury, UK.

Widmann, T. (2006) *Wohnmobiltourismus in Deutschland am Beispiel der Destination Mosel*. Selbstverlag der Universität Trier, Trier, Germany.

Wiezorek, B. (1998) *Strategien europäischer Fluggesellschaften in einem liberalisierten Weltluftverkehr*. Peter Lang Verlag, Frankfurt am Main, Germany.

Wöhe, G. (2010) *Einführung in die allgemeine Betriebswirtschaftslehre*, 24th edn. Vahlen, Munich, Germany.

Wolf, W. (1996) *Car Mania: A Critical History of Transport*. Pluto Press, Chicago, Illinois.

World Class Driving (2012) Tracks. Available at: http://www.worldclassdriving.com/drive-exotic-racecars-track (accessed 2 December 2012).

XCOR (2013) Ticket. Available at: http://www.xcor.com/contact/ticket.php (accessed 8 April 2013).

Xenellis, G. (2003) Maritime Transport of Goods and Passengers 1997-2001. Available at: http://www.eds-destatis.de/en/downloads/sif/nz_03_04.pdf (accessed 16 November 2012)

Zeppelin Luftschifftechnik GmbH & Co KG (2013) Übersicht. Available at: http://www.zeppelinflug.de/uebersicht.html (accessed 4 July 2013).

Zucker, S. & Goericke, T. (2004) Der Charterer - das unbekannte Risiko (anhand ausgewählter Schäden). Available at: http://www.tis-gdv.de/tis/tagungen/kasko/wsp_2004/2_zucker_goericke.pdf (accessed 13 February 2013).

Zukunftsinstitut GmbH (2011) *Travel Trends – wie wir in Zukunft reisen werden*. Kelkheim, Germany.

Index

Note: Page numbers in *italics* indicate figures and tables. Page numbers in **bold** indicate boxes.